LONG TERM ALMANAC 2000-2050

(Second Edition)

LONG TERM ALMANAC 2000-2050

(Second Edition)

by

Geoffrey Kolbe

STARPATH®

Seattle, Washington

Published by: Starpath Publications, 3050 NW 63rd Street, Seattle, WA 98107, USA

IBSN 978-0-914025-10-8

Mistakes and omissions

These tables have been carefully checked, but neither the author nor the publisher can accept any responsibility for the consequences of any mistake or omission.

TABLE OF CONTENTS

Section Headings and Main Tables · Page

Introduction — 1

Daily tables — 3 - 51

Star chart for Southern sky — 52

Star chart for Northern sky — 53

Year 2000 star positions — 54 - 59

Explanation of Daily tables — 60

Tables of GHA increments — 63

Explanation of tables of star positions — 64

Explanation of altitude correction tables — 67

Altitude correction tables — 68

Sight reduction using a calculator — 69

Explanation of the sight reduction tables — 70

Great Circle Route – course and distance — 77

Sight reduction tables — 79 - 111

List of Other Tables · Page

Values of *a* and *b* for any given year — 61

Minutes and seconds as decimal parts of an hour or degree — 62

Workform for GHA, Dec and observed altitude — 65

Monthly corrections for the sun's limbs — 67

Workform for the sight reduction tables — 76

INTRODUCTION

Aims

Today, celestial navigation is mainly used by the recreational sailing community. Even then, it is not usually used as the principal means of determining a position, but either as an emergency backup in case of malfunction in the electronic navigation, or for the pleasure of learning and practicing an ancient art. Either way, the use of celestial navigation is occasional and infrequent and so a long term almanac which does not need updating every year becomes attractive.

The aim has been to produce an almanac of small size and which will remain valid for a period of 50 years. Ease of use has been a prime consideration in the design of this almanac. Explanations are detailed and examples are given at every stage. However, a working knowledge of celestial navigation is assumed.

Arrangement

The main body of the Almanac consists of ephemerides from which the Greenwich Hour Angle (GHA) of the sun, the declination of the sun and the GHA of Aries may be determined for any time from the year 2000 to 2050. These are based on the fact that approximately correct values for the position of the sun and the GHA of Aries may be obtained from an almanac that is exactly four years out of date. By applying quadrennial correction factors, an ephemeris for any given year may be used to determine the position of the sun and the GHA of Aries to good accuracy exactly four years hence and multiples thereof.

The *Daily tables* for the four years 2000 to 2003 inclusive give the 00 hrs value for the GHA of the sun, the declination of the sun and the GHA of Aries. Quadrennial correction factors are also given so that positions for the sun may be determined for any subsequent year until 2050. Also tabulated are averages for the hourly rates of change for the sun's declination and the hourly acceleration of the sun's GHA for that day. A separate *Tables of GHA increments* allows the increment for any given time of day to be added to the GHA value from the *Daily tables*, so giving the sun's GHA for any time.

The period of validity for these tables has been set at fifty years, that being the period for which simple, linear, quadrennial correction factors for the sun will still give good accuracy for corrected table values. (In fact, good accuracy should be maintained until 2060, but accuracy will deteriorate rapidly thereafter.)

The GHA of Aries may be determined for any given time and date until the year 2060, using the *Daily tables* and the *Tables of GHA increments*.

Tables for the positions of 39 selected navigational stars, including Polaris, are given for the year 2000. Annual correction factors are also given to account for their subsequent apparent motion, so that their positions may be calculated for any subsequent year.

Star charts showing the positions of the selected stars are given. These stars are also shown in the context of prominent constellations and other stars.

Formulae are given for sight reduction using a calculator.

Finally, concise tables for sight reduction are given. The tables given here are a version of the "NAO Sight Reduction Tables" as used in the *Nautical Almanac* since 1989. The tables were originally created by Admiral Davies, founder of the Navigation Foundation, in collaboration with Dr. Paul Janiczek, former Head of the Astronomical Applications Department of the US Naval Observatory. Admiral Davies donated his work on the project to the Nautical Almanac Office in the name of the Navigation Foundation for the benefit of all mariners. An earlier form of the tables, called the *Davies Concise Tables*, was published by Cornell Maritime Press.

Data sources

The Nautical Almanacs for the years 1996 to 1999, published by HMSO, were used as a starting base for the ephemerides given in the *Daily tables*. Quadrennial corrections for the sun and annual corrections for the selected stars were determined using the *Stormy Weather Astro* program, written by Paul Adamthwaite of Stormy Weather Ltd., Picton, Ontario, Canada. This program uses algorithms based on the recent resolutions of the International Astronomical Union, the new standard epoch J2000.0, the FKS system and the new orbital data from the Bureau des Longitudes in Paris, France.

Accuracy

For the earlier years during which these tables are valid, the error of the values for the GHA and declination of the sun as tabulated in the *Daily tables* and corrected using the quadrennial correction should be of the order of 0.25'. In one percent of cases the error will be about 0.5' but the error should never exceed 0.7'. The GHA of Aries as tabulated and as corrected using a constant quadrennial correction factor of 1.84' should generally not be in error by more than 0.3'

However, during the later years for which these tables are valid, uncertainty in the future behaviour of delta T will start to dominate over other potential error sources. By 2050, this uncertainly will contribute errors in the GHA of the sun and Aries of about ±1', (but it could be as much as ±2.5'). See the section on *Time* below.

The Sidereal Hour Angle (SHA) and declination of the stars as tabulated should generally not be in error by more than 0.3' up until the year 2050. The SHA of the selected stars are given for the 15th of each month. A slight increase in accuracy may be achieved using interpolation to achieve the value for the day in question.

The calculated altitude derived using the *Sight reduction tables* will have a precision of 1' and in general the accuracy should also be 1'. The azimuth is calculated to a precision of 0.1°. The tables should not be used for latitudes higher than 80°.

Time

The time system to be used with this almanac is Greenwich Mean Time (GMT), also known as Universal Time, or more particularly UT1, which is based on the mean period of the earth's rotation with reference to the sun. But due to the gradual slowing of the earth's rotation, UT1 is slowly diverging from the broadcast time or Coordinated Universal Time system (UTC) used for civil time keeping, which is determined by atomic clocks.

The difference between UT1 and UTC is known as DUT1 (DUT1 = UT1 – UTC) and currently DUT1 is kept to ±0.9 seconds or less by inserting a "leap second" into UTC approximately once a year. While this practice continues, it is adequate to treat UTC as equivalent to UT1. But at the time of writing (2007) there are arguments that the insertion of leap seconds into UTC should cease. If that happens, it will be necessary to correct UTC by the current value of DUT1 so that UTC may be used with this almanac.

This almanac uses a prediction of how DUT1 (or strictly, the related function delta T) will vary in the future. But short term variations in the earth's rotational period are poorly understood. The result is that by 2050, the value of delta T may differ from that predicted by anything up to ten seconds, but more probably some four or five seconds.

DAILY TABLES

For the GHA and declination of the sun,
and the GHA of Aries

DAY	GHA SUN	HRLY ACCN	QUAD CORR	DEC SUN	HRLY RATE	QUAD CORR	GHA ARIES
01	179°13.9′	−0.30′	−0.02′	S 23°04.2′	−0.20′	−0.16′	99°58.1′
02	179 06.8	−0.30	−0.02	22 59.4	−0.22	−0.17	100 57.3
03	178 59.7	−0.29	−0.02	22 54.2	−0.24	−0.18	101 56.4
04	178 52.8	−0.28	−0.02	22 48.5	−0.25	−0.19	102 55.5
05	178 46.0	−0.28	−0.02	22 42.4	−0.27	−0.21	103 54.7
06	178 39.3	−0.28	−0.01	22 35.9	−0.30	−0.22	104 53.8
07	178 32.6	−0.27	−0.01	22 28.8	−0.31	−0.23	105 53.0
08	178 26.1	−0.26	−0.01	22 21.3	−0.33	−0.25	106 52.1
09	178 19.8	−0.26	−0.01	22 13.4	−0.35	−0.26	107 51.2
10	178 13.5	−0.25	−0.01	22 05.0	−0.36	−0.27	108 50.4
11	178 07.4	−0.25	0.00	21 56.3	−0.38	−0.29	109 49.5
12	178 01.4	−0.25	+0.01	21 47.1	−0.40	−0.30	110 48.7
13	177 55.5	−0.24	+0.02	21 37.5	−0.42	−0.31	111 47.8
14	177 49.8	−0.23	+0.03	21 27.4	−0.43	−0.32	112 46.9
15	177 44.3	−0.23	+0.03	21 17.0	−0.45	−0.33	113 46.1
16	177 38.9	−0.21	+0.04	21 06.1	−0.48	−0.34	114 45.2
17	177 33.8	−0.21	+0.05	20 54.7	−0.48	−0.35	115 44.3
18	177 28.8	−0.20	+0.06	20 43.1	−0.50	−0.36	116 43.5
19	177 23.9	−0.20	+0.06	20 31.0	−0.52	−0.37	117 42.6
20	177 19.2	−0.19	+0.06	20 18.6	−0.54	−0.38	118 41.8
21	177 14.7	−0.18	+0.07	20 05.7	−0.55	−0.39	119 40.9
22	177 10.4	−0.18	+0.08	19 52.5	−0.56	−0.40	120 40.0
23	177 06.2	−0.16	+0.08	19 39.0	−0.58	−0.41	121 39.2
24	177 02.3	−0.15	+0.09	19 25.0	−0.60	−0.42	122 38.3
25	176 58.6	−0.15	+0.09	19 10.7	−0.61	−0.43	123 37.5
26	176 55.0	−0.14	+0.10	18 56.1	−0.63	−0.44	124 36.6
27	176 51.7	−0.13	+0.10	18 41.0	−0.64	−0.45	125 35.7
28	176 48.6	−0.13	+0.11	18 25.6	−0.65	−0.46	126 34.9
29	176 45.6	−0.11	+0.11	18 10.0	−0.67	−0.46	127 34.0
30	176 42.9	−0.10	+0.11	17 54.0	−0.68	−0.47	128 33.1
31	176 40.4	−0.10	+0.12	17 37.7	−0.70	−0.48	129 32.3

VALID FOR THE YEARS	For an *Explanation of Daily tables*, see page 60
2000	For the *Tables of GHA increments*, see page 63
2004	
2008	
2012	
2016	
2020	
2024	
2028	
2032	
2036	
2040	
2044	
2048	

DAY	GHA SUN	HRLY ACCN	QUAD CORR	DEC SUN	HRLY RATE	QUAD CORR	GHA ARIES
01	176°38.1′	−0.09′	+0.12′	S 17°21.0′	−0.70′	−0.49′	130°31.4′
02	176 36.0	−0.08	+0.12	17 04.1	−0.72	−0.50	131 30.6
03	176 34.2	−0.07	+0.12	16 46.8	−0.73	−0.51	132 29.7
04	176 32.5	−0.06	+0.12	16 29.3	−0.74	−0.52	133 28.8
05	176 31.0	−0.05	+0.12	16 11.5	−0.75	−0.53	134 28.0
06	176 29.7	−0.04	+0.13	15 53.4	−0.77	−0.53	135 27.1
07	176 28.7	−0.04	+0.13	15 35.0	−0.78	−0.54	136 26.3
08	176 27.8	−0.03	+0.14	15 16.4	−0.79	−0.54	137 25.4
09	176 27.1	−0.02	+0.14	14 57.4	−0.80	−0.55	138 24.5
10	176 26.7	−0.01	+0.15	14 38.2	−0.81	−0.56	139 23.7
11	176 26.4	0.00	+0.15	14 18.8	−0.82	−0.56	140 22.8
12	176 26.3	0.00	+0.16	13 59.2	−0.83	−0.57	141 22.0
13	176 26.4	+0.01	+0.16	13 39.3	−0.84	−0.58	142 21.1
14	176 26.7	+0.02	+0.17	13 19.2	−0.85	−0.58	143 20.2
15	176 27.2	+0.03	+0.17	12 58.9	−0.85	−0.59	144 19.4
16	176 27.8	+0.03	+0.18	12 38.4	−0.86	−0.60	145 18.5
17	176 28.6	+0.04	+0.18	12 17.7	−0.88	−0.60	146 17.6
18	176 29.6	+0.05	+0.19	11 56.7	−0.88	−0.61	147 16.8
19	176 30.8	+0.05	+0.19	11 35.6	−0.89	−0.61	148 15.9
20	176 32.1	+0.06	+0.20	11 14.3	−0.89	−0.61	149 15.1
21	176 33.6	+0.07	+0.20	10 52.9	−0.90	−0.61	150 14.2
22	176 35.2	+0.08	+0.21	10 31.2	−0.91	−0.62	151 13.3
23	176 37.1	+0.09	+0.21	10 09.4	−0.91	−0.62	152 12.5
24	176 39.1	+0.08	+0.21	9 47.5	−0.92	−0.63	153 11.6
25	176 41.2	+0.10	+0.22	9 25.4	−0.93	−0.64	154 10.8
26	176 43.5	+0.10	+0.22	9 03.1	−0.94	−0.64	155 09.9
27	176 45.9	+0.11	+0.22	8 40.6	−0.94	−0.65	156 09.0
28	176 48.5	+0.11	+0.22	8 18.1	−0.94	−0.65	157 08.2
29	176 51.2	+0.12	+0.22	7 55.5	−0.95	−0.66	158 07.3
30							
31							

VALID FOR THE YEARS	
2000	For an *Explanation of Daily tables*, see page 60
2004	
2008	For the *Tables of GHA increments*, see page 63
2012	
2016	
2020	
2024	
2028	
2032	
2036	
2040	
2044	
2048	

DAY	GHA SUN	HRLY ACCN	QUAD CORR	DEC SUN	HRLY RATE	QUAD CORR	GHA ARIES
01	176°54.1′	+0.13′	+0.22′	S 7°32.7′	−0.95′	−0.66′	159 06.4
02	176 57.1	+0.13	+0.22	7 09.9	−0.96	−0.66	160 05.6
03	177 00.2	+0.13	+0.21	6 46.9	−0.96	−0.67	161 04.7
04	177 03.4	+0.14	+0.21	6 23.9	−0.97	−0.68	162 03.9
05	177 06.8	+0.15	+0.21	6 00.7	−0.97	−0.68	163 03.0
06	177 10.3	+0.15	+0.21	5 37.5	−0.97	−0.68	164 02.1
07	177 13.8	+0.15	+0.21	5 14.2	−0.97	−0.68	165 01.3
08	177 17.5	+0.15	+0.21	4 50.9	−0.98	−0.68	166 00.4
09	177 21.2	+0.16	+0.20	4 27.4	−0.98	−0.69	166 59.6
10	177 25.1	+0.16	+0.20	4 03.9	−0.98	−0.69	167 58.7
11	177 29.0	+0.17	+0.20	3 40.4	−0.98	−0.69	168 57.8
12	177 33.0	+0.17	+0.21	3 16.8	−0.98	−0.69	169 57.0
13	177 37.0	+0.18	+0.21	2 53.2	−0.99	−0.69	170 56.1
14	177 41.2	+0.17	+0.21	2 29.5	−0.99	−0.69	171 55.2
15	177 45.3	+0.18	+0.21	2 05.8	−0.99	−0.69	172 54.4
16	177 49.6	+0.18	+0.21	1 42.1	−0.99	−0.69	173 53.5
17	177 53.8	+0.18	+0.21	1 18.4	−0.99	−0.69	174 52.7
18	177 58.2	+0.18	+0.22	0 54.7	−0.99	−0.69	175 51.8
19	178 02.5	+0.18	+0.22	0 31.0	−0.99	−0.69	176 50.9
20	178 06.9	+0.18	+0.22	S 0 07.3	−0.99	−0.69	177 50.1
21	178 11.3	+0.19	+0.23	N 0 16.5	+0.98	+0.69	178 49.2
22	178 15.8	+0.19	+0.23	0 40.1	+0.99	+0.69	179 48.4
23	178 20.3	+0.19	+0.23	1 03.8	+0.99	+0.69	180 47.5
24	178 24.8	+0.19	+0.22	1 27.5	+0.98	+0.68	181 46.6
25	178 29.4	+0.19	+0.21	1 51.1	+0.98	+0.68	182 45.8
26	178 33.9	+0.19	+0.21	2 14.6	+0.98	+0.68	183 44.9
27	178 38.4	+0.19	+0.20	2 38.1	+0.98	+0.69	184 44.0
28	178 43.0	+0.19	+0.20	3 01.6	+0.98	+0.69	185 43.2
29	178 47.5	+0.19	+0.20	3 25.0	+0.97	+0.69	186 42.3
30	178 52.1	+0.19	+0.19	3 48.3	+0.97	+0.69	187 41.5
31	178 56.6	+0.19	+0.19	4 11.6	+0.96	+0.69	188 40.6

VALID FOR THE YEARS	
2000	For an *Explanation of Daily tables*, see page 60
2004	
2008	For the *Tables of GHA increments*, see page 63
2012	**Declinations for March 20th**
2016	If the summed corrections for the hourly rate and the quadrennial correction exceed −7.3′, then the declination has changed name. In this case, change the signs for the corrections to +, take 7.3′ from the summed corrections and change the name to North.
2020	
2024	
2028	
2032	**Declinations for March 19th (for 2044 and on)**
2036	For 2044 and the years following, the Equinox will fall on this date. Read as above for March 20th, but using 31.0′ in place of 7.3′.
2040	
2044	
2048	

DAY	GHA SUN	HRLY ACCN	QUAD CORR	DEC SUN	HRLY RATE	QUAD CORR	GHA ARIES
01	179°01.1'	+0.18'	+0.18'	N 4°34.7'	+0.96'	+0.69'	189°39.7'
02	179 05.5	+0.19	+0.18	4 57.8	+0.96	+0.69	190 38.9
03	179 10.0	+0.18	+0.17	5 20.9	+0.95	+0.68	191 38.0
04	179 14.4	+0.18	+0.16	5 43.8	+0.95	+0.68	192 37.2
05	179 18.8	+0.18	+0.16	6 06.6	+0.95	+0.68	193 36.3
06	179 23.1	+0.18	+0.15	6 29.3	+0.94	+0.68	194 35.4
07	179 27.3	+0.18	+0.14	6 51.9	+0.94	+0.68	195 34.6
08	179 31.5	+0.17	+0.14	7 14.4	+0.93	+0.67	196 33.7
09	179 35.6	+0.17	+0.13	7 36.8	+0.93	+0.67	197 32.9
10	179 39.7	+0.17	+0.13	7 59.0	+0.92	+0.66	198 32.0
11	179 43.7	+0.16	+0.13	8 21.1	+0.92	+0.66	199 31.1
12	179 47.6	+0.16	+0.12	8 43.1	+0.91	+0.65	200 30.3
13	179 51.5	+0.15	+0.12	9 04.9	+0.90	+0.65	201 29.4
14	179 55.2	+0.15	+0.12	9 26.6	+0.90	+0.65	202 28.5
15	179 58.9	+0.14	+0.11	9 48.1	+0.88	+0.65	203 27.7
16	180 02.3	+0.15	+0.11	10 09.3	+0.88	+0.64	204 26.8
17	180 05.9	+0.14	+0.11	10 30.5	+0.88	+0.63	205 26.0
18	180 09.3	+0.14	+0.11	10 51.5	+0.87	+0.62	206 25.1
19	180 12.6	+0.13	+0.11	11 12.4	+0.86	+0.61	207 24.2
20	180 15.8	+0.13	+0.11	11 33.0	+0.85	+0.61	208 23.4
21	180 18.9	+0.12	+0.10	11 53.5	+0.84	+0.60	209 22.5
22	180 21.8	+0.12	+0.10	12 13.7	+0.84	+0.60	210 21.7
23	180 24.7	+0.12	+0.09	12 33.8	+0.83	+0.59	211 20.8
24	180 27.5	+0.11	+0.09	12 53.6	+0.82	+0.59	212 19.9
25	180 30.1	+0.10	+0.08	13 13.3	+0.81	+0.58	213 19.1
26	180 32.6	+0.10	+0.07	13 32.7	+0.80	+0.58	214 18.2
27	180 35.1	+0.09	+0.06	13 51.9	+0.79	+0.57	215 17.3
28	180 37.3	+0.09	+0.05	14 10.9	+0.78	+0.56	216 16.5
29	180 39.4	+0.08	+0.04	14 29.6	+0.77	+0.55	217 15.6
30	180 41.4	+0.08	+0.03	14 48.1	+0.76	+0.55	218 14.8
31							

VALID FOR THE YEARS	For an *Explanation of Daily tables*, see page 60
2000	For the *Tables of GHA increments*, see page 63
2004	
2008	
2012	
2016	
2020	
2024	
2028	
2032	
2036	
2040	
2044	
2048	

DAY	GHA SUN	HRLY ACCN	QUAD CORR	DEC SUN	HRLY RATE	QUAD CORR	GHA ARIES
01	180°43.3'	+0.08'	+0.02'	N 15°06.3'	+0.75'	+0.54'	219°13.9'
02	180 45.1	+0.07	+0.01	15 24.3	+0.74	+0.54	220 13.0
03	180 46.8	+0.06	0.00	15 42.0	+0.73	+0.53	221 12.2
04	180 48.3	+0.05	−0.01	15 59.5	+0.72	+0.53	222 11.3
05	180 49.6	+0.05	−0.02	16 16.7	+0.71	+0.52	223 10.5
06	180 50.8	+0.05	−0.03	16 33.7	+0.70	+0.51	224 09.6
07	180 51.9	+0.04	−0.03	16 50.4	+0.68	+0.50	225 08.7
08	180 52.8	+0.03	−0.03	17 06.8	+0.67	+0.49	226 07.9
09	180 53.6	+0.03	−0.04	17 22.9	+0.66	+0.49	227 07.0
10	180 54.2	+0.02	−0.04	17 38.7	+0.65	+0.48	228 06.1
11	180 54.7	+0.01	−0.04	17 54.2	+0.64	+0.46	229 05.3
12	180 55.0	0.00	−0.05	18 09.5	+0.62	+0.45	230 04.4
13	180 55.1	0.00	−0.05	18 24.3	+0.61	+0.44	231 03.6
14	180 55.2	0.00	−0.05	18 38.9	+0.60	+0.43	232 02.7
15	180 55.1	−0.01	−0.06	18 53.2	+0.58	+0.42	233 01.8
16	180 54.8	−0.01	−0.06	19 07.2	+0.57	+0.41	234 01.0
17	180 54.5	−0.03	−0.07	19 20.9	+0.55	+0.40	235 00.1
18	180 53.9	−0.03	−0.07	19 34.2	+0.54	+0.39	235 59.3
19	180 53.3	−0.03	−0.08	19 47.2	+0.53	+0.38	236 58.4
20	180 52.5	−0.04	−0.09	19 59.8	+0.52	+0.37	237 57.5
21	180 51.5	−0.04	−0.09	20 12.2	+0.50	+0.36	238 56.7
22	180 50.5	−0.05	−0.10	20 24.1	+0.48	+0.35	239 55.8
23	180 49.3	−0.05	−0.11	20 35.7	+0.47	+0.34	240 54.9
24	180 48.0	−0.06	−0.11	20 46.9	+0.45	+0.33	241 54.1
25	180 46.5	−0.06	−0.12	20 57.8	+0.44	+0.32	242 53.2
26	180 45.0	−0.07	−0.13	21 08.4	+0.43	+0.31	243 52.4
27	180 43.3	−0.08	−0.13	21 18.6	+0.41	+0.30	244 51.5
28	180 41.5	−0.08	−0.14	21 28.4	+0.39	+0.28	245 50.6
29	180 39.5	−0.08	−0.15	21 37.8	+0.38	+0.27	246 49.8
30	180 37.5	−0.09	−0.16	21 46.9	+0.36	+0.26	247 48.9
31	180 35.4	−0.09	−0.17	21 55.6	+0.34	+0.25	248 48.1

VALID FOR THE YEARS	
2000	For an *Explanation of Daily tables*, see page 60
2004	
2008	For the *Tables of GHA increments*, see page 63
2012	
2016	
2020	
2024	
2028	
2032	
2036	
2040	
2044	
2048	

DAY	GHA SUN	HRLY ACCN	QUAD CORR	DEC SUN	HRLY RATE	QUAD CORR	GHA ARIES
01	180°33.2′	−0.10′	−0.18′	N 22°03.8′	+0.33′	+0.24′	249°47.2′
02	180 30.9	−0.10	−0.19	22 11.7	+0.32	+0.22	250 46.3
03	180 28.5	−0.10	−0.19	22 19.3	+0.30	+0.21	251 45.5
04	180 26.0	−0.11	−0.20	22 26.4	+0.28	+0.20	252 44.6
05	180 23.4	−0.11	−0.20	22 33.0	+0.28	+0.18	253 43.7
06	180 20.7	−0.11	−0.21	22 39.6	+0.25	+0.17	254 42.9
07	180 18.0	−0.12	−0.21	22 45.5	+0.23	+0.16	255 42.0
08	180 15.2	−0.12	−0.21	22 51.0	+0.22	+0.14	256 41.2
09	180 12.3	−0.13	−0.21	22 56.2	+0.20	+0.13	257 40.3
10	180 09.3	−0.13	−0.21	23 00.9	+0.18	+0.12	258 39.4
11	180 06.3	−0.13	−0.21	23 05.3	+0.16	+0.10	259 38.6
12	180 03.2	−0.13	−0.21	23 09.2	+0.15	+0.09	260 37.7
13	180 00.1	−0.13	−0.21	23 12.8	+0.13	+0.08	261 36.9
14	179 56.9	−0.13	−0.21	23 15.9	+0.11	+0.06	262 36.0
15	179 53.7	−0.13	−0.21	23 18.6	+0.09	+0.05	263 35.1
16	179 50.5	−0.14	−0.21	23 20.8	+0.08	+0.04	264 34.3
17	179 47.2	−0.13	−0.21	23 22.7	+0.06	+0.02	265 33.4
18	179 44.0	−0.14	−0.21	23 24.2	+0.05	+0.01	266 32.5
19	179 40.7	−0.14	−0.21	23 25.3	+0.03	0.00	267 31.7
20	179 37.4	−0.14	−0.21	23 26.0	+0.01	−0.01	268 30.8
21	179 34.1	−0.13	−0.21	23 26.2	−0.01	−0.03	269 30.0
22	179 30.9	−0.14	−0.21	23 26.0	−0.03	−0.05	270 29.1
23	179 27.6	−0.13	−0.21	23 25.4	−0.04	−0.07	271 28.2
24	179 24.4	−0.13	−0.22	23 24.4	−0.06	−0.09	272 27.4
25	179 21.2	−0.13	−0.22	23 23.0	−0.08	−0.11	273 26.5
26	179 18.0	−0.13	−0.22	23 21.2	−0.10	−0.11	274 25.7
27	179 14.9	−0.13	−0.23	23 18.9	−0.11	−0.12	275 24.8
28	179 11.9	−0.13	−0.23	23 16.3	−0.13	−0.12	276 23.9
29	179 08.8	−0.12	−0.23	23 13.3	−0.15	−0.14	277 23.1
30	179 05.9	−0.12	−0.23	23 09.7	−0.16	−0.15	278 22.2
31							

VALID FOR THE YEARS	For an *Explanation of Daily tables*, see page 60
2000	For the *Tables of GHA increments*, see page 63
2004	
2008	
2012	
2016	
2020	
2024	
2028	
2032	
2036	
2040	
2044	
2048	

DAY	GHA SUN	HRLY ACCN	QUAD CORR	DEC SUN	HRLY RATE	QUAD CORR	GHA ARIES
01	179°03.0′	−0.12′	−0.23′	N 23°05.9′	−0.18′	−0.17′	279°21.3′
02	179 00.1	−0.11	−0.23	23 01.6	−0.19	−0.18	280 20.5
03	178 57.4	−0.11	−0.23	22 57.0	−0.21	−0.20	281 19.6
04	178 54.7	−0.11	−0.23	22 51.9	−0.23	−0.21	282 18.8
05	178 52.0	−0.10	−0.23	22 46.4	−0.24	−0.22	283 17.9
06	178 49.5	−0.10	−0.22	22 40.6	−0.26	−0.23	284 17.0
07	178 47.0	−0.10	−0.22	22 34.3	−0.28	−0.24	285 16.2
08	178 44.7	−0.10	−0.22	22 27.6	−0.29	−0.25	286 15.3
09	178 42.4	−0.09	−0.21	22 20.6	−0.31	−0.27	287 14.5
10	178 40.3	−0.09	−0.21	22 13.1	−0.32	−0.28	288 13.6
11	178 38.2	−0.08	−0.20	22 05.4	−0.34	−0.29	289 12.7
12	178 36.2	−0.08	−0.20	21 57.2	−0.36	−0.30	290 11.9
13	178 34.4	−0.07	−0.19	21 48.6	−0.37	−0.31	291 11.0
14	178 32.7	−0.07	−0.19	21 39.7	−0.39	−0.32	292 10.1
15	178 31.1	−0.06	−0.18	21 30.4	−0.41	−0.34	293 09.3
16	178 29.6	−0.06	−0.17	21 20.6	−0.42	−0.35	294 08.4
17	178 28.2	−0.05	−0.16	21 10.6	−0.43	−0.36	295 07.6
18	178 27.0	−0.05	−0.16	21 00.2	−0.45	−0.38	296 06.7
19	178 25.9	−0.04	−0.15	20 49.5	−0.46	−0.39	297 05.8
20	178 25.0	−0.03	−0.14	20 38.4	−0.48	−0.40	298 05.0
21	178 24.2	−0.03	−0.14	20 27.0	−0.49	−0.41	299 04.1
22	178 23.6	−0.02	−0.13	20 15.2	−0.50	−0.42	300 03.3
23	178 23.1	−0.02	−0.13	20 03.1	−0.53	−0.43	301 02.4
24	178 22.7	−0.01	−0.12	19 50.5	−0.53	−0.45	302 01.5
25	178 22.5	0.00	−0.12	19 37.8	−0.55	−0.46	303 00.7
26	178 22.5	0.00	−0.12	19 24.7	−0.56	−0.47	303 59.8
27	178 22.6	+0.01	−0.12	19 11.2	−0.57	−0.48	304 58.9
28	178 22.8	+0.02	−0.12	18 57.5	−0.59	−0.49	305 58.1
29	178 23.3	+0.02	−0.12	18 43.4	−0.60	−0.50	306 57.2
30	178 23.8	+0.03	−0.12	18 29.1	−0.61	−0.51	307 56.4
31	178 24.5	+0.04	−0.11	18 14.4	−0.63	−0.52	308 55.5

VALID FOR THE YEARS	For an *Explanation of Daily tables*, see page 60
2000	For the *Tables of GHA increments*, see page 63
2004	
2008	
2012	
2016	
2020	
2024	
2028	
2032	
2036	
2040	
2044	
2048	

DAY	GHA SUN	HRLY ACCN	QUAD CORR	DEC SUN	HRLY RATE	QUAD CORR	GHA ARIES
01	178°25.4'	+0.04'	−0.11'	N 17°59.4'	−0.63'	−0.52'	309°54.6'
02	178 26.4	+0.05	−0.11	17 44.2	−0.65	−0.53	310 53.8
03	178 27.6	+0.05	−0.10	17 28.6	−0.66	−0.54	311 52.9
04	178 28.9	+0.06	−0.10	17 12.7	−0.67	−0.55	312 52.1
05	178 30.3	+0.07	−0.10	16 56.6	−0.68	−0.56	313 51.2
06	178 31.9	+0.08	−0.09	16 40.2	−0.70	−0.56	314 50.3
07	178 33.7	+0.08	−0.08	16 23.5	−0.70	−0.57	315 49.5
08	178 35.5	+0.09	−0.07	16 06.6	−0.72	−0.58	316 48.6
09	178 37.6	+0.09	−0.05	15 49.4	−0.73	−0.59	317 47.7
10	178 39.8	+0.10	−0.04	15 32.0	−0.74	−0.60	318 46.9
11	178 42.1	+0.10	−0.03	15 14.3	−0.75	−0.61	319 46.0
12	178 44.6	+0.11	−0.02	14 56.4	−0.76	−0.61	320 45.2
13	178 47.2	+0.11	−0.02	14 38.2	−0.77	−0.62	321 44.3
14	178 49.9	+0.12	−0.01	14 19.8	−0.78	−0.63	322 43.4
15	178 52.8	+0.13	−0.01	14 01.2	−0.78	−0.63	323 42.6
16	178 55.8	+0.13	0.00	13 42.4	−0.80	−0.64	324 41.7
17	178 58.9	+0.14	+0.01	13 23.3	−0.81	−0.64	325 40.9
18	179 02.2	+0.14	+0.01	13 03.9	−0.81	−0.65	326 40.0
19	179 05.5	+0.15	+0.02	12 44.4	−0.82	−0.65	327 39.1
20	179 09.1	+0.15	+0.02	12 24.7	−0.83	−0.66	328 38.3
21	179 12.7	+0.15	+0.03	12 04.9	−0.84	−0.67	329 37.4
22	179 16.4	+0.16	+0.03	11 44.8	−0.85	−0.68	330 36.5
23	179 20.3	+0.17	+0.03	11 24.5	−0.85	−0.68	331 35.7
24	179 24.3	+0.17	+0.03	11 04.1	−0.86	−0.69	332 34.8
25	179 28.4	+0.18	+0.03	10 43.5	−0.87	−0.69	333 34.0
26	179 32.6	+0.18	+0.03	10 22.7	−0.88	−0.69	334 33.1
27	179 36.9	+0.18	+0.03	10 01.7	−0.88	−0.70	335 32.2
28	179 41.3	+0.18	+0.03	9 40.6	−0.88	−0.70	336 31.4
29	179 45.7	+0.19	+0.03	9 19.4	−0.90	−0.71	337 30.5
30	179 50.3	+0.20	+0.03	8 57.9	−0.90	−0.71	338 29.7
31	179 55.0	+0.20	+0.04	8 36.4	−0.90	−0.72	339 28.8

VALID FOR THE YEARS	For an *Explanation of Daily tables*, see page 60
2000	For the *Tables of GHA increments*, see page 63
2004	
2008	
2012	
2016	
2020	
2024	
2028	
2032	
2036	
2040	
2044	
2048	

DAY	GHA SUN	HRLY ACCN	QUAD CORR	DEC SUN	HRLY RATE	QUAD CORR	GHA ARIES
01	179°59.7'	+0.20'	+0.04'	N 8°14.7'	-0.91'	-0.72'	340°27.9'
02	180 04.5	+0.20	+0.04	7 52.9	-0.92	-0.72	341 27.1
03	180 09.4	+0.21	+0.05	7 30.9	-0.92	-0.72	342 26.2
04	180 14.4	+0.20	+0.05	7 08.8	-0.92	-0.72	343 25.3
05	180 19.3	+0.21	+0.06	6 46.7	-0.93	-0.72	344 24.5
06	180 24.4	+0.21	+0.06	6 24.4	-0.94	-0.73	345 23.6
07	180 29.5	+0.21	+0.07	6 01.9	-0.94	-0.73	346 22.8
08	180 34.6	+0.22	+0.08	5 39.4	-0.94	-0.73	347 21.9
09	180 39.8	+0.22	+0.08	5 16.8	-0.95	-0.73	348 21.0
10	180 45.0	+0.22	+0.09	4 54.1	-0.95	-0.73	349 20.2
11	180 50.2	+0.22	+0.09	4 31.4	-0.95	-0.73	350 19.3
12	180 55.5	+0.22	+0.10	4 08.5	-0.95	-0.74	351 18.5
13	181 00.8	+0.22	+0.10	3 45.6	-0.96	-0.74	352 17.6
14	181 06.1	+0.22	+0.10	3 22.6	-0.96	-0.74	353 16.7
15	181 11.4	+0.22	+0.11	2 59.5	-0.96	-0.74	354 15.9
16	181 16.7	+0.23	+0.11	2 36.4	-0.97	-0.74	355 15.0
17	181 22.1	+0.22	+0.11	2 13.2	-0.97	-0.74	356 14.2
18	181 27.4	+0.22	+0.12	1 50.0	-0.97	-0.74	357 13.3
19	181 32.7	+0.22	+0.12	1 26.8	-0.97	-0.74	358 12.4
20	181 38.0	+0.23	+0.12	1 03.5	-0.97	-0.74	359 11.6
21	181 43.4	+0.22	+0.11	0 40.2	-0.98	-0.74	0 10.7
22	181 48.7	+0.22	+0.11	N 0 16.8	-0.97	-0.74	1 09.8
23	181 53.9	+0.22	+0.11	S 0 06.5	+0.98	+0.74	2 09.0
24	181 59.2	+0.22	+0.10	0 29.9	+0.98	+0.73	3 08.1
25	182 04.4	+0.22	+0.10	0 53.3	+0.97	+0.73	4 07.3
26	182 09.6	+0.21	+0.10	1 16.6	+0.98	+0.73	5 06.4
27	182 14.7	+0.21	+0.10	1 40.0	+0.97	+0.74	6 05.5
28	182 19.8	+0.21	+0.10	2 03.3	+0.98	+0.74	7 04.7
29	182 24.8	+0.21	+0.10	2 26.7	+0.97	+0.74	8 03.8
30	182 29.8	+0.20	+0.09	2 50.0	+0.97	+0.73	9 03.0
31							

VALID FOR THE YEARS	
2000	For an *Explanation of Daily tables*, see page 60
2004	
2008	For the *Tables of GHA increments*, see page 63
2012	**Declinations for September 22nd**
2016	If the summed corrections for the hourly rate and the
2020	quadrennial correction exceed –16.8', then the declination
2024	has changed name. In this case, change the signs for the
2028	corrections to +, take 16.8' from the summed corrections
2032	and change the name to South.
2036	
2040	
2044	
2048	

DAY	GHA SUN	HRLY ACCN	QUAD CORR	DEC SUN	HRLY RATE	QUAD CORR	GHA ARIES
01	182°34.7′	+0.20′	+0.09′	S 3°13.3′	+0.97′	+0.73′	10°02.1′
02	182 39.5	+0.20	+0.09	3 36.5	+0.97	+0.73	11 01.2
03	182 44.2	+0.20	+0.09	3 59.7	+0.97	+0.72	12 00.4
04	182 48.9	+0.19	+0.09	4 22.9	+0.96	+0.72	12 59.5
05	182 53.4	+0.19	+0.09	4 46.0	+0.96	+0.72	13 58.6
06	182 57.9	+0.18	+0.10	5 09.0	+0.96	+0.71	14 57.8
07	183 02.2	+0.18	+0.10	5 32.0	+0.95	+0.71	15 56.9
08	183 06.5	+0.17	+0.10	5 54.9	+0.95	+0.71	16 56.1
09	183 10.6	+0.17	+0.11	6 17.8	+0.95	+0.70	17 55.2
10	183 14.6	+0.16	+0.11	6 40.5	+0.95	+0.70	18 54.3
11	183 18.5	+0.16	+0.11	7 03.2	+0.94	+0.69	19 53.5
12	183 22.3	+0.15	+0.11	7 25.8	+0.94	+0.69	20 52.6
13	183 26.0	+0.15	+0.11	7 48.3	+0.93	+0.68	21 51.8
14	183 29.5	+0.14	+0.11	8 10.6	+0.93	+0.68	22 50.9
15	183 32.9	+0.13	+0.11	8 32.9	+0.92	+0.67	23 50.0
16	183 36.1	+0.13	+0.11	8 55.0	+0.92	+0.67	24 49.2
17	183 39.2	+0.13	+0.11	9 17.1	+0.91	+0.66	25 48.3
18	183 42.2	+0.12	+0.10	9 38.9	+0.90	+0.65	26 47.4
19	183 45.0	+0.11	+0.10	10 00.6	+0.90	+0.64	27 46.6
20	183 47.7	+0.10	+0.09	10 22.1	+0.90	+0.64	28 45.7
21	183 50.2	+0.10	+0.09	10 43.6	+0.89	+0.63	29 44.9
22	183 52.5	+0.09	+0.08	11 04.9	+0.88	+0.63	30 44.0
23	183 54.7	+0.08	+0.07	11 26.0	+0.87	+0.63	31 43.1
24	183 56.7	+0.08	+0.07	11 46.9	+0.86	+0.62	32 42.3
25	183 58.6	+0.07	+0.06	12 07.6	+0.86	+0.62	33 41.4
26	184 00.2	+0.06	+0.06	12 28.2	+0.85	+0.61	34 40.6
27	184 01.7	+0.05	+0.05	12 48.6	+0.84	+0.60	35 39.7
28	184 03.0	+0.05	+0.05	13 08.8	+0.83	+0.59	36 38.8
29	184 04.1	+0.04	+0.05	13 28.7	+0.83	+0.58	37 38.0
30	184 05.0	+0.03	+0.05	13 48.5	+0.81	+0.57	38 37.1
31	184 05.6	+0.02	+0.04	14 08.0	+0.81	+0.56	39 36.3

VALID FOR THE YEARS	For an *Explanation of Daily tables*, see page 60
2000	For the *Tables of GHA increments*, see page 63
2004	
2008	
2012	
2016	
2020	
2024	
2028	
2032	
2036	
2040	
2044	
2048	

DAY	GHA SUN	HRLY ACCN	QUAD CORR	DEC SUN	HRLY RATE	QUAD CORR	GHA ARIES
01	184°06.1′	+0.01′	+0.04′	S 14°27.4′	+0.79′	+0.56′	40°35.4′
02	184 06.4	0.00	+0.04	14 46.4	+0.79	+0.55	41 34.5
03	184 06.5	0.00	+0.03	15 05.3	+0.77	+0.55	42 33.7
04	184 06.4	−0.02	+0.03	15 23.8	+0.76	+0.54	43 32.8
05	184 06.1	−0.02	+0.03	15 42.1	+0.75	+0.53	44 31.9
06	184 05.6	−0.03	+0.03	16 00.2	+0.75	+0.51	45 31.1
07	184 04.8	−0.04	+0.03	16 18.1	+0.73	+0.50	46 30.2
08	184 03.9	−0.05	+0.03	16 35.6	+0.72	+0.49	47 29.4
09	184 02.7	−0.06	+0.03	16 52.9	+0.71	+0.49	48 28.5
10	184 01.3	−0.07	+0.03	17 09.9	+0.70	+0.48	49 27.6
11	183 59.7	−0.08	+0.03	17 26.6	+0.68	+0.47	50 26.8
12	183 57.9	−0.08	+0.02	17 43.0	+0.67	+0.46	51 25.9
13	183 55.9	−0.09	+0.02	17 59.0	+0.65	+0.45	52 25.1
14	183 53.7	−0.10	+0.02	18 14.7	+0.65	+0.44	53 24.2
15	183 51.2	−0.11	+0.01	18 30.2	+0.63	+0.43	54 23.3
16	183 48.6	−0.12	+0.01	18 45.3	+0.62	+0.42	55 22.5
17	183 45.7	−0.13	0.00	19 00.1	+0.60	+0.41	56 21.6
18	183 42.7	−0.14	0.00	19 14.6	+0.59	+0.39	57 20.7
19	183 39.4	−0.15	−0.01	19 28.7	+0.57	+0.38	58 19.9
20	183 35.9	−0.15	−0.01	19 42.4	+0.56	+0.37	59 19.0
21	183 32.3	−0.16	−0.02	19 55.8	+0.55	+0.36	60 18.2
22	183 28.4	−0.17	−0.02	20 08.9	+0.52	+0.35	61 17.3
23	183 24.4	−0.18	−0.03	20 21.4	+0.51	+0.34	62 16.4
24	183 20.2	−0.19	−0.03	20 33.7	+0.50	+0.33	63 15.6
25	183 15.7	−0.20	−0.04	20 45.6	+0.48	+0.32	64 14.7
26	183 11.0	−0.20	−0.05	20 57.2	+0.46	+0.31	65 13.9
27	183 06.2	−0.21	−0.05	21 08.3	+0.45	+0.30	66 13.0
28	183 01.2	−0.22	−0.06	21 19.0	+0.43	+0.29	67 12.1
29	182 56.0	−0.22	−0.06	21 29.4	+0.41	+0.28	68 11.3
30	182 50.7	−0.23	−0.07	21 39.3	+0.40	+0.26	69 10.4
31							

VALID FOR THE YEARS	
2000	For an *Explanation of Daily tables*, see page 60
2004	
2008	For the *Tables of GHA increments*, see page 63
2012	
2016	
2020	
2024	
2028	
2032	
2036	
2040	
2044	
2048	

DAY	GHA SUN	HRLY ACCN	QUAD CORR	DEC SUN	HRLY RATE	QUAD CORR	GHA ARIES
01	182°45.2′	−0.24′	−0.07′	S 21°48.8′	+0.38′	+0.25′	70°09.6′
02	182 39.5	−0.24	−0.07	21 57.8	+0.36	+0.24	71 08.7
03	182 33.7	−0.25	−0.07	22 06.5	+0.34	+0.22	72 07.8
04	182 27.7	−0.26	−0.07	22 14.7	+0.33	+0.21	73 07.0
05	182 21.5	−0.26	−0.07	22 22.5	+0.31	+0.20	74 06.1
06	182 15.3	−0.27	−0.07	22 29.9	+0.29	+0.17	75 05.2
07	182 08.9	−0.28	−0.07	22 36.9	+0.27	+0.16	76 04.4
08	182 02.3	−0.28	−0.07	22 43.4	+0.25	+0.15	77 03.5
09	181 55.6	−0.28	−0.06	22 49.3	+0.23	+0.14	78 02.7
10	181 48.9	−0.29	−0.06	22 54.9	+0.22	+0.13	79 01.8
11	181 42.0	−0.29	−0.06	23 00.1	+0.20	+0.12	80 00.9
12	181 35.0	−0.30	−0.05	23 04.8	+0.18	+0.10	81 00.1
13	181 27.9	−0.30	−0.05	23 09.0	+0.16	+0.09	81 59.2
14	181 20.8	−0.30	−0.05	23 12.8	+0.14	+0.07	82 58.4
15	181 13.6	−0.30	−0.05	23 16.1	+0.12	+0.06	83 57.5
16	181 06.3	−0.30	−0.05	23 18.9	+0.10	+0.04	84 56.6
17	180 59.0	−0.31	−0.05	23 21.3	+0.08	+0.03	85 55.8
18	180 51.6	−0.31	−0.05	23 23.2	+0.06	+0.02	86 54.9
19	180 44.2	−0.31	−0.05	23 24.6	+0.04	+0.01	87 54.1
20	180 36.8	−0.31	−0.05	23 25.6	+0.02	−0.01	88 53.2
21	180 29.4	−0.31	−0.06	23 26.1	0.00	−0.02	89 52.3
22	180 21.9	−0.31	−0.06	23 26.2	−0.02	−0.04	90 51.5
23	180 14.5	−0.31	−0.06	23 25.7	−0.04	−0.05	91 50.6
24	180 07.0	−0.31	−0.07	23 24.8	−0.06	−0.07	92 49.7
25	179 59.6	−0.31	−0.07	23 23.4	−0.08	−0.08	93 48.9
26	179 32.2	−0.31	−0.07	23 21.5	−0.10	−0.09	94 48.0
27	179 44.8	−0.30	−0.07	23 19.2	−0.11	−0.11	95 47.2
28	179 37.5	−0.30	−0.07	23 16.5	−0.14	−0.12	96 46.3
29	179 30.2	−0.30	−0.07	23 13.2	−0.16	−0.13	97 45.4
30	179 22.9	−0.30	−0.06	23 09.4	−0.18	−0.15	98 44.6
31	179 15.7	−0.30	−0.06	23 05.2	−0.19	−0.16	99 43.7

VALID FOR THE YEARS	
2000	For an *Explanation of Daily tables*, see page 60
2004	
2008	For the *Tables of GHA increments*, see page 63
2012	
2016	
2020	
2024	
2028	
2032	
2036	
2040	
2044	
2048	

DAY	GHA SUN	HRLY ACCN	QUAD CORR	DEC SUN	HRLY RATE	QUAD CORR	GHA ARIES
01	179°08.6′	−0.30′	−0.05′	S 23°00.6′	−0.21′	−0.17′	100°42.9′
02	179 01.5	−0.28	−0.05	22 55.5	−0.23	−0.18	101 42.0
03	178 54.7	−0.29	−0.04	22 49.9	−0.25	−0.19	102 41.1
04	178 47.8	−0.28	−0.04	22 43.9	−0.27	−0.20	103 40.3
05	178 41.0	−0.28	−0.03	22 37.5	−0.29	−0.21	104 39.4
06	178 34.3	−0.28	−0.02	22 30.6	−0.31	−0.23	105 38.6
07	178 27.7	−0.27	−0.01	22 23.2	−0.33	−0.24	106 37.7
08	178 21.3	−0.26	−0.01	22 15.3	−0.34	−0.25	107 36.8
09	178 15.0	−0.26	0.00	22 07.1	−0.36	−0.26	108 36.0
10	178 08.8	−0.25	0.00	21 58.4	−0.38	−0.27	109 35.1
11	178 02.7	−0.25	0.00	21 49.3	−0.40	−0.28	110 34.3
12	177 56.8	−0.24	+0.01	21 39.8	−0.41	−0.30	111 33.4
13	177 51.1	−0.23	+0.02	21 29.9	−0.43	−0.31	112 32.5
14	177 45.5	−0.23	+0.03	21 19.5	−0.45	−0.32	113 31.7
15	177 40.1	−0.22	+0.03	21 08.8	−0.47	−0.33	114 30.8
16	177 34.8	−0.21	+0.04	20 57.6	−0.49	−0.34	115 29.9
17	177 29.7	−0.20	+0.04	20 45.9	−0.50	−0.35	116 29.1
18	177 24.9	−0.20	+0.04	20 34.0	−0.52	−0.37	117 28.2
19	177 20.2	−0.19	+0.04	20 21.6	−0.53	−0.38	118 27.4
20	177 15.6	−0.18	+0.04	20 08.9	−0.55	−0.39	119 26.5
21	177 11.3	−0.17	+0.04	19 55.8	−0.56	−0.40	120 25.6
22	177 07.2	−0.16	+0.04	19 42.3	−0.58	−0.41	121 24.8
23	177 03.3	−0.15	+0.05	19 28.5	−0.60	−0.42	122 23.9
24	176 59.6	−0.15	+0.06	19 14.2	−0.60	−0.43	123 23.1
25	176 56.0	−0.14	+0.06	18 59.7	−0.63	−0.44	124 22.2
26	176 52.7	−0.13	+0.06	18 44.7	−0.64	−0.45	125 21.3
27	176 49.5	−0.12	+0.06	18 29.4	−0.65	−0.46	126 20.5
28	176 46.6	−0.12	+0.06	18 13.8	−0.66	−0.47	127 19.6
29	176 43.8	−0.10	+0.07	17 57.9	−0.68	−0.48	128 18.8
30	176 41.3	−0.10	+0.08	17 41.7	−0.69	−0.49	129 17.9
31	176 38.9	−0.09	+0.08	17 25.1	−0.70	−0.50	130 17.0

VALID FOR THE YEARS	
2001	For an *Explanation of Daily tables*, see page 60
2005	
2009	For the *Tables of GHA increments*, see page 63
2013	
2017	
2021	
2025	
2029	
2033	
2037	
2041	
2045	
2049	

DAY	GHA SUN	HRLY ACCN	QUAD CORR	DEC SUN	HRLY RATE	QUAD CORR	GHA ARIES
01	176°36.8′	−0.08′	+0.09′	S 17°08.3′	−0.72′	−0.5′1	131°16.2′
02	176 34.8	−0.08	+0.10	16 51.1	−0.73	−0.52	132 15.3
03	176 33.0	−0.06	+0.10	16 33.6	−0.74	−0.52	133 14.4
04	176 31.5	−0.06	+0.11	16 15.9	−0.75	−0.53	134 13.6
05	176 30.1	−0.05	+0.12	15 57.8	−0.76	−0.53	135 12.7
06	176 29.0	−0.04	+0.13	15 39.5	−0.78	−0.54	136 11.9
07	176 28.0	−0.03	+0.14	15 20.9	−0.79	−0.54	137 11.0
08	176 27.3	−0.02	+0.15	15 02.0	−0.80	−0.55	138 10.1
09	176 26.8	−0.02	+0.15	14 42.9	−0.80	−0.56	139 09.3
10	176 26.4	−0.01	+0.16	14 23.6	−0.82	−0.57	140 08.4
11	176 26.2	0.00	+0.16	14 04.0	−0.83	−0.57	141 07.6
12	176 26.3	+0.01	+0.17	13 44.2	−0.84	−0.58	142 06.7
13	176 26.5	+0.02	+0.17	13 24.1	−0.84	−0.58	143 05.8
14	176 26.9	+0.03	+0.17	13 03.9	−0.85	−0.59	144 05.0
15	176 27.5	+0.03	+0.17	12 43.4	−0.86	−0.59	145 04.1
16	176 28.3	+0.04	+0.17	12 22.7	−0.87	−0.60	146 03.2
17	176 29.3	+0.05	+0.17	12 01.9	−0.88	−0.61	147 02.4
18	176 30.4	+0.05	+0.18	11 40.8	−0.88	−0.62	148 01.5
19	176 31.7	+0.06	+0.18	11 19.6	−0.90	−0.63	149 00.7
20	176 33.2	+0.07	+0.18	10 58.1	−0.90	−0.63	149 59.8
21	176 34.9	+0.08	+0.18	10 36.5	−0.90	−0.64	150 58.9
22	176 36.7	+0.08	+0.18	10 14.8	−0.91	−0.64	151 58.1
23	176 38.7	+0.09	+0.18	9 52.9	−0.93	−0.64	152 57.2
24	176 40.0	+0.10	+0.18	9 30.7	−0.93	−0.65	153 56.4
25	176 43.1	+0.10	+0.18	9 08.5	−0.93	−0.65	154 55.5
26	176 45.6	+0.10	+0.18	8 46.2	−0.94	−0.66	155 54.6
27	176 48.1	+0.11	+0.19	8 23.7	−0.94	−0.66	156 53.8
28	176 50.8	+0.12	+0.19	8 01.1	−0.95	−0.67	157 52.9
29							
30							
31							

VALID FOR THE YEARS	
2001	For an *Explanation of Daily tables,* see page 60
2005	
2009	For the *Tables of GHA increments,* see page 63
2013	
2017	
2021	
2025	
2029	
2033	
2037	
2041	
2045	
2049	

1   MARCH   1

DAY	GHA SUN	HRLY ACCN	QUAD CORR	DEC SUN	HRLY RATE	QUAD CORR	GHA ARIES
01	176°53.7'	+0.12'	+0.19'	S 7°38.4'	−0.95'	−0.67'	158°52.0'
02	176 56.6	+0.13	+0.19	7 15.5	−0.95	−0.67	159 51.2
03	176 59.7	+0.13	+0.20	6 52.6	−0.96	−0.68	160 50.3
04	177 02.9	+0.13	+0.20	6 29.6	−0.97	−0.68	161 49.5
05	177 06.1	+0.14	+0.21	6 06.4	−0.97	−0.68	162 48.6
06	177 09.5	+0.15	+0.21	5 43.2	−0.97	−0.68	163 47.7
07	177 13.0	+0.15	+0.22	5 19.9	−0.97	−0.68	164 46.9
08	177 16.6	+0.15	+0.22	4 56.6	−0.98	−0.68	165 46.0
09	177 20.3	+0.16	+0.22	4 33.2	−0.98	−0.68	166 45.1
10	177 24.1	+0.16	+0.22	4 09.7	−0.98	−0.68	167 44.3
11	177 28.0	+0.16	+0.22	3 46.1	−0.98	−0.68	168 43.4
12	177 31.9	+0.17	+0.23	3 22.5	−0.98	−0.68	169 42.6
13	177 35.9	+0.17	+0.23	2 58.9	−0.98	−0.68	170 41.7
14	177 40.0	+0.18	+0.23	2 35.3	−0.99	−0.69	171 40.8
15	177 44.2	+0.18	+0.23	2 11.6	−0.99	−0.69	172 40.0
16	177 48.4	+0.18	+0.23	1 47.9	−0.99	−0.69	173 39.1
17	177 52.7	+0.18	+0.23	1 24.2	−0.99	−0.69	174 38.3
18	177 57.0	+0.18	+0.22	1 00.5	−0.99	−0.70	175 37.4
19	178 01.4	+0.19	+0.22	0 36.8	−0.99	−0.70	176 36.5
20	178 05.9	+0.18	+0.21	S 0 13.0	−0.99	−0.70	177 35.7
21	178 10.3	+0.19	+0.21	N 0 10.7	+0.98	+0.70	178 34.8
22	178 14.8	+0.19	+0.20	0 34.3	+0.99	+0.70	179 33.9
23	178 19.3	+0.19	+0.20	0 58.0	+0.98	+0.70	180 33.1
24	178 23.9	+0.19	+0.19	1 21.6	+0.98	+0.70	181 32.2
25	178 28.4	+0.19	+0.19	1 45.2	+0.98	+0.70	182 31.4
26	178 33.0	+0.19	+0.19	2 08.8	+0.98	+0.70	183 30.5
27	178 37.6	+0.19	+0.18	2 32.3	+0.98	+0.70	184 29.6
28	178 42.1	+0.19	+0.18	2 55.8	+0.98	+0.70	185 28.8
29	178 46.7	+0.19	+0.18	3 19.2	+0.97	+0.70	186 27.9
30	178 51.2	+0.19	+0.18	3 42.5	+0.97	+0.70	187 27.0
31	178 55.7	+0.19	+0.18	4 05.8	+0.97	+0.69	188 26.2

VALID FOR THE YEARS	
2001	For an *Explanation of Daily tables*, see page 60
2005	
2009	For the *Tables of GHA increments*, see page 63
2013	
2017	**Declinations for March 20th**
2021	If the summed corrections for the hourly rate and the quadrennial correction exceed −13.0', then the declination has changed name. In this case, change the signs for the corrections to +, take 13.0' from the summed corrections and change the name to North.
2025	
2029	
2033	
2037	
2041	
2045	
2049	

DAY	GHA SUN	HRLY ACCN	QUAD CORR	DEC SUN	HRLY RATE	QUAD CORR	GHA ARIES
01	179°00.2′	+0.19′	+0.18′	N 4°29.0′	+0.97′	+0.69′	189°25.3′
02	179 04.7	+0.18	+0.18	4 52.2	+0.96	+0.69	190 24.5
03	179 09.1	+0.18	+0.18	5 15.2	+0.95	+0.68	191 23.6
04	179 13.5	+0.18	+0.18	5 38.1	+0.95	+0.68	192 22.7
05	179 17.8	+0.18	+0.18	6 01.0	+0.95	+0.68	193 21.9
06	179 22.1	+0.18	+0.18	6 23.7	+0.95	+0.67	194 21.0
07	179 26.3	+0.18	+0.18	6 46.4	+0.94	+0.67	195 20.1
08	179 30.5	+0.17	+0.17	7 08.9	+0.93	+0.67	196 19.3
09	179 34.6	+0.17	+0.17	7 31.3	+0.93	+0.66	197 18.4
10	179 38.7	+0.17	+0.17	7 53.6	+0.92	+0.66	198 17.6
11	179 42.7	+0.16	+0.16	8 15.7	+0.92	+0.65	199 16.7
12	179 46.6	+0.16	+0.16	8 37.7	+0.91	+0.65	200 15.8
13	179 50.5	+0.16	+0.15	8 59.5	+0.90	+0.64	201 15.0
14	179 54.3	+0.15	+0.15	9 21.2	+0.90	+0.64	202 14.1
15	179 57.9	+0.15	+0.14	9 42.8	+0.89	+0.64	203 13.3
16	180 01.5	+0.15	+0.13	10 04.1	+0.89	+0.64	204 12.4
17	180 05.0	+0.15	+0.12	10 25.4	+0.88	+0.63	205 11.5
18	180 08.5	+0.14	+0.12	10 46.4	+0.87	+0.63	206 10.7
19	180 11.8	+0.14	+0.11	11 07.3	+0.86	+0.62	207 09.8
20	180 15.1	+0.13	+0.10	11 28.0	+0.85	+0.62	208 08.9
21	180 18.2	+0.13	+0.09	11 48.5	+0.85	+0.61	209 08.1
22	180 21.3	+0.12	+0.08	12 08.8	+0.84	+0.61	210 07.2
23	180 24.2	+0.12	+0.07	12 28.9	+0.83	+0.60	211 06.4
24	180 27.0	+0.11	+0.07	12 48.8	+0.82	+0.60	212 05.5
25	180 29.7	+0.11	+0.06	13 08.5	+0.81	+0.59	213 04.6
26	180 32.3	+0.10	+0.05	13 27.9	+0.80	+0.58	214 03.8
27	180 34.7	+0.10	+0.05	13 47.2	+0.79	+0.58	215 02.9
28	180 37.0	+0.09	+0.04	14 06.2	+0.78	+0.57	216 02.0
29	180 39.2	+0.08	+0.04	14 25.0	+0.78	+0.56	217 01.2
30	180 41.2	+0.08	+0.03	14 43.6	+0.76	+0.56	218 00.3
31							

VALID FOR THE YEARS	
2001	For an *Explanation of Daily tables*, see page 60
2005	
2009	For the *Tables of GHA increments*, see page 63
2013	
2017	
2021	
2025	
2029	
2033	
2037	
2041	
2045	
2049	

DAY	GHA SUN	HRLY ACCN	QUAD CORR	DEC SUN	HRLY RATE	QUAD CORR	GHA ARIES
01	180°43.1′	+0.08′	+0.03′	N 15°01.9′	+0.75′	+0.55′	218°59.5′
02	180 44.9	+0.07	+0.03	15 19.8	+0.75	+0.54	219 58.6
03	180 46.5	+0.06	+0.02	15 37.7	+0.73	+0.54	220 57.7
04	180 48.0	+0.06	+0.02	15 55.2	+0.72	+0.53	221 56.9
05	180 49.4	+0.05	+0.01	16 12.5	+0.71	+0.52	222 56.0
06	180 50.6	+0.05	+0.01	16 29.5	+0.70	+0.51	223 55.2
07	180 51.7	+0.04	0.00	16 46.3	+0.69	+0.50	224 54.3
08	180 52.6	+0.03	0.00	17 02.8	+0.68	+0.49	225 53.4
09	180 53.4	+0.03	0.00	17 19.0	+0.66	+0.48	226 52.6
10	180 54.0	+0.02	0.00	17 34.9	+0.65	+0.47	227 51.7
11	180 54.5	+0.02	-0.01	17 50.5	+0.64	+0.46	228 50.9
12	180 54.9	+0.01	-0.01	18 05.8	+0.62	+0.45	229 50.0
13	180 55.1	0.00	-0.02	18 20.7	+0.61	+0.44	230 49.1
14	180 55.2	0.00	-0.03	18 35.4	+0.60	+0.43	231 48.3
15	180 55.1	-0.01	-0.05	18 49.7	+0.59	+0.43	232 47.4
16	180 54.9	-0.01	-0.06	19 03.8	+0.57	+0.42	233 46.5
17	180 54.6	-0.02	-0.07	19 17.5	+0.56	+0.41	234 45.7
18	180 54.1	-0.03	-0.07	19 31.0	+0.54	+0.40	235 44.8
19	180 53.5	-0.03	-0.08	19 44.0	+0.53	+0.39	236 44.0
20	180 52.8	-0.04	-0.09	19 56.8	+0.52	+0.38	237 43.1
21	180 51.9	-0.04	-0.10	20 09.2	+0.50	+0.37	238 42.2
22	180 50.9	-0.05	-0.11	20 21.2	+0.49	+0.36	239 41.4
23	180 49.8	-0.05	-0.12	20 32.9	+0.47	+0.35	240 40.5
24	180 48.5	-0.05	-0.13	20 44.2	+0.46	+0.33	241 39.7
25	180 47.2	-0.07	-0.14	20 55.2	+0.44	+0.32	242 38.8
26	180 45.6	-0.07	-0.14	21 05.8	+0.43	+0.31	243 37.9
27	180 43.9	-0.07	-0.15	21 16.1	+0.41	+0.30	244 37.1
28	180 42.2	-0.08	-0.15	21 26.0	+0.40	+0.29	245 36.2
29	180 40.3	-0.08	-0.15	21 35.5	+0.38	+0.28	246 35.4
30	180 38.3	-0.09	-0.15	21 44.7	+0.37	+0.26	247 34.5
31	180 36.2	-0.09	-0.16	21 53.5	+0.35	+0.25	248 33.6

VALID FOR THE YEARS	
2001	For an *Explanation of Daily tables*, see page 60
2005	
2009	For the *Tables of GHA increments*, see page 63
2013	
2017	
2021	
2025	
2029	
2033	
2037	
2041	
2045	
2049	

DAY	GHA SUN	HRLY ACCN	QUAD CORR	DEC SUN	HRLY RATE	QUAD CORR	GHA ARIES
01	180°34.0′	−0.10′	−0.16′	N 22°01.8′	+0.33′	+0.24′	249°32.8′
02	180 31.6	−0.10	−0.16	22 09.8	+0.32	+0.23	250 31.9
03	180 29.2	−0.10	−0.16	22 17.5	+0.30	+0.21	251 31.0
04	180 26.7	−0.11	−0.16	22 24.7	+0.29	+0.20	252 30.2
05	180 24.1	−0.11	−0.16	22 31.6	+0.27	+0.19	253 29.3
06	180 21.4	−0.12	−0.16	22 38.0	+0.25	+0.17	254 28.5
07	180 18.6	−0.12	−0.16	22 44.1	+0.24	+0.16	255 27.6
08	180 15.8	−0.12	−0.16	22 49.8	+0.21	+0.15	256 26.7
09	180 12.9	−0.12	−0.17	22 54.9	+0.20	+0.13	257 25.9
10	180 10.0	−0.13	−0.18	22 59.8	+0.18	+0.12	258 25.0
11	180 06.9	−0.13	−0.18	23 04.2	+0.17	+0.12	259 24.2
12	180 03.9	−0.13	−0.19	23 08.3	+0.15	+0.11	260 23.3
13	180 00.8	−0.13	−0.19	23 11.9	+0.14	+0.11	261 22.4
14	179 57.6	−0.13	−0.20	23 15.2	+0.12	+0.09	262 21.6
15	179 54.5	−0.13	−0.20	23 18.0	+0.10	+0.07	263 20.7
16	179 51.3	−0.13	−0.21	23 20.4	+0.08	+0.05	264 19.9
17	179 48.1	−0.14	−0.21	23 22.3	+0.07	+0.03	265 19.0
18	179 44.8	−0.13	−0.22	23 23.9	+0.05	+0.01	266 18.1
19	179 41.6	−0.13	−0.22	23 25.1	+0.03	0.00	267 17.3
20	179 38.4	−0.14	−0.22	23 25.9	+0.03	−0.01	268 16.4
21	179 35.1	−0.13	−0.23	23 26.6	−0.02	−0.02	269 15.5
22	179 31.9	−0.13	−0.23	23 26.1	−0.02	−0.03	270 14.7
23	179 28.7	−0.13	−0.23	23 25.6	−0.04	−0.05	271 13.8
24	179 25.5	−0.13	−0.23	23 24.7	−0.05	−0.06	272 13.0
25	179 22.3	−0.13	−0.23	23 23.4	−0.07	−0.08	273 12.1
26	179 19.1	−0.13	−0.23	23 21.7	−0.09	−0.09	274 11.2
27	179 16.0	−0.13	−0.23	23 19.5	−0.10	−0.11	275 10.4
28	179 12.9	−0.13	−0.23	23 17.0	−0.12	−0.12	276 09.5
29	179 09.8	−0.13	−0.23	23 14.1	−0.14	−0.13	277 08.7
30	179 06.8	−0.12	−0.22	23 10.7	−0.16	−0.14	278 07.8
31							

VALID FOR THE YEARS	For an *Explanation of Daily tables*, see page 60
2001	For the *Tables of GHA increments*, see page 63
2005	
2009	
2013	
2017	
2021	
2025	
2029	
2033	
2037	
2041	
2045	
2049	

DAY	GHA SUN	HRLY ACCN	QUAD CORR	DEC SUN	HRLY RATE	QUAD CORR	GHA ARIES
01	179°03.9′	−0.12′	−0.22′	N 23°06.8′	−0.17′	−0.15′	279°06.9′
02	179 01.0	−0.12	−0.21	23 02.7	−0.19	−0.17	280 06.1
03	178 58.1	−0.11	−0.21	22 58.1	−0.20	−0.18	281 05.2
04	178 55.4	−0.11	−0.20	22 53.2	−0.23	−0.20	282 04.4
05	178 52.7	−0.11	−0.20	22 47.8	−0.24	−0.21	283 03.5
06	178 50.1	−0.10	−0.19	22 42.0	−0.25	−0.23	284 02.6
07	178 47.6	−0.10	−0.19	22 35.9	−0.28	−0.24	285 01.8
08	178 45.2	−0.10	−0.19	22 29.2	−0.29	−0.25	286 00.9
09	178 42.9	−0.09	−0.18	22 22.3	−0.30	−0.26	287 00.1
10	178 40.7	−0.09	−0.18	22 15.0	−0.32	−0.27	287 59.2
11	178 38.6	−0.08	−0.18	22 07.3	−0.34	−0.28	288 58.3
12	178 36.6	−0.08	−0.17	21 59.2	−0.35	−0.30	289 57.5
13	178 34.7	−0.07	−0.17	21 50.7	−0.37	−0.31	290 56.6
14	178 33.0	−0.07	−0.17	21 41.9	−0.38	−0.32	291 55.7
15	178 31.4	−0.06	−0.17	21 32.7	−0.40	−0.33	292 54.9
16	178 29.9	−0.05	−0.17	21 23.1	−0.42	−0.34	293 54.0
17	178 28.6	−0.05	−0.17	21 13.1	−0.43	−0.36	294 53.2
18	178 27.4	−0.05	−0.17	21 02.8	−0.44	−0.37	295 52.3
19	178 26.3	−0.04	−0.17	20 52.2	−0.46	−0.39	296 51.4
20	178 25.3	−0.03	−0.17	20 41.2	−0.48	−0.40	297 50.6
21	178 24.5	−0.03	−0.16	20 29.8	−0.49	−0.40	298 49.7
22	178 23.9	−0.02	−0.16	20 18.1	−0.50	−0.41	299 48.9
23	178 23.4	−0.02	−0.16	20 06.1	−0.52	−0.42	300 48.0
24	178 23.0	−0.01	−0.15	19 53.7	−0.53	−0.44	301 47.1
25	178 22.8	0.00	−0.15	19 40.9	−0.54	−0.45	302 46.3
26	178 22.8	0.00	−0.14	19 27.9	−0.55	−0.46	303 45.4
27	178 22.8	+0.01	−0.14	19 14.6	−0.57	−0.47	304 44.6
28	178 23.0	+0.01	−0.13	19 00.9	−0.58	−0.48	305 43.7
29	178 23.3	+0.02	−0.13	18 46.9	−0.60	−0.49	306 42.8
30	178 23.8	+0.03	−0.12	18 32.6	−0.61	−0.50	307 42.0
31	178 24.5	+0.03	−0.11	18 18.0	−0.62	−0.51	308 41.1

VALID FOR THE YEARS	For an *Explanation of Daily tables*, see page 60
2001	For the *Tables of GHA increments*, see page 63
2005	
2009	
2013	
2017	
2021	
2025	
2029	
2033	
2037	
2041	
2045	
2049	

DAY	GHA SUN	HRLY ACCN	QUAD CORR	DEC SUN	HRLY RATE	QUAD CORR	GHA ARIES
01	178°25.3′	+0.04′	−0.10′	N 18°03.1′	−0.63′	−0.52′	309°40.3′
02	178 26.2	+0.05	−0.09	17 47.9	−0.65	−0.53	310 39.4
03	178 27.3	+0.05	−0.08	17 32.4	−0.66	−0.54	311 38.5
04	178 28.5	+0.06	−0.07	17 16.6	−0.67	−0.55	312 37.7
05	178 29.9	+0.06	−0.06	17 00.5	−0.68	−0.56	313 36.8
06	178 31.4	+0.07	−0.06	16 44.2	−0.69	−0.56	314 35.9
07	178 33.1	+0.08	−0.05	16 27.6	−0.70	−0.57	315 35.1
08	178 35.0	+0.09	−0.05	16 10.7	−0.71	−0.58	316 34.2
09	178 37.1	+0.09	−0.04	15 53.6	−0.73	−0.58	317 33.4
10	178 39.2	+0.10	−0.04	15 36.2	−0.73	−0.59	318 32.5
11	178 41.5	+0.10	−0.04	15 18.6	−0.74	−0.60	319 31.6
12	178 43.9	+0.11	−0.03	15 00.8	−0.75	−0.61	320 30.8
13	178 46.5	+0.11	−0.03	14 42.7	−0.77	−0.62	321 29.9
14	178 49.2	+0.12	−0.03	14 24.3	−0.77	−0.63	322 29.0
15	178 52.1	+0.13	−0.03	14 05.8	−0.78	−0.63	323 28.2
16	178 55.1	+0.13	−0.03	13 47.0	−0.80	−0.64	324 27.3
17	178 58.2	+0.14	−0.03	13 27.9	−0.80	−0.65	325 26.5
18	179 01.5	+0.14	−0.03	13 08.6	−0.81	−0.65	326 25.6
19	179 04.8	+0.15	−0.03	12 49.2	−0.82	−0.66	327 24.7
20	179 08.4	+0.15	−0.02	12 29.6	−0.83	−0.67	328 23.9
21	179 12.0	+0.15	−0.01	12 09.8	−0.84	−0.69	329 23.0
22	179 15.7	+0.16	0.00	11 49.7	−0.84	−0.70	330 22.2
23	179 19.6	+0.16	0.00	11 29.5	−0.85	−0.70	331 21.3
24	179 23.5	+0.17	+0.01	11 09.1	−0.86	−0.70	332 20.4
25	179 27.6	+0.17	+0.01	10 48.5	−0.86	−0.70	333 19.6
26	179 31.7	+0.18	+0.02	10 27.8	−0.87	−0.70	334 18.7
27	179 36.0	+0.18	+0.02	10 06.9	−0.88	−0.70	335 17.9
28	179 40.3	+0.18	+0.03	9 45.8	−0.88	−0.70	336 17.0
29	179 44.7	+0.20	+0.04	9 24.6	−0.89	−0.70	337 16.1
30	179 49.4	+0.19	+0.05	9 03.2	−0.90	−0.70	338 15.3
31	179 53.9	+0.20	+0.05	8 41.7	−0.90	−0.71	339 14.4

VALID FOR THE YEARS	For an *Explanation of Daily tables*, see page 60
2001	For the *Tables of GHA increments*, see page 63
2005	
2009	
2013	
2017	
2021	
2025	
2029	
2033	
2037	
2041	
2045	
2049	

DAY	GHA SUN	HRLY ACCN	QUAD CORR	DEC SUN	HRLY RATE	QUAD CORR	GHA ARIES
01	179°58.6′	+0.20′	+0.06′	N 8°20.0′	−0.91′	−0.71′	340°13.5′
02	180 03.4	+0.20	+0.06	7 58.2	−0.91	−0.71	341 12.7
03	180 08.2	+0.20	+0.07	7 36.3	−0.92	−0.72	342 11.8
04	180 13.1	+0.20	+0.07	7 14.2	−0.92	−0.72	343 11.0
05	180 18.0	+0.21	+0.08	6 52.1	−0.93	−0.72	344 10.1
06	180 23.0	+0.21	+0.08	6 29.8	−0.93	−0.73	345 09.2
07	180 28.1	+0.21	+0.09	6 07.4	−0.94	−0.73	346 08.4
08	180 33.2	+0.22	+0.09	5 44.9	−0.94	−0.73	347 07.5
09	180 38.4	+0.22	+0.09	5 22.3	−0.95	−0.73	348 06.6
10	180 43.6	+0.22	+0.09	4 59.6	−0.95	−0.73	349 05.8
11	180 48.8	+0.22	+0.09	4 36.9	−0.95	−0.73	350 04.9
12	180 54.1	+0.22	+0.09	4 14.0	−0.95	−0.74	351 04.1
13	180 59.4	+0.22	+0.09	3 51.1	−0.95	−0.74	352 03.2
14	181 04.7	+0.23	+0.09	3 28.2	−0.96	−0.74	353 02.3
15	181 10.1	+0.23	+0.08	3 05.1	−0.96	−0.74	354 01.5
16	181 15.5	+0.22	+0.08	2 42.0	−0.96	−0.74	355 00.6
17	181 20.8	+0.23	+0.08	2 18.9	−0.97	−0.74	355 59.7
18	181 26.2	+0.23	+0.08	1 55.6	−0.97	−0.75	356 58.9
19	181 31.6	+0.22	+0.08	1 32.4	−0.97	−0.75	357 58.0
20	181 36.9	+0.22	+0.08	1 09.1	−0.97	−0.75	358 57.2
21	181 42.2	+0.23	+0.09	0 45.8	−0.97	−0.75	359 56.3
22	181 47.6	+0.22	+0.09	N 0 22.5	−0.98	−0.75	0 55.4
23	181 52.8	+0.22	+0.09	S 0 00.9	+0.97	+0.75	1 54.6
24	181 58.1	+0.22	+0.10	0 24.2	+0.98	+0.75	2 53.7
25	182 03.3	+0.21	+0.10	0 47.6	+0.98	+0.75	3 52.9
26	182 08.4	+0.22	+0.10	1 11.0	+0.97	+0.75	4 52.0
27	182 13.6	+0.21	+0.11	1 34.3	+0.97	+0.74	5 51.1
28	182 18.6	+0.21	+0.11	1 57.6	+0.98	+0.74	6 50.3
29	182 23.6	+0.20	+0.11	2 21.0	+0.97	+0.74	7 49.4
30	182 28.5	+0.20	+0.12	2 44.3	+0.97	+0.73	8 48.5
31							

VALID FOR THE YEARS	
2001	For an *Explanation of Daily tables*, see page 60
2005	
2009	For the *Tables of GHA increments*, see page 63
2013	
2017	**Declinations for September 22nd**
2021	If the summed corrections for the hourly rate and the quadrennial correction exceed −22.5′, then the declination has changed name. In this case, change the signs for the corrections to +, take 22.5′ from the summed corrections and change the name to South.
2025	
2029	
2033	
2037	
2041	
2045	
2049	

DAY	GHA SUN	HRLY ACCN	QUAD CORR	DEC SUN	HRLY RATE	QUAD CORR	GHA ARIES
01	182°33.4′	+0.20′	+0.12′	S 3°07.6′	+0.97′	+0.73′	9°47.7′
02	182 38.2	+0.20	+0.12	3 30.9	+0.97	+0.72	10 46.8
03	182 42.9	+0.20	+0.12	3 54.1	+0.97	+0.72	11 46.0
04	182 47.6	+0.19	+0.12	4 17.3	+0.96	+0.71	12 45.1
05	182 52.1	+0.19	+0.12	4 40.4	+0.96	+0.71	13 44.2
06	182 56.6	+0.18	+0.12	5 03.5	+0.96	+0.70	14 43.4
07	183 01.0	+0.18	+0.12	5 26.5	+0.95	+0.70	15 42.5
08	183 05.2	+0.18	+0.12	5 49.4	+0.95	+0.70	16 41.6
09	183 09.4	+0.17	+0.11	6 12.3	+0.95	+0.69	17 40.8
10	183 13.5	+0.16	+0.11	6 35.1	+0.94	+0.69	18 39.9
11	183 17.4	+0.16	+0.11	6 57.7	+0.94	+0.69	19 39.1
12	183 21.3	+0.15	+0.10	7 20.3	+0.94	+0.69	20 38.2
13	183 25.0	+0.15	+0.10	7 42.8	+0.93	+0.69	21 37.3
14	183 28.6	+0.15	+0.09	8 05.2	+0.93	+0.69	22 36.5
15	183 32.1	+0.14	+0.09	8 27.5	+0.92	+0.68	23 35.6
16	183 35.4	+0.13	+0.08	8 49.6	+0.92	+0.68	24 34.7
17	183 38.6	+0.13	+0.08	9 11.7	+0.91	+0.68	25 33.9
18	183 41.6	+0.12	+0.07	9 33.6	+0.90	+0.67	26 33.0
19	183 44.5	+0.11	+0.07	9 55.3	+0.90	+0.67	27 32.2
20	183 47.2	+0.11	+0.07	10 16.9	+0.90	+0.66	28 31.3
21	183 49.8	+0.10	+0.06	10 38.4	+0.89	+0.66	29 30.4
22	183 52.2	+0.09	+0.06	10 59.7	+0.88	+0.65	30 29.6
23	183 54.4	+0.08	+0.06	11 20.8	+0.87	+0.64	31 28.7
24	183 56.4	+0.08	+0.06	11 41.7	+0.87	+0.64	32 27.9
25	183 58.3	+0.07	+0.06	12 02.5	+0.86	+0.63	33 27.0
26	184 00.0	+0.06	+0.06	12 23.2	+0.85	+0.62	34 26.1
27	184 01.5	+0.05	+0.06	12 43.6	+0.84	+0.62	35 25.3
28	184 02.8	+0.05	+0.06	13 03.8	+0.84	+0.60	36 24.4
29	184 03.9	+0.04	+0.06	13 23.9	+0.83	+0.59	37 23.5
30	184 04.8	+0.03	+0.06	13 43.7	+0.82	+0.58	38 22.7
31	184 05.5	+0.02	+0.06	14 03.3	+0.81	+0.57	39 21.8

VALID FOR THE YEARS	For an *Explanation of Daily tables*, see page 60
2001	For the *Tables of GHA increments*, see page 63
2005	
2009	
2013	
2017	
2021	
2025	
2029	
2033	
2037	
2041	
2045	
2049	

DAY	GHA SUN	HRLY ACCN	QUAD CORR	DEC SUN	HRLY RATE	QUAD CORR	GHA ARIES
01	184°06.0′	+0.02′	+0.06′	S 14°22.7′	+0.80′	+0.56′	40°21.0′
02	184 06.4	0.00	+0.06	14 41.8	+0.79	+0.55	41 20.1
03	184 06.5	0.00	+0.06	15 00.7	+0.78	+0.55	42 19.2
04	184 06.4	−0.01	+0.06	15 19.3	+0.77	+0.54	43 18.4
05	184 06.2	−0.02	+0.05	15 37.7	+0.76	+0.53	44 17.5
06	184 05.7	−0.03	+0.05	15 55.9	+0.75	+0.52	45 16.7
07	184 04.9	−0.04	+0.04	16 13.8	+0.73	+0.51	46 15.8
08	184 04.0	−0.05	+0.03	16 31.4	+0.72	+0.50	47 14.9
09	184 02.9	−0.05	+0.03	16 48.7	+0.71	+0.49	48 14.1
10	184 01.6	−0.06	+0.02	17 05.8	+0.70	+0.48	49 13.2
11	184 00.1	−0.07	+0.01	17 22.5	+0.69	+0.47	50 12.3
12	183 58.4	−0.08	+0.01	17 39.0	+0.67	+0.47	51 11.5
13	183 56.5	−0.09	0.00	17 55.1	+0.66	+0.46	52 10.6
14	183 54.3	−0.10	−0.01	18 11.0	+0.64	+0.45	53 09.8
15	183 52.0	−0.10	−0.02	18 26.4	+0.63	+0.44	54 08.9
16	183 49.5	−0.12	−0.03	18 41.6	+0.62	+0.43	55 08.0
17	183 46.7	−0.13	−0.03	18 56.5	+0.60	+0.42	56 07.2
18	183 43.7	−0.13	−0.03	19 11.0	+0.59	+0.41	57 06.3
19	183 40.5	−0.14	−0.03	19 25.2	+0.58	+0.40	58 05.5
20	183 37.1	−0.15	−0.03	19 39.1	+0.56	+0.39	59 03.6
21	183 33.5	−0.16	−0.04	19 52.5	+0.55	+0.37	60 03.7
22	183 29.7	−0.17	−0.04	20 05.7	+0.53	+0.36	61 02.9
23	183 25.7	−0.18	−0.04	20 18.4	+0.51	+0.35	62 02.0
24	183 21.4	−0.18	−0.05	20 30.7	+0.50	+0.34	63 01.2
25	183 17.0	−0.20	−0.05	20 42.7	+0.48	+0.33	64 00.3
26	183 12.3	−0.20	−0.05	20 54.3	+0.47	+0.32	64 59.4
27	183 07.7	−0.20	−0.04	21 05.6	+0.45	+0.30	65 58.6
28	183 02.7	−0.22	−0.04	21 16.4	+0.43	+0.29	66 57.7
29	182 57.5	−0.22	−0.04	21 26.8	+0.42	+0.28	67 56.8
30	182 52.2	−0.23	−0.04	21 36.9	+0.40	+0.26	68 56.0
31							

VALID FOR THE YEARS	For an *Explanation of Daily tables*, see page 60
2001	For the *Tables of GHA increments*, see page 63
2005	
2009	
2013	
2017	
2021	
2025	
2029	
2033	
2037	
2041	
2045	
2049	

DAY	GHA SUN	HRLY ACCN	QUAD CORR	DEC SUN	HRLY RATE	QUAD CORR	GHA ARIES
01	182°46.7′	−0.24′	−0.04′	S 21°46.5′	+0.38′	+0.25′	69°55.1′
02	182 41.0	−0.24	−0.04	21 55.6	+0.37	+0.24	70 54.3
03	182 35.2	−0.25	−0.04	22 04.4	+0.35	+0.23	71 53.4
04	182 29.2	−0.25	−0.04	22 12.7	+0.33	+0.22	72 52.5
05	182 23.1	−0.26	−0.04	22 20.7	+0.31	+0.21	73 51.7
06	182 16.8	−0.27	−0.05	22 28.2	+0.29	+0.19	74 50.8
07	182 10.4	−0.27	−0.05	22 35.2	+0.28	+0.18	75 50.0
08	182 03.9	−0.28	−0.06	22 41.8	+0.26	+0.17	76 49.1
09	181 57.3	−0.28	−0.06	22 48.0	+0.23	+0.15	77 48.2
10	181 50.6	−0.28	−0.07	22 53.6	+0.22	+0.14	78 47.4
11	181 43.8	−0.29	−0.07	22 58.9	+0.20	+0.13	79 46.5
12	181 36.9	−0.29	−0.08	23 03.7	+0.18	+0.11	80 45.7
13	181 29.9	−0.30	−0.08	23 08.0	+0.16	+0.10	81 44.8
14	181 22.8	−0.30	−0.08	23 11.9	+0.15	+0.09	82 43.9
15	181 15.7	−0.30	−0.09	23 15.4	+0.12	+0.07	83 43.1
16	181 08.5	−0.30	−0.09	23 18.3	+0.10	+0.06	84 42.2
17	181 01.2	−0.30	−0.09	23 20.8	+0.08	+0.05	85 41.4
18	180 53.9	−0.31	−0.09	23 22.8	+0.06	+0.03	86 40.5
19	180 46.5	−0.31	−0.09	23 24.3	+0.05	+0.02	87 39.6
20	180 39.1	−0.31	−0.09	23 25.4	+0.03	+0.01	88 38.8
21	180 31.7	−0.31	−0.08	23 26.1	0.00	−0.01	89 37.9
22	180 24.2	−0.31	−0.08	23 26.2	−0.01	−0.02	90 37.1
23	180 16.8	−0.31	−0.08	23 25.9	−0.04	−0.04	91 36.2
24	180 09.3	−0.31	−0.07	23 25.0	−0.05	−0.05	92 35.3
25	180 01.8	−0.31	−0.07	23 23.8	−0.08	−0.07	93 34.5
26	179 54.4	−0.31	−0.06	23 22.0	−0.09	−0.08	94 33.6
27	179 46.9	−0.31	−0.06	23 19.8	−0.11	−0.10	95 32.7
28	179 39.5	−0.30	−0.05	23 17.2	−0.13	−0.11	96 31.9
29	179 32.2	−0.30	−0.05	23 14.0	−0.15	−0.12	97 31.0
30	179 24.9	−0.30	−0.05	23 10.5	−0.18	−0.13	98 30.2
31	179 17.7	−0.30	−0.04	23 06.3	−0.19	−0.15	99 29.3

VALID FOR THE YEARS	For an *Explanation of Daily tables*, see page 60
2001	For the *Tables of GHA increments*, see page 63
2005	
2009	
2013	
2017	
2021	
2025	
2029	
2033	
2037	
2041	
2045	
2049	

DAY	GHA SUN	HRLY ACCN	QUAD CORR	DEC SUN	HRLY RATE	QUAD CORR	GHA ARIES
01	179°10.6′	−0.30′	−0.04′	S 23°01.8′	−0.21′	−0.16′	100°28.4′
02	179 03.5	−0.29	−0.04	22 56.8	−0.23	−0.17	101 27.6
03	178 56.5	−0.29	−0.03	22 51.4	−0.25	−0.19	102 26.7
04	178 49.6	−0.28	−0.03	22 45.5	−0.27	−0.20	103 25.9
05	178 42.8	−0.28	−0.03	22 39.1	−0.28	−0.21	104 25.0
06	178 36.1	−0.28	−0.03	22 32.3	−0.30	−0.23	105 24.1
07	178 29.5	−0.27	−0.03	22 25.1	−0.33	−0.24	106 23.3
08	178 23.0	−0.26	−0.03	22 17.3	−0.34	−0.25	107 22.4
09	178 16.7	−0.26	−0.02	22 09.2	−0.36	−0.26	108 21.6
10	178 10.5	−0.25	−0.02	22 00.6	−0.37	−0.27	109 20.7
11	178 04.5	−0.25	−0.02	21 51.7	−0.40	−0.28	110 19.8
12	177 58.6	−0.24	−0.02	21 42.2	−0.41	−0.29	111 19.0
13	177 52.9	−0.23	−0.02	21 32.4	−0.43	−0.31	112 18.1
14	177 47.3	−0.23	−0.02	21 22.2	−0.45	−0.32	113 17.3
15	177 41.9	−0.22	−0.01	21 11.5	−0.46	−0.33	114 16.4
16	177 36.6	−0.21	−0.01	21 00.4	−0.48	−0.35	115 15.5
17	177 31.5	−0.20	0.00	20 48.9	−0.50	−0.36	116 14.7
18	177 26.6	−0.20	0.00	20 37.0	−0.51	−0.37	117 13.8
19	177 21.8	−0.19	+0.01	20 24.8	−0.53	−0.38	118 12.9
20	177 17.3	−0.18	+0.01	20 12.1	−0.54	−0.39	119 12.1
21	177 12.9	−0.18	+0.02	19 59.1	−0.56	−0.40	120 11.2
22	177 08.7	−0.17	+0.02	19 45.7	−0.57	−0.41	121 10.4
23	177 04.7	−0.16	+0.03	19 32.0	−0.59	−0.42	122 09.5
24	177 00.8	−0.15	+0.04	19 17.8	−0.60	−0.43	123 08.6
25	176 57.3	−0.14	+0.05	19 03.4	−0.63	−0.44	124 07.8
26	176 53.9	−0.14	+0.06	18 48.4	−0.63	−0.45	125 06.9
27	176 50.6	−0.13	+0.06	18 33.2	−0.65	−0.45	126 06.1
28	176 47.6	−0.12	+0.07	18 17.7	−0.66	−0.46	127 05.2
29	176 44.7	−0.11	+0.08	18 01.9	−0.68	−0.47	128 04.3
30	176 42.1	−0.10	+0.09	17 45.7	−0.69	−0.48	129 03.5
31	176 39.7	−0.10	+0.10	17 29.2	−0.70	−0.49	130 02.6

VALID FOR THE YEARS	
2002	For an *Explanation of Daily tables*, see page 60
2006	
2010	For the *Tables of GHA increments*, see page 63
2014	
2018	
2022	
2026	
2030	
2034	
2038	
2042	
2046	
2050	

DAY	GHA SUN	HRLY ACCN	QUAD CORR	DEC SUN	HRLY RATE	QUAD CORR	GHA ARIES
01	176°37.4′	−0.08′	+0.10′	S 17°12.5′	−0.71′	−0.51′	131°01.8′
02	176 35.4	−0.08	+0.10	16 55.4	−0.73	−0.52	132 00.9
03	176 33.6	−0.07	+0.11	16 38.0	−0.74	−0.52	133 00.0
04	176 32.0	−0.06	+0.11	16 20.3	−0.75	−0.53	133 59.2
05	176 30.6	−0.05	+0.11	16 02.3	−0.76	−0.54	134 58.2
06	176 29.4	−0.04	+0.11	15 44.1	−0.78	−0.54	135 57.4
07	176 28.5	−0.03	+0.11	15 25.5	−0.78	−0.55	136 56.6
08	176 27.7	−0.03	+0.11	15 06.7	−0.79	−0.56	137 55.7
09	176 27.1	−0.02	+0.12	14 47.7	−0.80	−0.56	138 54.9
10	176 26.7	0.00	+0.12	14 28.4	−0.81	−0.57	139 54.0
11	176 26.6	0.00	+0.12	14 08.9	−0.82	−0.58	140 53.1
12	176 26.6	+0.01	+0.12	13 49.2	−0.83	−0.59	141 52.3
13	176 26.8	+0.02	+0.12	13 29.2	−0.84	−0.60	142 51.4
14	176 27.2	+0.02	+0.12	13 09.0	−0.85	−0.61	143 50.6
15	176 27.7	+0.03	+0.13	12 48.6	−0.86	−0.61	144 49.7
16	176 28.5	+0.04	+0.13	12 28.0	−0.87	−0.62	145 48.8
17	176 29.4	+0.05	+0.13	12 07.1	−0.88	−0.62	146 48.0
18	176 30.5	+0.05	+0.14	11 46.1	−0.88	−0.63	147 47.1
19	176 31.8	+0.06	+0.14	11 24.9	−0.89	−0.63	148 46.2
20	176 33.3	+0.07	+0.15	11 03.5	−0.90	−0.64	149 45.4
21	176 34.9	+0.08	+0.15	10 42.0	−0.91	−0.64	150 44.5
22	176 36.7	+0.08	+0.16	10 20.2	−0.91	−0.65	151 43.7
23	176 38.6	+0.08	+0.16	9 58.3	−0.92	−0.65	152 42.8
24	176 40.6	+0.09	+0.16	9 36.2	−0.93	−0.65	153 41.9
25	176 42.8	+0.10	+0.16	9 14.0	−0.93	−0.65	154 41.1
26	176 45.2	+0.10	+0.17	8 51.7	−0.93	−0.66	155 40.2
27	176 47.7	+0.11	+0.18	8 29.3	−0.94	−0.66	156 39.4
28	176 50.3	+0.12	+0.19	8 06.7	−0.95	−0.67	157 38.5
29							
30							
31							

VALID FOR THE YEARS	
2002	For an *Explanation of Daily tables*, see page 60
2006	
2010	For the *Tables of GHA increments*, see page 63
2014	
2018	
2022	
2026	
2030	
2034	
2038	
2042	
2046	
2050	

DAY	GHA SUN	HRLY ACCN	QUAD CORR	DEC SUN	HRLY RATE	QUAD CORR	GHA ARIES
01	176′53.1′	+0.12′	+0.19′	S 7°44.0′	−0.95′	−0.67′	158°37.6′
02	176 56.0	+0.13	+0.19	7 21.2	−0.95	−0.67	159 36.8
03	176 59.0	+0.13	+0.20	6 58.3	−0.96	−0.67	160 35.9
04	177 02.1	+0.14	+0.20	6 35.2	−0.96	−0.67	161 35.0
05	177 05.4	+0.14	+0.20	6 12.1	−0.96	−0.68	162 34.2
06	177 08.8	+0.15	+0.19	5 49.0	−0.97	−0.68	163 33.3
07	177 12.3	+0.15	+0.19	5 25.7	−0.98	−0.69	164 32.5
08	177 15.9	+0.15	+0.19	5 02.3	−0.98	−0.69	165 31.6
09	177 19.6	+0.16	+0.19	4 38.9	−0.98	−0.70	166 30.7
10	177 23.4	+0.16	+0.19	4 15.5	−0.98	−0.70	167 29.9
11	177 27.2	+0.17	+0.19	3 52.0	−0.98	−0.70	168 29.0
12	177 31.2	+0.17	+0.19	3 28.4	−0.98	−0.71	169 28.2
13	177 35.2	+0.17	+0.19	3 04.8	−0.98	−0.71	170 27.3
14	177 39.3	+0.18	+0.19	2 41.2	−0.99	−0.71	171 26.4
15	177 43.5	+0.18	+0.18	2 17.5	−0.99	−0.71	172 25.6
16	177 47.7	+0.18	+0.18	1 53.8	−0.99	−0.71	173 24.7
17	177 52.0	+0.18	+0.18	1 30.1	−0.99	−0.71	174 23.8
18	177 56.3	+0.18	+0.18	1 06.4	−0.99	−0.72	175 23.0
19	178 00.7	+0.18	+0.18	0 42.7	−0.99	−0.72	176 22.1
20	178 05.1	+0.19	+0.18	S 0 19.0	−0.99	−0.72	177 21.2
21	178 09.6	+0.18	+0.18	N 0 04.7	+0.99	+0.72	178 20.4
22	178 14.0	+0.19	+0.18	0 28.4	+0.99	+0.72	179 19.5
23	178 18.5	+0.19	+0.18	0 52.1	+0.99	+0.72	180 18.7
24	178 23.0	+0.19	+0.19	1 15.8	+0.98	+0.71	181 17.8
25	178 27.5	+0.19	+0.19	1 39.4	+0.98	+0.71	182 16.9
26	178 32.0	+0.19	+0.19	2 03.0	+0.98	+0.71	183 16.1
27	178 36.6	+0.19	+0.19	2 26.5	+0.98	+0.70	184 15.2
28	178 41.1	+0.19	+0.19	2 50.0	+0.98	+0.70	185 14.4
29	178 45.6	+0.19	+0.19	3 13.5	+0.97	+0.70	186 13.5
30	178 50.1	+0.19	+0.19	3 36.8	+0.98	+0.70	187 12.6
31	178 54.6	+0.18	+0.19	4 00.2	+0.97	+0.69	188 11.8

VALID FOR THE YEARS	
2002	For an *Explanation of Daily tables*, see page 60
2006	
2010	For the *Tables of GHA increments*, see page 63
2014	
2018	**Declinations for March 20th**
2022	If the summed corrections for the hourly rate and the quadrennial correction exceed −19.0′, then the declination has changed name. In this case, change the signs for the corrections to +, take 19.0′ from the summed corrections and change the name to North.
2026	
2030	
2034	
2038	
2042	
2046	
2050	

APRIL

DAY	GHA SUN	HRLY ACCN	QUAD CORR	DEC SUN	HRLY RATE	QUAD CORR	GHA ARIES
01	178°59.0'	+0.19'	+0.19'	N 4°23.4'	+0.96'	+0.69'	189°10.9'
02	179 03.5	+0.18	+0.18	4 46.5	+0.96	+0.69	190 10.0
03	179 07.9	+0.18	+0.18	5 09.6	+0.96	+0.68	191 09.2
04	179 12.3	+0.18	+0.17	5 32.6	+0.95	+0.68	192 08.3
05	179 16.7	+0.18	+0.16	5 55.5	+0.95	+0.68	193 07.5
06	179 21.0	+0.18	+0.16	6 18.2	+0.95	+0.68	194 06.6
07	179 25.3	+0.17	+0.15	6 40.9	+0.94	+0.68	195 05.7
08	179 29.4	+0.18	+0.14	7 03.4	+0.94	+0.68	196 04.9
09	179 33.6	+0.17	+0.14	7 25.9	+0.93	+0.67	197 04.0
10	179 37.7	+0.17	+0.13	7 48.2	+0.92	+0.67	198 03.1
11	179 41.7	+0.17	+0.12	8 10.3	+0.92	+0.67	199 02.3
12	179 45.7	+0.16	+0.12	8 32.3	+0.91	+0.67	200 01.4
13	179 49.6	+0.16	+0.11	8 54.2	+0.91	+0.67	201 00.6
14	179 53.4	+0.16	+0.11	9 16.0	+0.90	+0.66	201 59.7
15	179 57.2	+0.15	+0.10	9 37.6	+0.89	+0.66	202 58.8
16	180 00.8	+0.15	+0.10	9 59.0	+0.88	+0.65	203 58.0
17	180 04.4	+0.14	+0.10	10 20.1	+0.88	+0.64	204 57.1
18	180 07.8	+0.14	+0.09	10 41.2	+0.88	+0.64	205 56.3
19	180 11.2	+0.13	+0.09	11 02.2	+0.86	+0.63	206 55.4
20	180 14.4	+0.13	+0.09	11 22.9	+0.85	+0.63	207 54.5
21	180 17.6	+0.13	+0.08	11 43.4	+0.85	+0.62	208 53.7
22	180 20.6	+0.12	+0.08	12 03.8	+0.84	+0.62	209 52.8
23	180 23.5	+0.12	+0.08	12 24.0	+0.83	+0.61	210 51.9
24	180 26.3	+0.11	+0.07	12 43.9	+0.83	+0.61	211 51.1
25	180 29.0	+0.10	+0.07	13 03.7	+0.81	+0.60	212 50.2
26	180 31.5	+0.10	+0.07	13 23.2	+0.80	+0.59	213 49.4
27	180 34.0	+0.10	+0.06	13 42.5	+0.80	+0.59	214 48.5
28	180 36.3	+0.09	+0.06	14 01.6	+0.79	+0.58	215 47.6
29	180 38.5	+0.08	+0.05	14 20.5	+0.78	+0.57	216 46.8
30	180 40.5	+0.08	+0.05	14 39.1	+0.77	+0.56	217 45.9
31							

VALID FOR THE YEARS	
2002	For an *Explanation of Daily tables*, see page 60
2006	
2010	For the *Tables of GHA increments*, see page 63
2014	
2018	
2022	
2026	
2030	
2034	
2038	
2042	
2046	
2050	

DAY	GHA SUN	HRLY ACCN	QUAD CORR	DEC SUN	HRLY RATE	QUAD CORR	GHA ARIES
01	180°42.4′	+0.08′	+0.04′	N 14°57.5′	+0.75′	+0.55′	218°45.1′
02	180 44.2	+0.07	+0.03	15 15.6	+0.74	+0.55	219 44.2
03	180 45.8	+0.07	+0.03	15 33.4	+0.73	+0.54	220 43.3
04	180 47.4	+0.06	+0.02	15 50.9	+0.73	+0.54	221 42.5
05	180 48.8	+0.05	+0.01	16 08.4	+0.71	+0.53	222 41.6
06	180 50.0	+0.05	0.00	16 25.5	+0.70	+0.52	223 40.7
07	180 51.2	+0.04	-0.01	16 42.3	+0.69	+0.51	224 39.9
08	180 52.2	+0.03	-0.02	16 58.8	+0.68	+0.50	225 39.0
09	180 53.0	+0.03	-0.02	17 15.1	+0.67	+0.49	226 38.2
10	180 53.7	+0.03	-0.03	17 31.1	+0.65	+0.48	227 37.3
11	180 54.3	+0.02	-0.04	17 46.7	+0.64	+0.47	228 36.4
12	180 54.7	+0.01	-0.04	18 02.1	+0.63	+0.47	229 35.6
13	180 54.9	+0.01	-0.05	18 17.2	+0.61	+0.46	230 34.7
14	180 55.1	0.00	-0.06	18 31.9	+0.60	+0.45	231 33.9
15	180 55.1	-0.01	-0.06	18 46.3	+0.59	+0.44	232 33.0
16	180 54.9	-0.01	-0.07	19 00.4	+0.58	+0.43	233 32.1
17	180 54.6	-0.02	-0.08	19 14.2	+0.54	+0.42	234 31.3
18	180 54.2	-0.03	-0.08	19 27.7	+0.57	+0.41	235 30.4
19	180 53.6	-0.03	-0.09	19 40.9	+0.53	+0.40	236 29.6
20	180 52.9	-0.04	-0.09	19 53.7	+0.52	+0.39	237 28.7
21	180 52.0	-0.04	-0.10	20 06.2	+0.50	+0.38	238 27.8
22	180 51.0	-0.05	-0.10	20 18.3	+0.49	+0.37	239 27.0
23	180 49.9	-0.05	-0.10	20 30.1	+0.48	+0.36	240 26.1
24	180 48.6	-0.06	-0.11	20 41.5	+0.48	+0.34	241 25.2
25	180 47.2	-0.06	-0.11	20 52.6	+0.45	+0.33	242 24.4
26	180 45.7	-0.07	-0.11	21 03.3	+0.43	+0.32	243 23.5
27	180 44.0	-0.08	-0.11	21 13.7	+0.42	+0.30	244 22.7
28	180 42.2	-0.08	-0.11	21 23.7	+0.40	+0.29	245 21.8
29	180 40.4	-0.08	-0.12	21 33.3	+0.39	+0.28	246 20.9
30	180 38.4	-0.09	-0.13	21 42.6	+0.37	+0.26	247 20.1
31	180 36.3	-0.09	-0.13	21 51.5	+0.35	+0.25	248 19.2

VALID FOR THE YEARS	
2002	For an *Explanation of Daily tables*, see page 60
2006	
2010	For the *Tables of GHA increments*, see page 63
2014	
2018	
2022	
2026	
2030	
2034	
2038	
2042	
2046	
2050	

DAY	GHA SUN	HRLY ACCN	QUAD CORR	DEC SUN	HRLY RATE	QUAD CORR	GHA ARIES
01	180°34.1'	−0.10'	−0.14'	N 21°59.9'	+0.34'	+0.24'	249°18.4'
02	180 31.8	−0.10	−0.14	22 08.0	+0.32	+0.23	250 17.5
03	180 29.3	−0.10	−0.15	22 15.7	+0.30	+0.22	251 16.6
04	180 26.8	−0.10	−0.15	22 23.0	+0.29	+0.21	252 15.8
05	180 24.3	−0.11	−0.16	22 30.0	+0.27	+0.20	253 14.9
06	180 21.6	−0.11	−0.16	22 36.5	+0.26	+0.18	254 14.0
07	180 18.9	−0.11	−0.17	22 42.7	+0.24	+0.17	255 13.2
08	180 16.2	−0.12	−0.18	22 48.5	+0.22	+0.16	256 12.3
09	180 13.3	−0.12	−0.18	22 53.7	+0.21	+0.14	257 11.5
10	180 10.4	−0.13	−0.19	22 58.7	+0.19	+0.13	258 10.6
11	180 07.4	−0.13	−0.19	23 03.2	+0.18	+0.12	259 09.7
12	180 04.4	−0.13	−0.19	23 07.4	+0.15	+0.11	260 08.9
13	180 01.3	−0.13	−0.20	23 11.1	+0.14	+0.10	261 08.0
14	179 58.2	−0.13	−0.20	23 14.4	+0.13	+0.08	262 07.2
15	179 55.1	−0.13	−0.20	23 17.4	+0.10	+0.07	263 06.3
16	179 51.9	−0.13	−0.21	23 19.9	+0.08	+0.05	264 05.4
17	179 48.7	−0.14	−0.21	23 21.9	+0.07	+0.04	265 04.6
18	179 45.4	−0.13	−0.21	23 23.6	+0.05	+0.03	266 03.7
19	179 42.2	−0.14	−0.21	23 24.8	+0.04	+0.02	267 02.9
20	179 38.9	−0.14	−0.21	23 25.7	+0.02	+0.01	268 02.0
21	179 35.6	−0.14	−0.20	23 26.1	0.00	−0.01	269 01.1
22	179 32.3	−0.14	−0.20	23 26.2	−0.02	−0.03	270 00.3
23	179 29.0	−0.13	−0.20	23 25.8	−0.04	−0.04	270 59.4
24	179 25.8	−0.14	−0.19	23 24.9	−0.05	−0.06	271 58.6
25	179 22.5	−0.13	−0.19	23 23.7	−0.07	−0.07	272 57.7
26	179 19.3	−0.13	−0.19	23 22.1	−0.08	−0.08	273 56.8
27	179 16.2	−0.13	−0.19	23 20.1	−0.10	−0.10	274 56.0
28	179 13.0	−0.13	−0.19	23 17.6	−0.12	−0.11	275 55.1
29	179 09.9	−0.13	−0.19	23 14.8	−0.14	−0.12	276 54.3
30	179 06.9	−0.12	−0.19	23 11.5	−0.15	−0.14	277 53.4
31							

VALID FOR THE YEARS	
2002	For an *Explanation of Daily tables*, see page 60
2006	
2010	For the *Tables of GHA increments*, see page 63
2014	
2018	
2022	
2026	
2030	
2034	
2038	
2042	
2046	
2050	

DAY	GHA SUN	HRLY ACCN	QUAD CORR	DEC SUN	HRLY RATE	QUAD CORR	GHA ARIES
01	179°04.0'	−0.12'	−0.19'	N 23°07.8'	−0.17'	−0.15'	278°52.5'
02	179 01.1	−0.12	−0.19	23 03.7	−0.19	−0.16	279 51.7
03	178 58.2	−0.11	−0.19	22 59.2	−0.20	−0.18	280 50.8
04	178 55.5	−0.11	−0.19	22 54.4	−0.22	−0.19	281 49.9
05	178 52.8	−0.10	−0.19	22 49.1	−0.24	−0.20	282 49.1
06	178 50.3	−0.10	−0.20	22 43.4	−0.25	−0.22	283 48.2
07	178 47.8	−0.10	−0.20	22 37.4	−0.27	−0.23	284 47.4
08	178 45.4	−0.10	−0.20	22 30.9	−0.29	−0.24	285 46.5
09	178 43.1	−0.09	−0.20	22 24.0	−0.30	−0.26	286 45.6
10	178 40.9	−0.09	−0.20	22 16.8	−0.32	−0.27	287 44.8
11	178 38.8	−0.08	−0.20	22 09.2	−0.33	−0.28	288 43.9
12	178 36.8	−0.08	−0.19	22 01.2	−0.35	−0.29	289 43.1
13	178 35.0	−0.08	−0.19	21 52.8	−0.36	−0.30	290 42.2
14	178 33.2	−0.07	−0.19	21 44.1	−0.38	−0.32	291 41.3
15	178 31.6	−0.06	−0.18	21 34.9	−0.40	−0.33	292 40.5
16	178 30.1	−0.06	−0.18	21 25.4	−0.41	−0.35	293 39.6
17	178 28.7	−0.05	−0.17	21 15.5	−0.43	−0.36	294 38.8
18	178 27.4	−0.05	−0.16	21 05.3	−0.44	−0.36	295 37.9
19	178 26.2	−0.04	−0.15	20 54.7	−0.45	−0.37	296 37.0
20	178 25.3	−0.03	−0.14	20 43.8	−0.47	−0.38	297 36.2
21	178 24.5	−0.03	−0.14	20 32.5	−0.48	−0.39	298 35.3
22	178 23.7	−0.03	−0.13	20 20.9	−0.50	−0.40	299 34.5
23	178 23.1	−0.02	−0.12	20 09.0	−0.51	−0.41	300 33.6
24	178 22.7	−0.01	−0.12	19 56.7	−0.53	−0.43	301 32.7
25	178 22.4	−0.01	−0.11	19 44.1	−0.55	−0.44	302 31.9
26	178 22.2	0.00	−0.11	19 31.0	−0.55	−0.45	303 31.0
27	178 22.2	+0.01	−0.10	19 17.7	−0.57	−0.46	304 30.2
28	178 22.4	+0.01	−0.10	19 04.1	−0.58	−0.47	305 29.3
29	178 22.7	+0.02	−0.09	18 50.2	−0.59	−0.48	306 28.4
30	178 23.1	+0.03	−0.09	18 36.0	−0.60	−0.49	307 27.6
31	178 23.7	+0.03	−0.09	18 21.5	−0.63	−0.50	308 26.7

VALID FOR THE YEARS	For an *Explanation of Daily tables*, see page 60
2002	For the *Tables of GHA increments*, see page 63
2006	
2010	
2014	
2018	
2022	
2026	
2030	
2034	
2038	
2042	
2046	
2050	

DAY	GHA SUN	HRLY ACCN	QUAD CORR	DEC SUN	HRLY RATE	QUAD CORR	GHA ARIES
01	178°24.5′	+0.04′	−0.08′	N 18°06.7′	−0.63′	−0.51′	309°25.8′
02	178 25.4	+0.05	−0.08	17 51.5	−0.64	−0.52	310 25.0
03	178 26.5	+0.05	−0.07	17 36.1	−0.65	−0.53	311 24.1
04	178 27.7	+0.06	−0.07	17 20.4	−0.67	−0.54	312 23.3
05	178 29.1	+0.07	−0.07	17 04.4	−0.68	−0.55	313 22.4
06	178 30.7	+0.07	−0.07	16 48.1	−0.69	−0.56	314 21.5
07	178 32.4	+0.08	−0.07	16 31.6	−0.70	−0.57	315 20.7
08	178 34.2	+0.08	−0.07	16 14.8	−0.71	−0.58	316 19.8
09	178 36.2	+0.09	−0.06	15 57.7	−0.72	−0.58	317 19.0
10	178 38.4	+0.09	−0.06	15 40.4	−0.73	−0.59	318 18.1
11	178 40.6	+0.10	−0.05	15 22.9	−0.74	−0.60	319 17.2
12	178 43.0	+0.11	−0.05	15 05.1	−0.75	−0.60	320 16.4
13	178 45.7	+0.11	−0.04	14 47.0	−0.76	−0.61	321 15.5
14	178 48.4	+0.12	−0.03	14 28.8	−0.78	−0.62	322 14.6
15	178 51.2	+0.13	−0.03	14 10.2	−0.78	−0.62	323 13.8
16	178 54.2	+0.13	−0.02	13 51.5	−0.79	−0.63	324 12.9
17	178 57.2	+0.13	−0.01	13 32.5	−0.80	−0.64	325 12.1
18	179 00.4	+0.14	0.00	13 13.4	−0.81	−0.64	326 11.2
19	179 03.7	+0.15	+0.01	12 53.9	−0.82	−0.65	327 10.3
20	179 07.2	+0.15	+0.02	12 34.3	−0.83	−0.66	328 09.5
21	179 10.7	+0.15	+0.02	12 14.5	−0.83	−0.66	329 08.6
22	179 14.4	+0.16	+0.03	11 54.5	−0.84	−0.67	330 07.8
23	179 18.2	+0.16	+0.04	11 34.3	−0.85	−0.67	331 06.9
24	179 22.1	+0.17	+0.04	11 14.0	−0.86	−0.68	332 06.0
25	179 26.2	+0.17	+0.05	10 53.4	−0.86	−0.68	333 05.2
26	179 30.3	+0.18	+0.05	10 32.7	−0.87	−0.68	334 04.3
27	179 34.6	+0.18	+0.06	10 11.8	−0.88	−0.69	335 03.4
28	179 38.9	+0.18	+0.06	9 50.8	−0.88	−0.69	336 02.6
29	179 43.3	+0.19	+0.06	9 29.6	−0.89	−0.69	337 01.7
30	179 47.8	+0.19	+0.06	9 08.3	−0.90	−0.70	338 00.9
31	179 52.4	+0.20	+0.06	8 46.8	−0.90	−0.70	339 00.0

VALID FOR THE YEARS	For an *Explanation of Daily tables*, see page 60
2002	For the *Tables of GHA increments*, see page 63
2006	
2010	
2014	
2018	
2022	
2026	
2030	
2034	
2038	
2042	
2046	
2050	

DAY	GHA SUN	HRLY ACCN	QUAD CORR	DEC SUN	HRLY RATE	QUAD CORR	GHA ARIES
01	179°57.1′	+0.20′	+0.06′	N 8°25.2′	−0.91′	−0.71′	339°59.1′
02	180 01.8	+0.20	+0.06	8 03.4	−0.91	−0.71	340 58.3
03	180 06.7	+0.20	+0.07	7 41.5	−0.92	−0.72	341 57.4
04	180 11.6	+0.21	+0.07	7 19.5	−0.92	−0.72	342 56.5
05	180 16.6	+0.21	+0.07	6 57.4	−0.93	−0.73	343 55.7
06	180 21.6	+0.21	+0.07	6 35.1	−0.93	−0.73	344 54.8
07	180 26.7	+0.21	+0.07	6 12.8	−0.94	−0.74	345 54.0
08	180 31.8	+0.22	+0.07	5 50.3	−0.94	−0.74	346 53.1
09	180 37.0	+0.22	+0.08	5 27.8	−0.95	−0.74	347 52.2
10	180 42.2	+0.22	+0.08	5 05.1	−0.95	−0.74	348 51.4
11	180 47.5	+0.22	+0.08	4 42.4	−0.95	−0.74	349 50.5
12	180 52.7	+0.22	+0.09	4 19.5	−0.95	−0.75	350 49.6
13	180 58.0	+0.23	+0.09	3 56.6	−0.96	−0.75	351 48.8
14	181 03.4	+0.22	+0.09	3 33.6	−0.95	−0.75	352 47.9
15	181 08.7	+0.22	+0.10	3 10.7	−0.96	−0.74	353 47.1
16	181 14.0	+0.23	+0.10	2 47.6	−0.96	−0.74	354 46.2
17	181 19.4	+0.22	+0.11	2 24.5	−0.97	−0.74	355 45.3
18	181 24.7	+0.22	+0.11	2 01.3	−0.97	−0.74	356 44.5
19	181 30.0	+0.22	+0.12	1 38.0	−0.97	−0.74	357 43.6
20	181 35.3	+0.22	+0.12	1 14.8	−0.97	−0.74	358 42.8
21	181 40.6	+0.22	+0.13	0 51.5	−0.98	−0.74	359 41.9
22	181 45.9	+0.22	+0.13	0 28.1	−0.97	−0.74	0 41.0
23	181 51.2	+0.22	+0.13	N 0 04.8	−0.98	−0.74	1 40.2
24	181 56.4	+0.22	+0.13	S 0 18.6	+0.98	+0.73	2 39.3
25	182 01.6	+0.22	+0.13	0 42.0	+0.97	+0.73	3 38.4
26	182 06.8	+0.21	+0.13	1 05.3	+0.98	+0.73	4 37.6
27	182 11.9	+0.21	+0.13	1 28.7	+0.98	+0.73	5 36.7
28	182 17.0	+0.21	+0.13	1 52.1	+0.97	+0.73	6 35.9
29	182 22.0	+0.21	+0.13	2 15.4	+0.97	+0.73	7 35.0
30	182 27.0	+0.20	+0.12	2 38.7	+0.97	+0.73	8 34.1
31							

VALID FOR THE YEARS	
2002	For an *Explanation of Daily tables*, see page 60
2006	For the *Tables of GHA increments*, see page 63
2010	**Declinations for September 23rd**
2014	If the summed corrections for the hourly rate and the quadrennial correction exceed −4.8′ then the declination has changed name. In this case, change the signs for the corrections to +, take 4.8′ from the summed corrections and change the name to South.
2018	
2022	
2026	
2030	
2034	**Declinations for September 22nd (for 2030 and on)**
2038	For 2030 and the years following, the Equinox will fall on this date. Read as above for September 23rd, but using 28.1′ in place of 4.8′.
2042	
2046	
2050	

DAY	GHA SUN	HRLY ACCN	QUAD CORR	DEC SUN	HRLY RATE	QUAD CORR	GHA ARIES
01	182°31.9′	+0.20′	+0.12′	S 3°02.0′	+0.97′	+0.73′	9°33.3′
02	182 36.8	+0.20	+0.12	3 25.3	+0.97	+0.73	10 32.4
03	182 41.6	+0.20	+0.11	3 48.5	+0.97	+0.72	11 31.5
04	182 46.3	+0.19	+0.11	4 11.7	+0.96	+0.72	12 30.7
05	182 50.9	+0.19	+0.11	4 34.8	+0.96	+0.72	13 29.8
06	182 55.4	+0.19	+0.10	4 57.9	+0.96	+0.72	14 29.0
07	182 59.9	+0.18	+0.10	5 20.9	+0.96	+0.72	15 28.1
08	183 04.2	+0.18	+0.10	5 43.9	+0.95	+0.72	16 27.2
09	183 08.4	+0.17	+0.10	6 06.7	+0.95	+0.71	17 26.4
10	183 12.5	+0.17	+0.10	6 29.5	+0.95	+0.71	18 25.5
11	183 16.5	+0.16	+0.10	6 52.2	+0.94	+0.70	19 24.7
12	183 20.4	+0.15	+0.10	7 14.8	+0.94	+0.70	20 23.8
13	183 24.1	+0.15	+0.10	7 37.4	+0.93	+0.69	21 22.9
14	183 27.7	+0.15	+0.10	7 59.8	+0.93	+0.69	22 22.1
15	183 31.2	+0.14	+0.10	8 22.1	+0.93	+0.68	23 21.2
16	183 34.5	+0.13	+0.10	8 44.3	+0.92	+0.68	24 20.3
17	183 37.7	+0.13	+0.10	9 06.3	+0.92	+0.67	25 19.5
18	183 40.8	+0.12	+0.11	9 28.3	+0.91	+0.67	26 18.6
19	183 43.6	+0.12	+0.11	9 50.1	+0.90	+0.66	27 17.8
20	183 46.4	+0.10	+0.11	10 11.7	+0.90	+0.65	28 16.9
21	183 48.9	+0.10	+0.11	10 33.3	+0.88	+0.65	29 16.0
22	183 51.3	+0.10	+0.11	10 54.5	+0.88	+0.64	30 15.2
23	183 53.6	+0.09	+0.10	11 15.7	+0.88	+0.63	31 14.3
24	183 55.7	+0.08	+0.10	11 36.7	+0.87	+0.63	32 13.4
25	183 57.6	+0.07	+0.09	11 57.6	+0.86	+0.62	33 12.6
26	183 59.3	+0.06	+0.09	12 18.3	+0.85	+0.61	34 11.7
27	184 00.8	+0.06	+0.08	12 38.7	+0.85	+0.61	35 10.9
28	184 02.2	+0.05	+0.08	12 59.0	+0.84	+0.60	36 10.0
29	184 03.4	+0.04	+0.08	13 19.1	+0.83	+0.60	37 09.1
30	184 04.4	+0.03	+0.07	13 39.0	+0.82	+0.59	38 08.3
31	184 05.2	+0.03	+0.06	13 58.6	+0.81	+0.58	39 07.4

VALID FOR THE YEARS	For an *Explanation of Daily tables*, see page 60
2002	For the *Tables of GHA increments*, see page 63
2006	
2010	
2014	
2018	
2022	
2026	
2030	
2034	
2038	
2042	
2046	
2050	

DAY	GHA SUN	HRLY ACCN	QUAD CORR	DEC SUN	HRLY RATE	QUAD CORR	GHA ARIES
01	184°05.8'	+0.01'	+0.05'	S 14°18.0'	+0.80'	+0.57'	40°06.6'
02	184 06.1	+0.01	+0.04	14 37.2	+0.80	+0.56	41 05.7
03	184 06.3	0.00	+0.04	14 56.1	+0.79	+0.54	42 04.8
04	184 06.4	−0.01	+0.03	15 14.8	+0.78	+0.53	43 04.0
05	184 06.2	−0.02	+0.03	15 33.3	+0.76	+0.53	44 03.1
06	184 05.8	−0.03	+0.02	15 51.5	+0.75	+0.53	45 02.2
07	184 05.2	−0.03	+0.02	16 09.4	+0.74	+0.53	46 01.4
08	184 04.4	−0.05	+0.02	16 27.1	+0.73	+0.52	47 00.5
09	184 03.3	−0.05	+0.01	16 44.5	+0.71	+0.51	47 59.7
10	184 02.1	−0.06	+0.01	17 01.6	+0.70	+0.50	48 58.8
11	184 00.6	−0.07	+0.01	17 18.4	+0.69	+0.49	49 57.9
12	183 59.0	−0.08	0.00	17 35.0	+0.68	+0.48	50 57.1
13	183 57.1	−0.09	0.00	17 51.2	+0.66	+0.47	51 56.2
14	183 55.0	−0.10	0.00	18 07.1	+0.64	+0.46	52 55.4
15	183 52.6	−0.10	0.00	18 22.5	+0.64	+0.45	53 54.5
16	183 50.1	−0.11	0.00	18 37.9	+0.63	+0.44	54 53.6
17	183 47.4	−0.13	0.00	18 52.9	+0.61	+0.43	55 52.8
18	183 44.4	−0.13	0.00	19 07.5	+0.60	+0.41	56 51.9
19	183 41.2	−0.14	0.00	19 21.8	+0.58	+0.40	57 51.0
20	183 37.8	−0.15	0.00	19 35.7	+0.57	+0.39	58 50.2
21	183 34.3	−0.16	−0.01	19 49.3	+0.55	+0.38	59 49.3
22	183 30.5	−0.17	−0.01	20 02.5	+0.54	+0.37	60 48.5
23	183 26.5	−0.18	−0.01	20 15.4	+0.52	+0.36	61 47.6
24	183 22.3	−0.18	−0.02	20 27.8	+0.50	+0.34	62 46.7
25	183 18.0	−0.19	−0.02	20 39.9	+0.49	+0.33	63 45.9
26	183 13.4	−0.20	−0.03	20 51.6	+0.47	+0.32	64 45.0
27	183 08.7	−0.20	−0.03	21 02.9	+0.45	+0.31	65 44.2
28	183 03.8	−0.21	−0.04	21 13.8	+0.44	+0.30	66 43.3
29	182 58.7	−0.23	−0.04	21 24.4	+0.42	+0.29	67 42.4
30	182 53.3	−0.23	−0.05	21 34.5	+0.40	+0.27	68 41.6
31							

VALID FOR THE YEARS	
2002	For an *Explanation of Daily tables*, see page 60
2006	
2010	For the *Tables of GHA increments*, see page 63
2014	
2018	
2022	
2026	
2030	
2034	
2038	
2042	
2046	
2050	

DAY	GHA SUN	HRLY ACCN	QUAD CORR	DEC SUN	HRLY RATE	QUAD CORR	GHA ARIES
01	182°47.9′	−0.23′	−0.05′	S 21°44.2′	+0.39′	+0.26′	69°40.7′
02	182 42.4	−0.24	−0.06	21 53.5	+0.37	+0.25	70 39.9
03	182 36.6	−0.24	−0.06	22 02.3	+0.35	+0.24	71 39.0
04	182 30.8	−0.25	−0.07	22 10.7	+0.34	+0.23	72 38.1
05	182 24.7	−0.25	−0.08	22 18.8	+0.32	+0.22	73 37.3
06	182 18.6	−0.26	−0.08	22 26.4	+0.30	+0.20	74 36.4
07	182 12.3	−0.27	−0.09	22 33.5	+0.28	+0.19	75 35.6
08	182 05.8	−0.28	−0.09	22 40.2	+0.26	+0.18	76 34.7
09	181 59.2	−0.28	−0.09	22 46.5	+0.24	+0.16	77 33.8
10	181 52.6	−0.28	−0.09	22 52.3	+0.22	+0.15	78 33.0
11	181 45.8	−0.29	−0.09	22 57.6	+0.20	+0.13	79 32.1
12	181 38.9	−0.29	−0.08	23 02.5	+0.19	+0.12	80 31.3
13	181 31.9	−0.30	−0.08	23 07.0	+0.17	+0.10	81 30.4
14	181 24.8	−0.30	−0.08	23 11.0	+0.15	+0.09	82 29.5
15	181 17.6	−0.30	−0.07	23 14.5	+0.13	+0.08	83 28.7
16	181 10.4	−0.30	−0.07	23 17.6	+0.11	+0.07	84 27.8
17	181 03.1	−0.31	−0.07	23 20.3	+0.08	+0.05	85 26.9
18	180 55.7	−0.31	−0.06	23 22.3	+0.07	+0.04	86 26.1
19	180 48.3	−0.31	−0.06	23 24.0	+0.05	+0.02	87 25.2
20	180 40.9	−0.31	−0.06	23 25.2	+0.03	+0.01	88 24.4
21	180 33.5	−0.31	−0.06	23 26.0	−0.01	−0.01	89 23.5
22	180 26.0	−0.31	−0.06	23 26.2	−0.01	−0.02	90 22.6
23	180 18.5	−0.31	−0.06	23 26.0	−0.03	−0.03	91 21.8
24	180 11.0	−0.31	−0.06	23 25.3	−0.05	−0.05	92 20.9
25	180 03.6	−0.31	−0.06	23 24.1	−0.07	−0.06	93 20.1
26	179 56.1	−0.31	−0.06	23 22.5	−0.09	−0.07	94 19.2
27	179 48.7	−0.31	−0.06	23 20.4	−0.10	−0.09	95 18.3
28	179 41.3	−0.30	−0.06	23 17.9	−0.13	−0.10	96 17.5
29	179 34.0	−0.30	−0.06	23 14.9	−0.15	−0.12	97 16.6
30	179 26.7	−0.30	−0.06	23 11.4	−0.16	−0.13	98 15.8
31	179 19.5	−0.29	−0.07	23 07.5	−0.19	−0.14	99 14.9

VALID FOR THE YEARS	For an *Explanation of Daily tables*, see page 60
2002	For the *Tables of GHA increments*, see page 63
2006	
2010	
2014	
2018	
2022	
2026	
2030	
2034	
2038	
2042	
2046	
2050	

DAY	GHA SUN	HRLY ACCN	QUAD CORR	DEC SUN	HRLY RATE	QUAD CORR	GHA ARIES
01	179°12.6'	−0.30'	−0.07'	S 23°03.0'	−0.20'	−0.16'	100°14.0'
02	179 05.3	−0.29	−0.07	22 58.1	−0.22	−0.17	101 13.2
03	178 58.4	−0.29	−0.07	22 52.8	−0.24	−0.19	102 12.3
04	178 51.5	−0.28	−0.07	22 47.0	−0.26	−0.20	103 11.5
05	178 44.7	−0.28	−0.07	22 40.7	−0.28	−0.21	104 10.6
06	178 38.0	−0.28	−0.06	22 34.1	−0.30	−0.22	105 09.7
07	178 31.4	−0.27	−0.06	22 26.9	−0.31	−0.23	106 08.9
08	178 24.9	−0.26	−0.05	22 19.4	−0.34	−0.24	107 08.0
09	178 18.6	−0.26	−0.05	22 11.3	−0.35	−0.26	108 07.2
10	178 12.4	−0.25	−0.04	22 02.8	−0.37	−0.27	109 06.3
11	178 06.3	−0.25	−0.04	21 53.9	−0.39	−0.28	110 05.4
12	178 00.4	−0.24	−0.03	21 44.6	−0.40	−0.30	111 04.6
13	177 54.6	−0.24	−0.03	21 34.9	−0.43	−0.31	112 03.7
14	177 48.9	−0.23	−0.02	21 24.7	−0.44	−0.32	113 02.8
15	177 43.4	−0.22	−0.01	21 14.2	−0.46	−0.33	114 02.0
16	177 38.1	−0.22	0.00	21 03.2	−0.48	−0.34	115 01.1
17	177 32.9	−0.21	0.00	20 51.8	−0.49	−0.35	116 00.3
18	177 27.9	−0.20	+0.01	20 40.0	−0.51	−0.36	116 59.4
19	177 23.1	−0.20	+0.02	20 27.8	−0.52	−0.37	117 58.6
20	177 18.4	−0.18	+0.03	20 15.3	−0.54	−0.38	118 57.7
21	177 14.0	−0.18	+0.03	20 02.4	−0.56	−0.39	119 56.8
22	177 09.7	−0.17	+0.04	19 49.0	−0.57	−0.40	120 56.0
23	177 05.6	−0.16	+0.04	19 35.4	−0.59	−0.41	121 55.1
24	177 01.8	−0.15	+0.04	19 21.3	−0.60	−0.43	122 54.2
25	176 58.1	−0.15	+0.04	19 07.0	−0.62	−0.44	123 53.4
26	176 54.6	−0.13	+0.04	18 52.1	−0.63	−0.45	124 52.5
27	176 51.5	−0.13	+0.05	18 37.0	−0.64	−0.46	125 51.7
28	176 48.4	−0.12	+0.05	18 21.6	−0.66	−0.47	126 50.8
29	176 45.6	−0.11	+0.05	18 05.8	−0.67	−0.48	127 49.9
30	176 42.9	−0.10	+0.05	17 49.8	−0.68	−0.49	128 49.1
31	176 40.5	−0.09	+0.05	17 33.4	−0.70	−0.50	129 48.2

VALID FOR THE YEARS	For an *Explanation of Daily tables*, see page 60
2003	For the *Tables of GHA increments*, see page 63
2007	
2011	
2015	
2019	
2023	
2027	
2031	
2035	
2039	
2043	
2047	
2051	

DAY	GHA SUN	HRLY ACCN	QUAD CORR	DEC SUN	HRLY RATE	QUAD CORR	GHA ARIES
01	176°38.3′	−0.09′	+0.05′	S 17°16.7′	−0.71′	−0.51′	130°47.4′
02	176 36.2	−0.08	+0.05	16 59.7	−0.73	−0.52	131 46.5
03	176 34.4	−0.07	+0.06	16 42.3	−0.73	−0.52	132 45.6
04	176 32.8	−0.06	+0.06	16 24.7	−0.75	−0.53	133 44.8
05	176 31.4	−0.05	+0.07	16 06.8	−0.76	−0.54	134 43.9
06	176 30.1	−0.04	+0.07	15 48.6	−0.77	−0.55	135 43.1
07	176 29.1	−0.03	+0.08	15 30.1	−0.78	−0.56	136 42.2
08	176 28.3	−0.03	+0.09	15 11.4	−0.79	−0.57	137 41.3
09	176 27.6	−0.02	+0.09	14 52.5	−0.80	−0.57	138 40.5
10	176 27.1	−0.01	+0.10	14 33.3	−0.81	−0.58	139 39.6
11	176 26.9	0.00	+0.11	14 13.8	−0.82	−0.59	140 38.7
12	176 26.9	0.00	+0.11	13 54.1	−0.83	−0.59	141 37.9
13	176 27.0	+0.01	+0.12	13 34.2	−0.84	−0.60	142 37.0
14	176 27.3	+0.02	+0.13	13 14.0	−0.85	−0.61	143 36.2
15	176 27.8	+0.03	+0.13	12 53.6	−0.85	−0.61	144 35.3
16	176 28.4	+0.04	+0.14	12 33.1	−0.87	−0.62	145 34.4
17	176 29.4	+0.04	+0.15	12 12.3	−0.88	−0.62	146 33.6
18	176 30.4	+0.05	+0.15	11 51.3	−0.88	−0.63	147 32.7
19	176 31.6	+0.06	+0.16	11 30.1	−0.89	−0.63	148 31.8
20	176 33.0	+0.06	+0.16	11 08.8	−0.90	−0.64	149 31.0
21	176 34.5	+0.08	+0.16	10 47.1	−0.90	−0.64	150 30.1
22	176 36.3	+0.08	+0.16	10 25.5	−0.91	−0.65	151 29.3
23	176 38.1	+0.09	+0.16	10 03.6	−0.91	−0.65	152 28.4
24	176 40.2	+0.09	+0.16	9 41.7	−0.93	−0.65	153 27.5
25	176 42.4	+0.10	+0.16	9 19.5	−0.93	−0.66	154 26.7
26	176 44.7	+0.10	+0.16	8 57.2	−0.93	−0.67	155 25.8
27	176 47.2	+0.11	+0.16	8 34.8	−0.94	−0.67	156 25.0
28	176 49.8	+0.12	+0.16	8 12.3	−0.95	−0.68	157 24.1
29							
30							
31							

VALID FOR THE YEARS	
2003	For an *Explanation of Daily tables*, see page 60
2007	
2011	For the *Tables of GHA increments*, see page 63
2015	
2019	
2023	
2027	
2031	
2035	
2039	
2043	
2047	
2051	

DAY	GHA SUN	HRLY ACCN	QUAD CORR	DEC SUN	HRLY RATE	QUAD CORR	GHA ARIES
01	176°52.6′	+0.12′	+0.16′	S 7°49.6′	−0.95′	−0.68′	158°23.2′
02	176 55.5	+0.13	+0.16	7 26.8	−0.95	−0.69	159 22.4
03	176 58.6	+0.13	+0.16	7 04.0	−0.96	−0.69	160 21.5
04	177 01.7	+0.14	+0.16	6 41.0	−0.96	−0.70	161 20.6
05	177 05.0	+0.14	+0.16	6 17.9	−0.96	−0.70	162 19.8
06	177 08.3	+0.15	+0.16	5 54.8	−0.97	−0.71	163 18.9
07	177 11.8	+0.15	+0.16	5 31.5	−0.98	−0.71	164 18.1
08	177 15.4	+0.15	+0.16	5 08.1	−0.97	−0.72	165 17.2
09	177 19.0	+0.16	+0.16	4 44.8	−0.98	−0.72	166 16.3
10	177 22.8	+0.16	+0.16	4 21.4	−0.98	−0.72	167 15.5
11	177 26.6	+0.16	+0.17	3 57.8	−0.98	−0.72	168 14.6
12	177 30.5	+0.17	+0.17	3 34.3	−0.98	−0.72	169 13.7
13	177 34.5	+0.17	+0.18	3 10.7	−0.98	−0.72	170 12.9
14	177 38.6	+0.17	+0.18	2 47.1	−0.99	−0.72	171 12.0
15	177 42.7	+0.18	+0.18	2 23.4	−0.99	−0.72	172 11.2
16	177 46.9	+0.18	+0.18	1 59.7	−0.99	−0.72	173 10.3
17	177 51.1	+0.18	+0.18	1 36.0	−0.99	−0.72	174 09.4
18	177 55.4	+0.18	+0.19	1 12.2	−0.99	−0.71	175 08.6
19	177 59.7	+0.18	+0.19	0 48.5	−0.99	−0.71	176 07.7
20	178 04.1	+0.18	+0.19	0 24.8	−0.99	−0.71	177 06.8
21	178 08.5	+0.18	+0.19	S 0 01.1	−0.99	−0.71	178 06.0
22	178 12.9	+0.19	+0.19	N 0 22.7	+0.98	+0.71	179 05.1
23	178 17.4	+0.19	+0.19	0 46.3	+0.99	+0.71	180 04.3
24	178 21.9	+0.19	+0.18	1 10.0	+0.98	+0.72	181 03.4
25	178 26.4	+0.19	+0.18	1 33.6	+0.98	+0.72	182 02.5
26	178 31.0	+0.19	+0.17	1 57.2	+0.98	+0.72	183 01.7
27	178 35.5	+0.19	+0.17	2 20.8	+0.98	+0.71	184 00.8
28	178 40.1	+0.19	+0.16	2 44.3	+0.98	+0.71	185 00.0
29	178 44.6	+0.19	+0.16	3 07.7	+0.98	+0.71	185 59.1
30	178 49.2	+0.18	+0.15	3 31.1	+0.97	+0.71	186 58.2
31	178 53.6	+0.19	+0.14	3 54.4	+0.97	+0.71	187 57.4

VALID FOR THE YEARS	
2003	For an *Explanation of Daily tables*, see page 60
2007	
2011	For the *Tables of GHA increments*, see page 63
2015	
2019	**Declinations for March 21st**
2023	If the summed corrections for the hourly rate and the quadrennial correction exceed −1.1′ then the declination has changed name. In this case, change the signs for the corrections to +, take 1.1′ from the summed corrections and change the name to North.
2027	
2031	
2035	
2039	**Declinations for March 20th (for 2011 and on)**
2043	For 2011 and the years following, the Equinox will fall on this date. Read as above for March 21st, but using 24.8′ in place of 1.1′.
2047	
2051	

DAY	GHA SUN	HRLY ACCN	QUAD CORR	DEC SUN	HRLY RATE	QUAD CORR	GHA ARIES
01	178°58.1′	+0.19′	+0.14′	N 4°17.7′	+0.96′	+0.71′	188°56.5′
02	179 02.6	+0.18	+0.14	4 40.8	+0.96	+0.71	189 55.6
03	179 07.0	+0.19	+0.14	5 03.9	+0.96	+0.71	190 54.8
04	179 11.5	+0.18	+0.13	5 26.9	+0.95	+0.71	191 53.9
05	179 15.9	+0.18	+0.13	5 49.8	+0.95	+0.70	192 53.1
06	179 20.2	+0.18	+0.12	6 12.6	+0.95	+0.70	193 52.2
07	179 24.5	+0.18	+0.12	6 35.3	+0.94	+0.69	194 51.3
08	179 28.7	+0.18	+0.12	6 57.8	+0.94	+0.69	195 50.5
09	179 32.9	+0.17	+0.11	7 20.3	+0.93	+0.69	196 49.6
10	179 37.0	+0.17	+0.11	7 42.6	+0.93	+0.69	197 48.8
11	179 41.0	+0.17	+0.11	8 04.8	+0.92	+0.69	198 47.9
12	179 45.0	+0.16	+0.11	8 26.9	+0.91	+0.68	199 47.0
13	179 48.9	+0.16	+0.11	8 48.8	+0.91	+0.68	200 46.2
14	179 52.7	+0.15	+0.11	9 10.6	+0.90	+0.67	201 45.3
15	179 56.4	+0.15	+0.11	9 32.3	+0.89	+0.67	202 44.4
16	180 00.0	+0.15	+0.11	9 53.7	+0.89	+0.66	203 43.6
17	180 03.5	+0.15	+0.11	10 15.1	+0.88	+0.65	204 42.7
18	180 07.0	+0.14	+0.10	10 36.2	+0.87	+0.65	205 41.9
19	180 10.3	+0.14	+0.10	10 57.1	+0.87	+0.64	206 41.0
20	180 13.6	+0.13	+0.09	11 17.9	+0.86	+0.63	207 40.1
21	180 16.8	+0.13	+0.09	11 38.5	+0.85	+0.63	208 39.3
22	180 19.8	+0.13	+0.08	11 58.9	+0.84	+0.62	209 38.4
23	180 22.8	+0.12	+0.07	12 19.1	+0.83	+0.62	210 37.6
24	180 25.6	+0.11	+0.07	12 39.1	+0.83	+0.61	211 36.7
25	180 28.3	+0.11	+0.06	12 58.9	+0.82	+0.61	212 35.8
26	180 31.0	+0.10	+0.05	13 18.5	+0.81	+0.60	213 35.0
27	180 33.5	+0.09	+0.05	13 37.9	+0.80	+0.60	214 34.1
28	180 35.7	+0.10	+0.04	13 57.0	+0.79	+0.59	215 33.2
29	180 38.0	+0.09	+0.03	14 15.9	+0.78	+0.58	216 32.4
30	180 40.1	+0.08	+0.02	14 34.6	+0.77	+0.58	217 31.5
31							

VALID FOR THE YEARS	For an *Explanation of Daily tables*, see page 60
2003	For the *Tables of GHA increments*, see page 63
2007	
2011	
2015	
2019	
2023	
2027	
2031	
2035	
2039	
2043	
2047	
2051	

DAY	GHA SUN	HRLY ACCN	QUAD CORR	DEC SUN	HRLY RATE	QUAD CORR	GHA ARIES
01	180°42.1′	+0.08′	+0.01′	N 14°53.0′	+0.76′	+0.57′	218°30.7′
02	180 44.0	+0.07	0.00	15 11.2	+0.75	+0.56	219 29.8
03	180 45.7	+0.07	0.00	15 29.1	+0.74	+0.56	220 28.9
04	180 47.3	+0.06	−0.01	15 46.8	+0.72	+0.55	221 28.1
05	180 48.7	+0.05	−0.02	16 04.1	+0.72	+0.54	222 27.2
06	180 50.0	+0.05	−0.02	16 21.3	+0.70	+0.53	223 26.3
07	180 51.2	+0.04	−0.03	16 38.2	+0.69	+0.52	224 25.5
08	180 52.2	+0.04	−0.03	16 54.8	+0.68	+0.51	225 24.6
09	180 53.1	+0.03	−0.04	17 11.1	+0.67	+0.50	226 23.8
10	180 53.8	+0.03	−0.04	17 27.2	+0.65	+0.49	227 22.9
11	180 54.4	+0.01	−0.04	17 42.9	+0.65	+0.48	228 22.0
12	180 54.7	+0.01	−0.05	17 58.4	+0.63	+0.48	229 21.2
13	180 55.0	0.00	−0.05	18 13.5	+0.62	+0.47	230 20.3
14	180 55.1	0.00	−0.05	18 28.4	+0.60	+0.46	231 19.5
15	180 55.1	−0.01	−0.05	18 42.9	+0.59	+0.45	232 18.6
16	180 54.9	−0.01	−0.05	18 57.0	+0.58	+0.44	233 17.7
17	180 54.6	−0.02	−0.06	19 10.9	+0.57	+0.43	234 16.9
18	180 54.2	−0.03	−0.06	19 24.5	+0.55	+0.42	235 16.0
19	180 53.6	−0.03	−0.07	19 37.7	+0.54	+0.41	236 15.2
20	180 52.9	−0.03	−0.08	19 50.7	+0.52	+0.40	237 14.3
21	180 52.1	−0.04	−0.08	20 03.2	+0.51	+0.38	238 13.4
22	180 51.1	−0.05	−0.09	20 15.5	+0.49	+0.37	239 12.6
23	180 50.0	−0.05	−0.10	20 27.3	+0.48	+0.36	240 11.7
24	180 48.8	−0.05	−0.11	20 38.8	+0.47	+0.34	241 10.8
25	180 47.5	−0.06	−0.12	20 50.0	+0.45	+0.33	242 10.0
26	180 46.0	−0.07	−0.12	21 00.8	+0.43	+0.32	243 09.1
27	180 44.4	−0.07	−0.13	21 11.2	+0.42	+0.31	244 08.3
28	180 42.7	−0.08	−0.13	21 21.3	+0.40	+0.30	245 07.4
29	180 40.9	−0.08	−0.13	21 31.0	+0.39	+0.29	246 06.5
30	180 39.0	−0.09	−0.14	21 40.4	+0.37	+0.28	247 05.7
31	180 36.9	−0.09	−0.15	21 49.3	+0.36	+0.27	248 04.8

VALID FOR THE YEARS	
2003	For an *Explanation of Daily tables*, see page 60
2007	
2011	For the *Tables of GHA increments*, see page 63
2015	
2019	
2023	
2027	
2031	
2035	
2039	
2043	
2047	
2051	

DAY	GHA SUN	HRLY ACCN	QUAD CORR	DEC SUN	HRLY RATE	QUAD CORR	GHA ARIES
01	180°34.7′	−0.09′	−0.16′	N 21°57.9′	+0.34′	+0.26′	249 04.0′
02	180 32.5	−0.10	−0.17	22 06.1	+0.32	+0.25	250 03.1
03	180 30.1	−0.10	−0.17	22 13.8	+0.31	+0.23	251 02.2
04	180 27.7	−0.11	−0.18	22 21.3	+0.29	+0.22	252 01.4
05	180 25.1	−0.11	−0.18	22 28.3	+0.28	+0.21	253 00.5
06	180 22.5	−0.11	−0.18	22 35.0	+0.26	+0.19	253 59.7
07	180 19.8	−0.12	−0.18	22 41.2	+0.25	+0.18	254 58.8
08	180 17.0	−0.12	−0.18	22 47.1	+0.23	+0.17	255 57.9
09	180 14.2	−0.13	−0.18	22 52.6	+0.20	+0.15	256 57.1
10	180 11.2	−0.13	−0.18	22 57.5	+0.20	+0.14	257 56.2
11	180 08.2	−0.13	−0.18	23 02.2	+0.18	+0.12	258 55.3
12	180 05.2	−0.13	−0.18	23 06.4	+0.16	+0.11	259 54.5
13	180 02.1	−0.13	−0.18	23 10.3	+0.14	+0.09	260 53.6
14	179 58.9	−0.13	−0.18	23 13.7	+0.13	+0.08	261 52.8
15	179 55.7	−0.13	−0.18	23 16.7	+0.11	+0.07	262 51.9
16	179 52.5	−0.13	−0.18	23 19.3	+0.09	+0.06	263 51.1
17	179 49.3	−0.14	−0.18	23 21.5	+0.07	+0.05	264 50.2
18	179 46.0	−0.14	−0.18	23 23.2	+0.06	+0.03	265 49.3
19	179 42.7	−0.13	−0.18	23 24.6	+0.04	+0.02	266 48.5
20	179 39.5	−0.14	−0.18	23 25.6	+0.02	0.00	267 47.6
21	179 36.2	−0.14	−0.19	23 26.1	+0.01	−0.01	268 46.7
22	179 32.9	−0.13	−0.19	23 26.3	−0.01	−0.03	269 45.9
23	179 29.7	−0.13	−0.19	23 26.0	−0.03	−0.04	270 45.0
24	179 26.5	−0.13	−0.20	23 25.2	−0.05	−0.06	271 44.2
25	179 23.3	−0.13	−0.21	23 24.1	−0.06	−0.07	272 43.3
26	179 20.1	−0.13	−0.21	23 22.6	−0.08	−0.08	273 42.4
27	179 17.0	−0.13	−0.22	23 20.6	−0.10	−0.09	274 41.6
28	179 13.9	−0.13	−0.22	23 18.3	−0.12	−0.10	275 40.7
29	179 10.8	−0.13	−0.22	23 15.5	−0.13	−0.11	276 39.9
30	179 07.8	−0.13	−0.21	23 12.4	−0.15	−0.13	277 39.0
31							

VALID FOR THE YEARS	
2003	For an *Explanation of Daily tables*, see page 60
2007	
2011	For the *Tables of GHA increments*, see page 63
2015	
2019	
2023	
2027	
2031	
2035	
2039	
2043	
2047	
2051	

DAY	GHA SUN	HRLY ACCN	QUAD CORR	DEC SUN	HRLY RATE	QUAD CORR	GHA ARIES
01	179 04.8′	−0.12′	−0.21′	N 23°08.8′	−0.17′	−0.14′	278°38.1′
02	179 02.0	−0.12	−0.21	23 04.8	−0.18	−0.15	279 37.3
03	178 59.1	−0.11	−0.21	23 00.4	−0.20	−0.17	280 36.4
04	178 56.4	−0.11	−0.21	22 55.6	−0.21	−0.18	281 35.6
05	178 53.7	−0.11	−0.20	22 50.5	−0.23	−0.19	282 34.7
06	178 51.1	−0.11	−0.20	22 44.9	−0.25	−0.21	283 33.8
07	178 48.5	−0.10	−0.19	22 38.9	−0.26	−0.22	284 33.0
08	178 46.1	−0.10	−0.19	22 32.6	−0.29	−0.23	285 32.1
09	178 43.8	−0.10	−0.18	22 25.7	−0.30	−0.25	286 31.2
10	178 41.5	−0.09	−0.18	22 18.6	−0.31	−0.26	287 30.4
11	178 39.3	−0.08	−0.17	22 11.1	−0.33	−0.27	288 29.5
12	178 37.3	−0.08	−0.16	22 03.2	−0.35	−0.29	289 28.7
13	178 35.3	−0.08	−0.15	21 54.9	−0.36	−0.30	290 27.8
14	178 33.5	−0.07	−0.15	21 46.2	−0.38	−0.31	291 27.0
15	178 31.9	−0.06	−0.14	21 37.2	−0.39	−0.32	292 26.1
16	178 30.4	−0.06	−0.14	21 27.8	−0.40	−0.33	293 25.2
17	178 28.9	−0.05	−0.14	21 18.1	−0.43	−0.34	294 24.4
18	178 27.6	−0.05	−0.13	21 07.8	−0.43	−0.36	295 23.5
19	178 26.4	−0.04	−0.13	20 57.4	−0.45	−0.37	296 22.6
20	178 25.4	−0.04	−0.13	20 46.5	−0.47	−0.38	297 21.8
21	178 24.5	−0.03	−0.13	20 35.3	−0.48	−0.39	298 20.9
22	178 23.8	−0.03	−0.13	20 23.8	−0.50	−0.40	299 20.1
23	178 23.2	−0.02	−0.13	20 11.9	−0.51	−0.41	300 19.2
24	178 22.7	−0.01	−0.12	19 59.7	−0.52	−0.43	301 18.3
25	178 22.4	0.00	−0.12	19 47.2	−0.54	−0.44	302 17.5
26	178 22.3	0.00	−0.12	19 34.2	−0.55	−0.45	303 16.6
27	178 22.3	0.00	−0.11	19 21.0	−0.56	−0.46	304 15.8
28	178 22.4	+0.01	−0.11	19 07.5	−0.58	−0.47	305 14.9
29	178 22.7	+0.02	−0.11	18 53.7	−0.59	−0.48	306 14.0
30	178 23.2	+0.03	−0.10	18 39.5	−0.60	−0.49	307 13.2
31	178 23.8	+0.03	−0.09	18 25.1	−0.61	−0.50	308 12.3

VALID FOR THE YEARS	
2003	For an *Explanation of Daily tables*, see page 60
2007	
2011	For the *Tables of GHA increments*, see page 63
2015	
2019	
2023	
2027	
2031	
2035	
2039	
2043	
2047	
2051	

DAY	GHA SUN	HRLY ACCN	QUAD CORR	DEC SUN	HRLY RATE	QUAD CORR	GHA ARIES
01	178°24.5′	+0.04′	−0.09′	N 18°10.4′	−0.63′	−0.51′	309°11.4′
02	178 25.4	+0.05	−0.09	17 55.3	−0.64	−0.52	310 10.6
03	178 26.5	+0.05	−0.08	17 40.0	−0.65	−0.52	311 09.7
04	178 27.7	+0.05	−0.08	17 24.3	−0.66	−0.53	312 08.9
05	178 29.0	+0.06	−0.07	17 08.4	−0.68	−0.54	313 08.0
06	178 30.5	+0.07	−0.06	16 52.1	−0.68	−0.55	314 07.1
07	178 32.1	+0.08	−0.05	16 35.7	−0.70	−0.56	315 06.3
08	178 34.0	+0.08	−0.04	16 19.0	−0.71	−0.57	316 05.4
09	178 35.9	+0.09	−0.04	16 02.0	−0.72	−0.57	317 04.6
10	178 38.0	+0.09	−0.03	15 44.7	−0.73	−0.58	318 03.7
11	178 40.2	+0.10	−0.02	15 27.2	−0.74	−0.59	319 02.8
12	178 42.5	+0.10	−0.01	15 09.5	−0.75	−0.60	320 02.0
13	178 45.0	+0.11	0.00	14 51.5	−0.76	−0.61	321 01.1
14	178 47.6	+0.12	0.00	14 33.2	−0.77	−0.62	322 00.3
15	178 50.4	+0.12	+0.01	14 14.8	−0.78	−0.62	322 59.4
16	178 53.3	+0.13	+0.01	13 56.1	−0.79	−0.63	323 58.5
17	178 56.4	+0.13	+0.02	13 37.2	−0.80	−0.63	324 57.7
18	178 59.5	+0.14	+0.02	13 18.0	−0.80	−0.64	325 56.8
19	179 02.8	+0.15	+0.03	12 58.7	−0.82	−0.64	326 55.9
20	179 06.3	+0.15	+0.03	12 39.1	−0.83	−0.65	327 55.1
21	179 09.8	+0.15	+0.03	12 19.3	−0.83	−0.65	328 54.2
22	179 13.5	+0.16	+0.03	11 59.4	−0.84	−0.66	329 53.4
23	179 17.3	+0.16	+0.03	11 39.3	−0.85	−0.67	330 52.5
24	179 21.2	+0.17	+0.04	11 19.0	−0.85	−0.67	331 51.6
25	179 25.2	+0.18	+0.04	10 58.5	−0.86	−0.68	332 50.8
26	179 29.4	+0.18	+0.04	10 37.8	−0.87	−0.69	333 49.9
27	179 33.6	+0.18	+0.04	10 17.0	−0.88	−0.69	334 49.1
28	179 37.9	+0.19	+0.04	9 56.0	−0.88	−0.70	335 48.2
29	179 42.4	+0.19	+0.04	9 34.9	−0.89	−0.70	336 47.3
30	179 46.9	+0.20	+0.04	9 13.6	−0.90	−0.70	337 46.5
31	179 51.6	+0.19	+0.05	8 52.1	−0.90	−0.71	338 45.6

VALID FOR THE YEARS	
2003	For an *Explanation of Daily tables*, see page 60
2007	
2011	For the *Tables of GHA increments*, see page 63
2015	
2019	
2023	
2027	
2031	
2035	
2039	
2043	
2047	
2051	

DAY	GHA SUN	HRLY ACCN	QUAD CORR	DEC SUN	HRLY RATE	QUAD CORR	GHA ARIES
01	179°56.2'	+0.20'	+0.05'	N 8°30.5'	−0.90'	−0.71'	339°44.7'
02	180 01.0	+0.20	+0.05	8 08.8	−0.91	−0.72	340 43.9
03	180 05.8	+0.20	+0.06	7 47.0	−0.92	−0.72	341 43.0
04	180 10.7	+0.20	+0.06	7 25.0	−0.92	−0.73	342 42.2
05	180 15.6	+0.21	+0.07	7 02.9	−0.93	−0.73	343 41.3
06	180 20.6	+0.21	+0.08	6 40.6	−0.93	−0.73	344 40.4
07	180 25.6	+0.21	+0.09	6 18.3	−0.93	−0.73	345 39.6
08	180 30.7	+0.21	+0.09	5 55.9	−0.94	−0.73	346 38.7
09	180 35.8	+0.22	+0.09	5 33.3	−0.94	−0.73	347 37.8
10	180 41.0	+0.22	+0.10	5 10.7	−0.95	−0.73	348 37.0
11	180 46.2	+0.22	+0.11	4 48.0	−0.95	−0.73	349 36.1
12	180 51.5	+0.22	+0.11	4 25.2	−0.95	−0.74	350 35.3
13	180 56.7	+0.22	+0.12	4 02.3	−0.96	−0.74	351 34.4
14	181 02.0	+0.22	+0.12	3 39.3	−0.96	−0.74	352 33.5
15	181 07.3	+0.23	+0.12	3 16.3	−0.96	−0.74	353 32.7
16	181 12.7	+0.22	+0.12	2 53.2	−0.96	−0.74	354 31.8
17	181 18.0	+0.23	+0.12	2 30.1	−0.97	−0.74	355 30.9
18	181 23.4	+0.22	+0.12	2 06.9	−0.97	−0.74	356 30.1
19	181 28.7	+0.23	+0.12	1 43.7	−0.97	−0.74	357 29.2
20	181 34.1	+0.22	+0.12	1 20.5	−0.97	−0.74	358 28.4
21	181 39.4	+0.22	+0.12	0 57.2	−0.98	−0.74	359 27.5
22	181 44.7	+0.22	+0.12	0 33.8	−0.97	−0.74	0 26.6
23	181 50.0	+0.22	+0.11	N 0 10.5	−0.98	−0.74	1 25.8
24	181 55.3	+0.22	+0.11	S 0 12.9	+0.98	+0.75	2 24.9
25	182 00.6	+0.22	+0.10	0 36.3	+0.98	+0.75	3 24.1
26	182 05.8	+0.22	+0.10	0 59.7	+0.97	+0.75	4 23.2
27	182 11.0	+0.21	+0.10	1 22.9	+0.98	+0.74	5 22.3
28	182 16.1	+0.21	+0.10	1 46.3	+0.97	+0.74	6 21.5
29	182 21.1	+0.21	+0.10	2 09.6	+0.97	+0.74	7 20.6
30	182 26.1	+0.21	+0.10	2 32.9	+0.97	+0.74	8 19.7
31							

VALID FOR THE YEARS	
2003	For an *Explanation of Daily tables*, see page 60
2007	
2011	For the *Tables of GHA increments*, see page 63
2015	**Declinations for September 23rd**
2019	If the summed corrections for the hourly rate and the quadrennial correction exceed −10.5', then the declination has changed name. In this case, change the signs for the corrections to +, take 10.5' from the summed corrections and change the name to South.
2023	
2027	
2031	
2035	
2039	
2043	
2047	
2051	

DAY	GHA SUN	HRLY ACCN	QUAD CORR	DEC SUN	HRLY RATE	QUAD CORR	GHA ARIES
01	182°31.1′	+0.20′	+0.10′	S 2°56.2′	+0.97′	+0.74′	9°18.9′
02	182 35.9	+0.20	+0.10	3 19.5	+0.97	+0.74	10 18.0
03	182 40.7	+0.20	+0.11	3 42.8	+0.96	+0.74	11 17.2
04	182 45.4	+0.19	+0.11	4 05.9	+0.97	+0.74	12 16.3
05	182 50.0	+0.19	+0.11	4 29.1	+0.96	+0.73	13 15.4
06	182 54.5	+0.18	+0.12	4 52.2	+0.96	+0.73	14 14.6
07	182 58.9	+0.18	+0.12	5 15.2	+0.96	+0.72	15 13.7
08	183 03.3	+0.18	+0.12	5 38.2	+0.95	+0.72	16 12.8
09	183 07.5	+0.17	+0.12	6 01.1	+0.95	+0.71	17 12.0
10	183 11.6	+0.17	+0.12	6 23.9	+0.95	+0.71	18 11.1
11	183 15.6	+0.16	+0.12	6 46.7	+0.94	+0.70	19 10.3
12	183 19.4	+0.16	+0.12	7 09.3	+0.94	+0.70	20 09.4
13	183 23.2	+0.15	+0.12	7 31.9	+0.93	+0.69	21 08.5
14	183 26.8	+0.15	+0.12	7 54.3	+0.93	+0.69	22 07.7
15	183 30.3	+0.14	+0.11	8 16.7	+0.93	+0.68	23 06.8
16	183 33.7	+0.13	+0.11	8 38.9	+0.92	+0.68	24 06.0
17	183 36.9	+0.13	+0.11	9 01.0	+0.92	+0.68	25 05.1
18	183 40.0	+0.12	+0.10	9 23.0	+0.91	+0.67	26 04.2
19	183 42.9	+0.12	+0.10	9 44.8	+0.90	+0.67	27 03.4
20	183 45.7	+0.11	+0.09	10 06.5	+0.90	+0.66	28 02.5
21	183 48.4	+0.10	+0.09	10 28.0	+0.90	+0.66	29 01.6
22	183 50.8	+0.10	+0.08	10 49.5	+0.88	+0.65	30 00.8
23	183 53.2	+0.09	+0.07	11 10.6	+0.88	+0.64	30 59.9
24	183 55.3	+0.08	+0.07	11 31.6	+0.87	+0.64	31 59.1
25	183 57.3	+0.08	+0.06	11 52.5	+0.86	+0.63	32 58.2
26	183 59.1	+0.07	+0.06	12 13.2	+0.85	+0.63	33 57.3
27	184 00.7	+0.06	+0.05	12 33.7	+0.85	+0.62	34 56.5
28	184 02.1	+0.05	+0.05	12 54.0	+0.84	+0.62	35 55.6
29	184 03.4	+0.04	+0.05	13 14.1	+0.83	+0.61	36 54.8
30	184 04.4	+0.04	+0.05	13 34.1	+0.82	+0.60	37 53.9
31	184 05.3	+0.03	+0.05	13 53.8	+0.81	+0.59	38 53.0

VALID FOR THE YEARS	
2003	For an *Explanation of Daily tables*, see page 60
2007	
2011	For the *Tables of GHA increments*, see page 63
2015	
2019	
2023	
2027	
2031	
2035	
2039	
2043	
2047	
2051	

DAY	GHA SUN	HRLY ACCN	QUAD CORR	DEC SUN	HRLY RATE	QUAD CORR	GHA ARIES
01	184°05.9′	+0.02′	+0.05′	S 14°13.2′	+0.80′	+0.59′	39°52.2′
02	184 06.3	+0.01	+0.05	14 32.5	+0.79	+0.58	40 51.3
03	184 06.5	0.00	+0.04	14 51.5	+0.78	+0.57	41 50.4
04	184 06.5	−0.01	+0.04	15 10.3	+0.78	+0.56	42 49.6
05	184 06.3	−0.02	+0.04	15 28.9	+0.75	+0.55	43 48.7
06	184 05.9	−0.02	+0.03	15 47.0	+0.75	+0.53	44 47.9
07	184 05.4	−0.04	+0.03	16 05.1	+0.74	+0.52	45 47.0
08	184 04.5	−0.04	+0.03	16 22.8	+0.73	+0.51	46 46.1
09	184 03.5	−0.05	+0.03	16 40.3	+0.72	+0.51	47 45.3
10	184 02.3	−0.06	+0.03	16 57.5	+0.70	+0.50	48 44.4
11	184 00.9	−0.07	+0.03	17 14.4	+0.69	+0.49	49 43.6
12	183 59.2	−0.08	+0.02	17 31.0	+0.68	+0.48	50 42.7
13	183 57.4	−0.09	+0.02	17 47.3	+0.67	+0.47	51 41.8
14	183 55.3	−0.10	+0.02	18 03.3	+0.65	+0.46	52 41.0
15	183 53.0	−0.10	+0.01	18 19.0	+0.64	+0.45	53 40.1
16	183 50.6	−0.11	0.00	18 34.3	+0.63	+0.44	54 39.2
17	183 47.9	−0.12	−0.01	18 49.3	+0.62	+0.43	55 38.4
18	183 45.0	−0.13	−0.02	19 04.1	+0.60	+0.42	56 37.5
19	183 41.9	−0.14	−0.02	19 18.4	+0.58	+0.41	57 36.7
20	183 38.6	−0.15	−0.03	19 32.4	+0.57	+0.40	58 35.8
21	183 35.1	−0.15	−0.03	19 46.1	+0.55	+0.39	59 34.9
22	183 31.4	−0.16	−0.04	19 59.4	+0.54	+0.38	60 34.1
23	183 27.5	−0.18	−0.04	20 12.3	+0.53	+0.37	61 33.2
24	183 23.3	−0.18	−0.05	20 24.9	+0.50	+0.35	62 32.4
25	183 19.0	−0.19	−0.05	20 37.0	+0.49	+0.34	63 31.5
26	183 14.5	−0.20	−0.05	20 48.8	+0.48	+0.33	64 30.6
27	183 09.8	−0.20	−0.06	21 00.2	+0.46	+0.32	65 29.8
28	183 05.0	−0.21	−0.06	21 11.2	+0.44	+0.31	66 28.9
29	183 00.0	−0.22	−0.06	21 21.8	+0.43	+0.30	67 28.1
30	182 54.8	−0.23	−0.07	21 32.1	+0.41	+0.28	68 27.2
31							

VALID FOR THE YEARS	For an *Explanation of Daily tables*, see page 60
2003	For the *Tables of GHA increments*, see page 63
2007	
2011	
2015	
2019	
2023	
2027	
2031	
2035	
2039	
2043	
2047	
2051	

DAY	GHA SUN	HRLY ACCN	QUAD CORR	DEC SUN	HRLY RATE	QUAD CORR	GHA ARIES
01	182°49.4'	−0.23'	−0.07'	S 21°41.9'	+0.39'	+0.27'	69°26.3'
02	182 43.8	−0.24	−0.07	21 51.3	+0.37	+0.26	70 25.5
03	182 38.1	−0.25	−0.07	22 00.2	+0.35	+0.24	71 24.6
04	182 32.2	−0.25	−0.07	22 08.7	+0.34	+0.23	72 23.8
05	182 26.1	−0.26	−0.07	22 16.9	+0.32	+0.22	73 22.9
06	182 19.9	−0.26	−0.06	22 24.6	+0.30	+0.20	74 22.0
07	182 13.6	−0.27	−0.06	22 31.8	+0.29	+0.19	75 21.2
08	182 07.2	−0.28	−0.06	22 38.7	+0.27	+0.18	76 20.3
09	182 00.6	−0.28	−0.06	22 45.1	+0.25	+0.16	77 19.4
10	181 53.9	−0.28	−0.06	22 51.0	+0.23	+0.15	78 18.6
11	181 47.1	−0.29	−0.06	22 56.4	+0.21	+0.14	79 17.7
12	181 40.2	−0.29	−0.06	23 01.4	+0.19	+0.12	80 16.9
13	181 33.2	−0.30	−0.06	23 06.0	+0.17	+0.11	81 16.0
14	181 26.1	−0.30	−0.06	23 10.1	+0.15	+0.09	82 15.1
15	181 19.0	−0.30	−0.07	23 13.8	+0.13	+0.08	83 14.3
16	181 11.8	−0.30	−0.07	23 17.0	+0.11	+0.06	84 13.4
17	181 04.5	−0.30	−0.07	23 19.7	+0.09	+0.05	85 12.6
18	180 57.2	−0.30	−0.08	23 21.9	+0.08	+0.03	86 11.7
19	180 49.9	−0.31	−0.08	23 23.7	+0.05	+0.02	87 10.8
20	180 42.5	−0.31	−0.08	23 25.0	+0.03	+0.01	88 10.0
21	180 35.1	−0.31	−0.09	23 25.8	+0.02	0.00	89 09.1
22	180 27.6	−0.31	−0.09	23 26.2	0.00	−0.01	90 08.3
23	180 20.2	−0.31	−0.09	23 26.1	−0.02	−0.03	91 07.4
24	180 12.8	−0.31	−0.09	23 25.6	−0.05	−0.04	92 06.5
25	180 05.3	−0.31	−0.09	23 24.5	−0.06	−0.06	93 05.7
26	179 57.9	−0.31	−0.09	23 23.0	−0.08	−0.07	94 04.8
27	179 50.5	−0.31	−0.09	23 21.0	−0.10	−0.09	95 04.0
28	179 43.1	−0.30	−0.09	23 18.6	−0.12	−0.10	96 03.1
29	179 35.8	−0.30	−0.09	23 15.7	−0.14	−0.12	97 02.2
30	179 28.5	−0.30	−0.08	23 12.3	−0.16	−0.13	98 01.4
31	179 21.2	−0.30	−0.07	23 08.5	−0.19	−0.14	99 00.5

VALID FOR THE YEARS	
2003	For an *Explanation of Daily tables*, see page 60
2007	
2011	For the *Tables of GHA increments*, see page 63
2015	
2019	
2023	
2027	
2031	
2035	
2039	
2043	
2047	
2051	

STAR CHART FOR THE SOUTHERN SKY

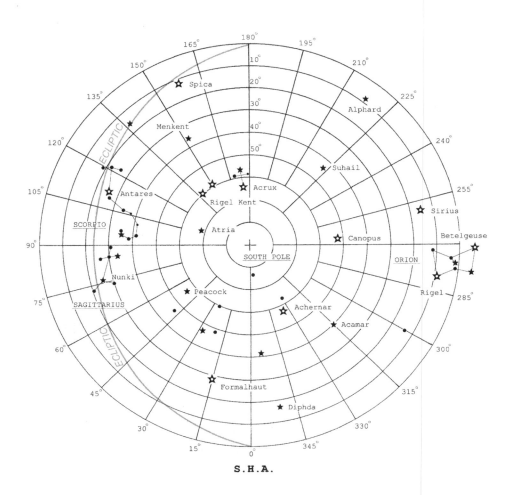

S.H.A.

The view as seen from the South Pole looking up at the sky

Do not confuse stars near the line of the Ecliptic with planets, which will transit the sky on or near the Ecliptic. In general, stars "twinkle", whereas planets do not.

STAR CHART FOR THE NORTHERN SKY

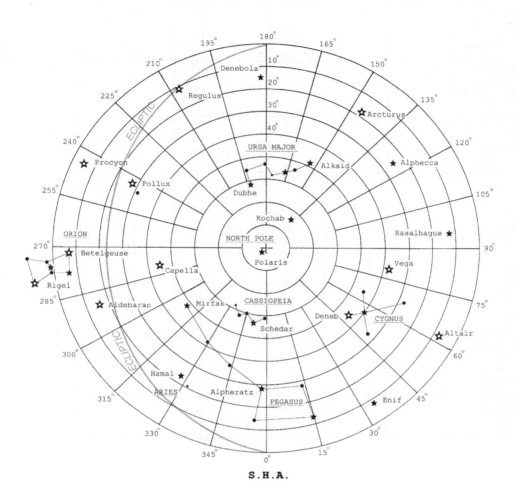

S.H.A.

The view as seen from the North Pole looking up at the sky.

Do not confuse stars near the line of the Ecliptic with planets, which transit the sky on or near the Ecliptic. In general, stars "twinkle", whereas planets do not.

YEAR 2000 STAR POSITIONS

STAR	SHA			DECLINATION		
	JANUARY	FEBUARY	ANN.COR.	JANUARY	FEBUARY	ANN.COR.
Acamar	315°26.0′	315°26.2′	-0.573′	S 40°18.6′	S 40°18.6′	-0.240′
Achernar	335 34.4	335 34.6	-0.560	S 57 14.6	S 57 14.6	-0.305
Acrux	173 20.7	173 20.3	-0.843	S 63 05.6	S 63 05.7	+0.330
Aldebaran	291 01.0	291 01.1	-0.860	N 16 30.5	N 16 30.5	+0.118
Alkaid	153 07.2	153 06.7	-0.600	N 49 18.6	N 49 18.6	-0.300
Alphard	218 06.0	218 05.9	-0.735	S 8 39.6	S 8 39.7	+0.260
Alphecca	126 20.1	126 19.9	-0.638	N 26 42.8	N 26 42.7	-0.230
Alpheratz	357 54.3	357 54.4	-0.778	N 29 05.4	N 29 05.4	+0.330
Altair	62 18.7	62 18.6	-0.730	N 8 52.2	N 8 52.1	+0.160
Antares	112 39.3	112 39.0	-0.923	S 26 25.7	S 26 25.7	+0.130
Arcturus	146 05.3	146 05.0	-0.688	N 19 10.9	N 19 10.8	-0.313
Atria	107 50.9	107 50.4	-1.600	S 69 01.3	S 69 01.3	+0.103
Betelgeuse	271 12.2	271 12.3	-0.813	N 7 24.2	N 7 24.2	+0.010
Canopus	264 00.2	264 00.4	-0.333	S 52 41.9	S 52 42.1	+0.030
Capella	280 48.9	280 49.0	-1.110	N 45 59.9	N 45 59.9	+0.058
Deneb	49 39.0	49 38.9	-0.508	N 45 16.9	N 45 16.8	+0.215
Denebola	182 44.1	182 43.9	-0.765	N 14 34.3	N 14 34.2	-0.335
Diphda	349 06.3	349 06.4	-0.753	S 17 59.5	S 17 59.5	-0.328
Dubhe	194 04.1	194 03.8	-0.920	N 61 44.8	N 61 44.9	-0.325
Enif	33 57.6	33 57.6	-0.735	N 9 52.5	N 9 52.5	+0.275
Fomalhaut	15 35.7	15 35.7	-0.825	S 29 37.6	S 29 37.6	-0.320
Hamal	328 12.4	328 12.5	-0.848	N 23 27.7	N 23 27.7	+0.283
Kochab	137 20.4	137 19.7	+0.015	N 74 09.1	N 74 09.0	-0.248
Menkent	148 19.9	148 19.6	-0.888	S 36 21.9	S 36 22.0	+0.293
Mirfak	308 54.9	308 55.1	-1.075	N 49 51.7	N 49 51.7	+0.210
Nunki	76 11.6	76 11.4	-0.930	S 26 17.7	S 26 17.7	-0.078
Peacock	53 36.2	53 36.0	-1.180	S 56 44.1	S 56 44.0	-0.195
Polaris	321 46.0	321 55.0	-21.54	N 89 16.0	N 89 16.0	+0.240
Pollux	243 40.1	243 40.0	-0.918	N 28 01.4	N 28 01.4	-0.153
Procyon	245 10.2	245 10.2	-0.785	N 5 13.3	N 5 13.3	-0.155
Rasalhague	96 16.4	96 16.2	-0.695	N 12 33.7	N 12 33.6	-0.043
Regulus	207 54.3	207 54.2	-0.798	N 11 57.9	N 11 57.9	-0.295
Rigel	281 21.8	281 21.9	-0.720	S 8 12.3	S 8 12.3	-0.070
Rigil Kent.	140 06.1	140 05.6	-1.090	S 60 49.8	S 60 49.8	+0.248
Schedar	349 52.4	349 52.6	-0.858	N 56 32.4	N 56 32.3	+0.328
Sirius	258 42.5	258 42.5	-0.660	S 16 43.2	S 16 43.2	+0.085
Spica	158 42.2	158 42.0	-0.793	S 11 09.3	S 11 09.4	+0.313
Suhail	222 59.6	222 59.5	-0.550	S 43 25.9	S 43 26.1	+0.243
Vega	80 46.4	80 46.2	-0.508	N 38 47.1	N 38 46.9	+0.055

YEAR 2000 STAR POSITIONS

STAR	SHA			DECLINATION		
	MARCH	APRIL	ANN.COR.	MARCH	APRIL	ANN.COR.
Acamar	315°26.4'	315°26.5'	-0.573'	S 40°18.6'	S 40°18.4'	-0.240'
Achernar	335 34.8	335 34.9	-0.560	S 57 14.5	S 57 14.3	-0.305
Acrux	173 20.1	173 20.1	-0.843	S 63 05.9	S 63 06.1	+0.330
Aldebaran	291 01.2	291 01.4	-0.860	N 16 30.5	N 16 30.5	+0.118
Alkaid	153 06.7	153 06.6	-0.600	N 49 18.6	N 49 18.7	-0.300
Alphard	218 05.9	218 06.0	-0.735	S 8 39.8	S 8 39.8	+0.260
Alphecca	126 19.7	126 19.5	-0.638	N 26 42.7	N 26 42.8	-0.230
Alpheratz	357 54.5	357 54.4	-0.778	N 29 05.3	N 29 05.2	+0.330
Altair	62 18.5	62 18.3	-0.730	N 08 52.1	N 08 52.1	+0.160
Antares	112 38.8	112 38.6	-0.923	S 26 25.8	S 26 25.8	+0.130
Arcturus	146 04.9	146 04.7	-0.688	N 19 10.8	N 19 10.9	-0.313
Atria	107 49.8	107 49.3	-1.600	S 69 01.3	S 69 01.4	+0.103
Betelgeuse	271 12.4	271 12.5	-0.813	N 7 24.2	N 7 24.2	+0.010
Canopus	264 00.6	264 00.9	-0.333	S 52 42.1	S 52 42.1	+0.030
Capella	280 49.2	280 49.4	-1.110	N 45 59.9	N 45 59.9	+0.058
Deneb	49 38.8	49 38.6	-0.508	N 45 16.6	N 45 16.6	+0.215
Denebola	182 43.8	182 43.8	-0.765	N 14 34.2	N 14 34.3	-0.335
Diphda	349 06.5	349 06.4	-0.753	S 17 59.4	S 17 59.3	-0.328
Dubhe	194 03.7	194 03.8	-0.920	N 61 45.0	N 61 45.2	-0.325
Enif	33 57.5	33 57.4	-0.735	N 9 52.4	N 9 52.4	+0.275
Fomalhaut	15 35.7	15 35.6	-0.825	S 29 37.5	S 29 37.4	-0.320
Hamal	328 12.6	328 12.6	-0.848	N 23 27.7	N 23 27.6	+0.283
Kochab	137 19.1	137 18.8	+0.015	N 74 09.1	N 74 09.2	-0.248
Menkent	148 19.4	148 19.3	-0.888	S 36 22.1	S 36 22.2	+0.293
Mirfak	308 55.3	308 55.5	-1.075	N 49 51.7	N 49 51.6	+0.210
Nunki	76 11.2	76 11.0	-0.930	S 26 17.7	S 26 17.6	-0.078
Peacock	53 35.8	53 35.4	-1.180	S 56 43.9	S 56 43.8	-0.195
Polaris	322 05.0	322 10.0	-21.54	N 89 15.9	N 89 15.8	+0.240
Pollux	243 40.1	243 40.3	-0.918	N 28 01.4	N 28 01.5	-0.153
Procyon	245 10.3	245 10.4	-0.785	N 5 13.2	N 5 13.3	-0.155
Rasalhague	96 16.0	96 15.8	-0.695	N 12 33.5	N 12 33.6	-0.043
Regulus	207 54.1	207 54.2	-0.798	N 11 57.9	N 11 57.9	-0.295
Rigel	281 22.0	281 22.1	-0.720	S 8 12.4	S 8 12.3	-0.070
Rigil Kent.	140 05.3	140 05.1	-1.090	S 60 49.9	S 60 50.1	+0.248
Schedar	349 52.7	349 52.7	-0.858	N 56 32.2	N 56 32.1	+0.328
Sirius	258 42.7	258 42.8	-0.660	S 16 43.3	S 16 43.3	+0.085
Spica	158 41.8	158 41.7	-0.793	S 11 09.4	S 11 09.5	+0.313
Suhail	222 59.6	222 59.8	-0.550	S 43 26.2	S 43 26.3	+0.243
Vega	80 46.0	80 45.8	-0.508	N 38 46.9	N 38 46.9	+0.055

YEAR 2000 STAR POSITIONS

STAR	SHA			DECLINATION		
	MAY	JUNE	ANN.COR.	MAY	JUNE	ANN.COR.
Acamar	315°26.5'	315°26.3'	-0.573'	S 40°18.3'	S 40°18.1'	-0.240'
Achernar	335 34.8	335 34.5	-0.560	S 57 14.1	S 57 14.0	-0.305
Acrux	173 20.2	173 20.4	-0.843	S 63 06.2	S 63 06.3	+0.330
Aldebaran	291 01.4	291 01.3	-0.860	N 16 30.5	N 16 30.5	+0.118
Alkaid	153 06.6	153 06.7	-0.600	N 49 18.9	N 49 19.0	-0.300
Alphard	218 06.2	218 06.2	-0.735	S 8 39.8	S 8 39.7	+0.260
Alphecca	126 19.4	126 19.4	-0.638	N 26 42.9	N 26 43.0	-0.230
Alpheratz	357 54.2	357 54.0	-0.778	N 29 05.2	N 29 05.3	+0.330
Altair	62 18.0	62 17.8	-0.730	N 08 52.1	N 08 52.2	+0.160
Antares	112 38.4	112 38.3	-0.923	S 26 25.8	S 26 25.9	+0.130
Arcturus	146 04.7	146 04.7	-0.688	N 19 10.9	N 19 11.0	-0.313
Atria	107 48.9	107 48.7	-1.600	S 69 01.5	S 69 01.6	+0.103
Betelgeuse	271 12.6	271 12.6	-0.813	N 7 24.2	N 7 24.3	+0.010
Canopus	264 01.1	264 01.2	-0.333	S 52 42.0	S 52 41.9	+0.030
Capella	280 49.5	280 49.4	-1.110	N 45 59.9	N 45 59.8	+0.058
Deneb	49 38.3	49 38.0	-0.508	N 45 16.6	N 45 16.8	+0.215
Denebola	182 43.8	182 43.9	-0.765	N 14 34.3	N 14 34.4	-0.335
Diphda	349 06.3	349 06.1	-0.753	S 17 59.2	S 17 59.1	-0.328
Dubhe	194 04.1	194 04.3	-0.920	N 61 45.2	N 61 45.3	-0.325
Enif	33 57.2	33 56.9	-0.735	N 9 52.5	N 9 52.6	+0.275
Fomalhaut	15 35.4	15 35.1	-0.825	S 29 37.3	S 29 37.2	-0.320
Hamal	328 12.5	328 12.4	-0.848	N 23 27.6	N 23 27.6	+0.283
Kochab	137 18.7	137 19.0	+0.015	N 74 09.4	N 74 09.5	-0.248
Menkent	148 19.2	148 19.2	-0.888	S 36 22.3	S 36 22.4	+0.293
Mirfak	308 55.4	308 55.3	-1.075	N 49 51.5	N 49 51.5	+0.210
Nunki	76 10.7	76 10.5	-0.930	S 26 17.6	S 26 17.6	-0.078
Peacock	53 35.1	53 34.7	-1.180	S 56 43.8	S 56 43.8	-0.195
Polaris	322 08.0	322 00.0	-21.54	N 89 15.6	N 89 15.5	+0.240
Pollux	243 40.4	243 40.4	-0.918	N 28 01.5	N 28 01.5	-0.153
Procyon	245 10.6	245 10.6	-0.785	N 5 13.3	N 5 13.3	-0.155
Rasalhague	96 15.6	96 15.5	-0.695	N 12 33.6	N 12 33.7	-0.043
Regulus	207 54.3	207 54.4	-0.798	N 11 57.9	N 11 58.0	-0.295
Rigel	281 22.2	281 22.1	-0.720	S 8 12.3	S 8 12.2	-0.070
Rigil Kent.	140 05.0	140 05.1	-1.090	S 60 50.2	S 60 50.3	+0.248
Schedar	349 52.5	349 52.2	-0.858	N 56 32.0	N 56 32.0	+0.328
Sirius	258 42.9	258 42.9	-0.660	S 16 43.2	S 16 43.1	+0.085
Spica	158 41.7	158 41.8	-0.793	S 11 09.5	S 11 09.5	+0.313
Suhail	222 59.9	223 00.1	-0.550	S 43 26.3	S 43 26.2	+0.243
Vega	80 45.6	80 45.4	-0.508	N 38 47.0	N 38 47.1	+0.055

YEAR 2000 STAR POSITIONS

STAR	SHA			DECLINATION		
	JULY	AUGUST	ANN.COR.	JULY	AUGUST	ANN.COR.
Acamar	315°26.1′	315°25.8′	−0.573′	S 40°18.0′	S 40°17.9′	−0.240′
Achernar	335 34.2	335 33.8	−0.560	S 57 13.9	S 57 13.8	−0.305
Acrux	173 20.7	173 21.0	−0.843	S 63 06.3	S 63 06.2	+0.330
Aldebaran	291 01.1	291 00.9	−0.860	N 16 30.6	N 16 30.6	+0.118
Alkaid	153 06.9	153 07.1	−0.600	N 49 19.0	N 49 19.0	−0.300
Alphard	218 06.3	218 06.3	−0.735	S 8 39.7	S 8 39.6	+0.260
Alphecca	126 19.5	126 19.6	−0.638	N 26 43.1	N 26 43.1	−0.230
Alpheratz	357 53.7	357 53.5	−0.778	N 29 05.4	N 29 05.5	+0.330
Altair	62 17.7	62 17.7	−0.730	N 08 52.3	N 08 52.4	+0.160
Antares	112 38.3	112 38.4	−0.923	S 26 25.9	S 26 25.9	+0.130
Arcturus	146 04.8	146 04.9	−0.688	N 19 11.1	N 19 11.1	−0.313
Atria	107 48.7	107 49.0	−1.600	S 69 01.8	S 69 01.8	+0.103
Betelgeuse	271 12.5	271 12.3	−0.813	N 7 24.3	N 7 24.4	+0.010
Canopus	264 01.2	264 01.0	−0.333	S 52 41.7	S 52 41.6	+0.030
Capella	280 49.2	280 48.9	−1.110	N 45 59.7	N 45 59.7	+0.058
Deneb	49 37.9	49 37.8	−0.508	N 45 16.9	N 45 17.1	+0.215
Denebola	182 44.0	182 44.1	−0.765	N 14 34.4	N 14 34.4	−0.335
Diphda	349 05.9	349 05.6	−0.753	S 17 59.0	S 17 58.9	−0.328
Dubhe	194 04.5	194 04.6	−0.920	N 61 45.2	N 61 45.1	−0.325
Enif	33 56.7	33 56.6	−0.735	N 9 52.7	N 9 52.8	+0.275
Fomalhaut	15 34.8	15 34.7	−0.825	S 29 37.1	S 29 37.1	−0.320
Hamal	328 12.1	328 11.9	−0.848	N 23 27.7	N 23 27.8	+0.283
Kochab	137 19.4	137 20.0	+0.015	N 74 09.6	N 74 09.6	−0.248
Menkent	148 19.3	148 19.5	−0.888	S 36 22.4	S 36 22.4	+0.293
Mirfak	308 55.0	308 54.7	−1.075	N 49 51.5	N 49 51.5	+0.210
Nunki	76 10.4	76 10.4	−0.930	S 26 17.6	S 26 17.6	−0.078
Peacock	53 34.4	53 34.3	−1.180	S 56 43.8	S 56 44.0	−0.195
Polaris	321 58.0	321 37.0	−21.54	N 89 15.5	N 89 15.5	+0.240
Pollux	243 40.4	243 40.3	−0.918	N 28 01.4	N 28 01.4	−0.153
Procyon	245 10.6	245 10.4	−0.785	N 5 13.4	N 5 13.4	−0.155
Rasalhague	96 15.5	96 15.5	−0.695	N 12 33.8	N 12 33.9	−0.043
Regulus	207 54.5	207 54.4	−0.798	N 11 58.0	N 11 58.0	−0.295
Rigel	281 22.0	281 21.8	−0.720	S 8 12.1	S 8 12.0	−0.070
Rigil Kent.	140 05.2	140 05.5	−1.090	S 60 50.4	S 60 50.4	+0.248
Schedar	349 51.8	349 51.5	−0.858	N 56 32.0	N 56 32.2	+0.328
Sirius	258 42.9	258 42.8	−0.660	S 16 43.0	S 16 42.9	+0.085
Spica	158 41.8	158 42.9	−0.793	S 11 09.4	S 11 09.4	+0.313
Suhail	223 00.2	223 00.2	−0.550	S 43 26.1	S 43 26.0	+0.243
Vega	80 45.3	80 45.4	−0.508	N 38 47.3	N 38 47.4	+0.055

YEAR 2000 STAR POSITIONS

STAR	SHA			DECLINATION		
	SEPTEMBER	OCTOBER	ANN.COR.	SEPTEMBER	OCTOBER	ANN.COR.
Acamar	315°25.6'	315°25.4'	-0.573'	S 40°17.9'	S 40°18.0'	-0.240'
Achernar	335 33.5	335 33.4	-0.560	S 57 13.9	S 57 14.0	-0.305
Acrux	173 21.1	173 21.1	-0.843	S 63 06.1	S 63 05.9	+0.330
Aldebaran	291 00.7	291 00.5	-0.860	N 16 30.6	N 16 30.7	+0.118
Alkaid	153 07.2	153 07.3	-0.600	N 49 18.9	N 49 19.8	-0.300
Alphard	218 06.2	218 06.0	-0.735	S 8 39.6	S 8 39.6	+0.260
Alphecca	126 19.7	126 19.8	-0.638	N 26 43.1	N 26 43.0	-0.230
Alpheratz	357 53.4	357 53.4	-0.778	N 29 05.6	N 29 05.7	+0.330
Altair	62 17.8	62 17.9	-0.730	N 08 52.5	N 08 52.5	+0.160
Antares	112 38.6	112 38.7	-0.923	S 26 25.9	S 26 25.9	+0.130
Arcturus	146 05.0	146 05.1	-0.688	N 19 11.1	N 19 11.0	-0.313
Atria	107 49.4	107 49.8	-1.600	S 69 01.9	S 69 01.8	+0.103
Betelgeuse	271 12.1	271 11.9	-0.813	N 7 24.4	N 7 24.4	+0.010
Canopus	264 00.7	264 00.4	-0.333	S 52 41.5	S 52 41.5	+0.030
Capella	280 48.6	280 48.3	-1.110	N 45 59.7	N 45 59.8	+0.058
Deneb	49 37.9	49 38.1	-0.508	N 45 17.2	N 45 17.3	+0.215
Denebola	182 44.1	182 44.0	-0.765	N 14 34.3	N 14 34.3	-0.335
Diphda	349 05.5	349 05.4	-0.753	S 17 58.9	S 17 59.0	-0.328
Dubhe	194 04.6	194 04.4	-0.920	N 61 44.9	N 61 44.8	-0.325
Enif	33 56.6	33 56.7	-0.735	N 9 52.8	N 9 52.9	+0.275
Fomalhaut	15 34.6	15 34.6	-0.825	S 29 37.2	S 29 37.3	-0.320
Hamal	328 11.7	328 11.6	-0.848	N 23 27.9	N 23 28.0	+0.283
Kochab	137 20.6	137 20.9	+0.015	N 74 09.5	N 74 09.3	-0.248
Menkent	148 19.6	148 19.6	-0.888	S 36 22.3	S 36 22.2	+0.293
Mirfak	308 54.3	308 54.1	-1.075	N 49 51.6	N 49 51.7	+0.210
Nunki	76 10.5	76 10.7	-0.930	S 26 17.7	S 26 17.7	-0.078
Peacock	53 34.4	53 34.6	-1.180	S 56 44.1	S 56 44.1	-0.195
Polaris	321 26.0	321 18.0	-21.54	N 89 15.6	N 89 15.8	+0.240
Pollux	243 40.1	243 39.9	-0.918	N 28 01.4	N 28 01.3	-0.153
Procyon	245 10.3	245 10.1	-0.785	N 5 13.4	N 5 13.4	-0.155
Rasalhague	96 15.7	96 15.8	-0.695	N 12 33.9	N 12 33.9	-0.043
Regulus	207 54.4	207 54.2	-0.798	N 11 58.0	N 11 57.9	-0.295
Rigel	281 21.6	281 21.4	-0.720	S 8 11.9	S 8 12.0	-0.070
Rigil Kent.	140 05.8	140 05.9	-1.090	S 60 50.3	S 60 50.2	+0.248
Schedar	349 51.3	349 51.2	-0.858	N 56 32.3	N 56 32.5	+0.328
Sirius	258 42.6	258 42.3	-0.660	S 16 42.9	S 16 42.9	+0.085
Spica	158 42.0	158 42.0	-0.793	S 11 09.4	S 11 09.4	+0.313
Suhail	223 00.1	222 59.8	-0.550	S 43 25.9	S 43 25.8	+0.243
Vega	80 45.6	80 45.8	-0.508	N 38 47.5	N 38 47.5	+0.055

YEAR 2000 STAR POSITIONS

STAR	SHA			DECLINATION		
	NOVEMBER	DECEMBER	ANN.COR.	NOVEMBER	DECEMBER	ANN.COR.
Acamar	315°25.3'	315°25.4'	−0.573'	S 40°18.1'	S 40°18.3'	−0.240'
Achernar	335 33.4	335 33.6	−0.560	S 57 14.2	S 57 14.3	−0.305
Acrux	173 20.8	173 20.4	−0.843	S 63 05.8	S 63 05.8	+0.330
Aldebaran	291 00.3	291 00.2	−0.860	N 16 30.7	N 16 30.7	+0.118
Alkaid	153 07.2	153 07.0	−0.600	N 49 18.6	N 49 18.4	−0.300
Alphard	218 05.8	218 05.5	−0.735	S 8 39.6	S 8 39.7	+0.260
Alphecca	126 19.9	126 19.8	−0.638	N 26 42.9	N 26 42.8	−0.230
Alpheratz	357 53.4	357 53.5	−0.778	N 29 05.8	N 29 05.8	+0.330
Altair	62 18.0	62 18.1	−0.730	N 08 52.4	N 08 52.4	+0.160
Antares	112 38.7	112 38.7	−0.923	S 26 25.8	S 26 25.8	+0.130
Arcturus	146 05.0	146 04.9	−0.688	N 19 10.9	N 19 10.7	−0.313
Atria	107 49.9	107 49.8	−1.600	S 69 01.7	S 69 01.6	+0.103
Betelgeuse	271 11.7	271 11.5	−0.813	N 7 24.4	N 7 24.3	+0.010
Canopus	264 00.1	264 00.0	−0.333	S 52 41.6	S 52 41.8	+0.030
Capella	280 48.1	280 47.9	−1.110	N 45 59.8	N 45 59.9	+0.058
Deneb	49 38.3	49 38.5	−0.508	N 45 17.3	N 45 17.2	+0.215
Denebola	182 43.8	182 43.6	−0.765	N 14 34.2	N 14 34.1	−0.335
Diphda	349 05.5	349 05.5	−0.753	S 17 59.1	S 17 59.1	−0.328
Dubhe	194 04.1	194 03.7	−0.920	N 61 44.6	N 61 44.5	−0.325
Enif	33 56.8	33 56.9	−0.735	N 9 52.9	N 9 52.8	+0.275
Fomalhaut	15 34.7	15 34.8	−0.825	S 29 37.3	S 29 37.4	−0.320
Hamal	328 11.5	328 11.5	−0.848	N 23 28.0	N 23 28.0	+0.283
Kochab	137 21.0	137 20.8	+0.015	N 74 09.2	N 74 09.0	−0.248
Menkent	148 19.6	148 19.4	−0.888	S 36 22.2	S 36 22.2	+0.293
Mirfak	308 53.9	308 53.9	−1.075	N 49 51.8	N 49 51.9	+0.210
Nunki	76 10.8	76 10.8	−0.930	S 26 17.7	S 26 17.7	−0.078
Peacock	53 34.9	53 35.0	−1.180	S 56 44.1	S 56 44.1	−0.195
Polaris	321 16.0	321 21.0	−21.54	N 89 16.0	N 89 16.1	+0.240
Pollux	243 39.6	243 39.4	−0.918	N 28 01.3	N 28 01.3	−0.153
Procyon	245 09.8	245 09.6	−0.785	N 5 13.3	N 5 13.3	−0.155
Rasalhague	96 15.9	96 15.9	−0.695	N 12 33.8	N 12 33.7	−0.043
Regulus	207 54.0	207 53.8	−0.798	N 11 57.8	N 11 57.7	−0.295
Rigel	281 21.2	281 21.1	−0.720	S 8 12.0	S 8 12.1	−0.070
Rigil Kent.	140 05.9	140 05.6	−1.090	S 60 50.1	S 60 50.0	+0.248
Schedar	349 51.3	349 51.4	−0.858	N 56 32.6	N 56 32.7	+0.328
Sirius	258 42.1	258 42.0	−0.660	S 16 43.0	S 16 43.1	+0.085
Spica	158 41.9	158 41.7	−0.793	S 11 09.4	S 11 09.5	+0.313
Suhail	223 59.6	222 59.3	−0.550	S 43 25.8	S 43 25.9	+0.243
Vega	80 45.9	80 46.0	−0.508	N 38 47.4	N 38 47.3	+0.055

EXPLANATION OF DAILY TABLES

Overview

The *Daily tables* give the GHA and declination of the sun, and the GHA of Aries at 00 hrs every day for the four years 2000 to 2003.

For the GHA of the sun, an hourly acceleration is also given for each day. This is the average amount by which the GHA advances on a standard increment of 15° per hour for that day. For the declination of the sun, an hourly rate is given for each day, which is the average amount by which the declination changes for each hour of that day.

Quadrennial corrections are given for each daily value of the GHA and declination of the sun. These quadrennial corrections are used to determine the GHA and declination of the sun at multiples of exactly four years after the date of tabulation, valid up to the year 2050.

For the GHA of Aries, the quadrennial correction is a constant +1.84'. Based on this value, the correction required to give the GHA of Aries for any year up to 2060 are given in the *Tables of GHA increments* on page 63.

To find the GHA of the sun

1. Subtract 2000 from the year in question and divide by four, obtaining the whole number *a* with a remainder *b*. (See the table *Values of a and b for any given year* on page 61.) Enter the *Daily tables* for the month in question which also has the number *b* at the top left and right hand corners. Note the 00 hrs GHA for the day in question.

2. Multiply the hourly acceleration listed for that day by the number of hours and add this to the 00 hrs GHA. (To convert minutes and seconds to decimal parts of an hour, see the table *Minutes and seconds as decimal parts of an hour or degree* on page 62.)

3. Multiply the quadrennial correction for the GHA of the sun by *a* and add this to the GHA.

4. Turn to the *Tables of GHA increments* on page 63, and note the increments required for the time in question and add these to the GHA to give the final GHA for the date and time in question.

Example. Find the GHA of the sun for 11h 27m 39s on July 18th 2014.

1. Taking 2000 from 2014 leaves 14. Dividing 14 by 4 gives 3 remainder 2, so *a* = 3 and *b* = 2. (Or, look up 2014 in the body of *Values of a and b for any given year* on page 61 and note the corresponding values of *a* and *b*.) Entering the *Daily tables* with '2' in the top left and right corners for the month of July, the 00 hrs value for the GHA on the 18th is given as 178° 27.4'.

2. The hourly acceleration tabulated for the 18th is –0.05'. This is multiplied by 11.46 (11 hrs plus 0.46 for the 27 mins 39 secs from the table *Minutes and seconds as decimal parts of an hour or degree* on page 62) to give a total acceleration of –0.58', which is about–0.6'

3. The quadrennial correction for the day is –0.16'. Multiplying by *a*, which is 3, then gives –0.48', which is about –0.5'.

	The GHA becomes	178° 27.4'	from 1
	–	00.6'	from 2
	–	00.5'	from 3
	giving	178° 26.3'	

60

4. Turning to the *Tables of GHA increments*, page 63, the increment for 11 hours is 165°, for 27 minutes it is 6° 45′ and for 39 seconds it is 9.8′. This gives a total increment of 171° 54.8′.

        The final GHA is then   178° 26.3′ from 3
                          +   171° 54.8′ from 4
            Final GHA   350° 21.1′

To find the declination of the sun

1. Proceed as for step 1 in *To find the GHA of the sun* above to find the correct page in the *Daily tables* and note the 00 hrs value of the declination for the day in question.

2. Multiply the hourly rate tabulated for that day by the number of hours and add this to 00 hrs declination. (To convert minutes and seconds to decimal parts of an hour, see the table *Minutes and seconds as decimal parts of an hour or degree* on page 62.)

3. Multiply the quadrennial correction for the declination of the sun by *a* and add this to the declination. This will give the final corrected declination for date and time in question.

Example. Find the declination of the sun for 11h 27m 39s on July 18th 2014.

1. In the '2' tables for the 18th of July, the 00 hrs declination of the sun is N 21° 05.3′

2. The hourly rate is given as –0.44′. Multiply this by 11.46 giving –5.1′.

3. The quadrennial correction is given as –0.36′. Multiply this by *a*, which is 3, to give a correction of –1.1′

      The final declination is then   21° 05.3′ from 1
                            –   05.1′ from 2
                            –   01.1′ from 3
         Final declination   N   20° 59.1′

VALUES OF *a* AND *b* FOR ANY GIVEN YEAR

a	*b* = 0	*b* = 1	*b* = 2	*b* = 3
0	2000	2001	2002	2003
1	2004	2005	2006	2007
2	2008	2009	2010	2111
3	2012	2013	2014	2015
4	2016	2017	2018	2019
5	2020	2021	2022	2023
6	2024	2025	2026	2027
7	2028	2029	2030	2031
8	2032	2033	2034	2035
9	2036	2037	2038	2039
10	2040	2041	2042	2043
11	2044	2045	2046	2047
12	2048	2049	2050	2051
13	2052	2053	2054	2055

Workform for GHA, dec and observed altitudes

A workform to facilitate calculation of the final GHA, declination and observed altitude for the sun and stars is given on page 65. The examples above for the GHA and declination of the sun are set out on the workform as an example on page 66.

To find the GHA of Aries

1. Proceed as for step 1 in *To find the GHA of the sun* above to find the correct page in the *Daily tables* and note the 00 hrs value of the GHA of Aries for the day in question.

2. Using the *Tables of GHA increments* on page 63, find the increments needed for *a*, the hours, the minutes and the seconds. Add these to the 00 hrs. GHA of Aries.

Example. Find the GHA of Aries for 19h 13m 6s on the 12th of May 2036.

1. Subtracting 2000 from 2036 leaves 36. Dividing 36 by 4 gives 9 remainder 0, so *a* = 9 and *b* = 0. Entering the '0' tables for the month of May, the 00 hrs. value of the GHA of Aries for the 12th day is 230° 04.4'.

2. From the *Tables of GHA increments*;

Increment for *a* = 9,	16.6'	00 hrs GHA	230° 04.4'
Increment for 19 hours	+ 285° 46.8'	Total Increment	+ 289° 20.4'
Increment for 13 minutes	+ 3° 15.5'	Total > 360°, so	519° 24.8'
Increment for 6 seconds	+ 1.5'	minus 360°	– 360°
Total Increment	289° 20.4'	Final GHA of Aries	159° 24.8'

MINUTES AND SECONDS AS DECIMAL PARTS OF AN HOUR OR DEGREE

MINUTES	SECONDS					MINUTES	SECONDS				
	0	15	30	45	60		0	15	30	45	60
0	0.00	0.00	0.01	0.01	0.02	30	0.50	0.50	0.51	0.51	0.52
1	0.02	0.02	0.03	0.03	0.03	31	0.52	0.52	0.53	0.53	0.53
2	0.03	0.04	0.04	0.05	0.05	32	0.53	0.54	0.54	0.55	0.55
3	0.05	0.05	0.06	0.06	0.07	33	0.55	0.55	0.56	0.56	0.57
4	0.07	0.07	0.08	0.08	0.08	34	0.57	0.57	0.58	0.58	0.58
5	0.08	0.09	0.09	0.10	0.10	35	0.58	0.59	0.59	0.60	0.60
6	0.10	0.10	0.11	0.11	0.12	36	0.60	0.60	0.61	0.61	0.62
7	0.12	0.12	0.13	0.13	0.13	37	0.62	0.62	0.63	0.63	0.63
8	0.13	0.14	0.14	0.15	0.15	38	0.63	0.64	0.64	0.65	0.65
9	0.15	0.15	0.16	0.16	0.17	39	0.65	0.65	0.66	0.66	0.67
10	0.17	0.17	0.18	0.18	0.18	40	0.67	0.67	0.68	0.68	0.68
11	0.18	0.19	0.19	0.20	0.20	41	0.68	0.69	0.68	0.70	0.70
12	0.20	0.20	0.21	0.21	0.22	42	0.70	0.70	0.71	0.71	0.72
13	0.22	0.22	0.23	0.23	0.23	43	0.72	0.72	0.73	0.73	0.73
14	0.23	0.24	0.24	0.25	0.25	44	0.73	0.74	0.74	0.75	0.75
15	0.25	0.25	0.26	0.26	0.27	45	0.75	0.75	0.76	0.76	0.77
16	0.27	0.27	0.28	0.28	0.28	46	0.77	0.77	0.78	0.78	0.78
17	0.28	0.29	0.29	0.30	0.30	47	0.78	0.79	0.79	0.80	0.80
18	0.30	0.30	0.31	0.31	0.32	48	0.80	0.80	0.81	0.81	0.82
19	0.32	0.32	0.33	0.33	0.33	49	0.82	0.82	0.83	0.83	0.83
20	0.33	0.34	0.34	0.35	0.35	50	0.83	0.84	0.84	0.85	0.85
21	0.35	0.35	0.36	0.36	0.37	51	0.85	0.85	0.86	0.86	0.87
22	0.37	0.37	0.38	0.38	0.38	52	0.87	0.87	0.88	0.88	0.88
23	0.38	0.39	0.39	0.40	0.40	53	0.88	0.89	0.89	0.90	0.90
24	0.40	0.40	0.41	0.41	0.42	54	0.90	0.90	0.91	0.91	0.92
25	0.42	0.42	0.43	0.43	0.43	55	0.92	0.92	0.93	0.93	0.93
26	0.43	0.44	0.44	0.45	0.45	56	0.93	0.94	0.94	0.95	0.95
27	0.45	0.45	0.46	0.46	0.47	57	0.95	0.95	0.96	0.96	0.97
28	0.47	0.47	0.48	0.48	0.48	58	0.97	0.97	0.98	0.98	0.98
29	0.48	0.49	0.49	0.50	0.50	59	0.98	0.99	0.99	1.00	1.00

TABLES OF GHA INCREMENTS

No	SUN HOURS	SUN MINUTES	SUN SECONDS	a	ARIES HOURS	ARIES MINUTES	ARIES SECONDS
1	15°	0° 15′	0.2′	1.8′	15° 02.5′	0° 15.0′	0.2′
2	30	0 30	0.5	3.7	30 04.9	0 30.1	0.5
3	45	0 45	0.8	5.5	45 07.4	0 45.1	0.8
4	60	1 00	1.0	7.4	60 09.9	1 00.2	1.0
5	75	1 15	1.2	9.2	75 12.3	1 15.2	1.2
6	90	1 30	1.5	11.0	90 14.8	1 30.2	1.5
7	105	1 45	1.8	12.9	105 17.2	1 45.3	1.8
8	120	2 00	2.0	14.7	120 19.7	2 00.3	2.0
9	135	2 15	2.2	16.6	135 22.2	2 15.4	2.2
10	150	2 30	2.5	18.4	150 24.6	2 30.4	2.5
11	165	2 45	2.8	20.2	165 27.1	2 45.5	2.8
12	180	3 00	3.0	22.1	180 29.6	3 00.5	3.0
13	195	3 15	3.2	23.9	195 32.0	3 15.5	3.2
14	210	3 30	3.5	25.8	210 34.5	3 30.6	3.5
15	225	3 45	3.8	27.6	225 37.0	3 45.6	3.8
16	240	4 00	4.0		240 39.4	4 00.7	4.0
17	255	4 15	4.2		255 41.9	4 15.7	4.2
18	270	4 30	4.5		270 44.4	4 30.7	4.5
19	285	4 45	4.8		285 46.8	4 45.8	4.8
20	300	5 00	5.0		300 49.3	5 00.8	5.0
21	315	5 15	5.2		315 51.7	5 15.9	5.2
22	330	5 30	5.5		330 54.2	5 30.9	5.5
23	345	5 45	5.8		345 56.7	5 45.9	5.8
24	360	6 00	6.0		360 59.1	6 01.0	6.0
25		6 15	6.2			6 16.0	6.2
26		6 30	6.5			6 31.1	6.5
27		6 45	6.8			6 46.1	6.8
28		7 00	7.0			7 01.1	7.0
29		7 15	7.2			7 16.2	7.2
30		7 30	7.5			7 31.2	7.5
31		7 45	7.8			7 46.3	7.8
32		8 00	8.0			8 01.3	8.0
33		8 15	8.2			8 16.4	8.2
34		8 30	8.5			8 31.4	8.5
35		8 45	8.8			8 46.4	8.8
36		9 00	9.0			9 01.5	9.0
37		9 15	9.2			9 16.5	9.2
38		9 30	9.5			9 31.6	9.5
39		9 45	9.8			9 46.6	9.8
40		10 00	10.0			10 01.6	10.0
41		10 15	10.2			10 16.7	10.2
42		10 30	10.5			10 31.7	10.5
43		10 45	10.8			10 46.8	10.8
44		11 00	11.0			11 01.8	11.0
45		11 15	11.2			11 16.8	11.2
46		11 30	11.5			11 31.9	11.5
47		11 45	11.8			11 46.9	11.8
48		12 00	12.0			12 02.0	12.0
49		12 15	12.2			12 17.0	12.2
50		12 30	12.5			12 32.1	12.5
51		12 45	12.8			12 47.1	12.8
52		13 00	13.0			13 02.1	13.0
53		13 15	13.2			13 17.2	13.2
54		13 30	13.5			13 32.2	13.5
55		13 45	13.8			13 47.3	13.8
56		14 00	14.0			14 02.3	14.0
57		14 15	14.2			14 17.3	14.2
58		14 30	14.5			14 32.4	14.5
59		14 45	14.8			14 47.4	14.8
60		15 00	15.0			15 02.5	15.0

EXPLANATION OF TABLES OF STAR POSITIONS

Overview

The tables of star positions give the Sidereal Hour Angle (SHA) and the declination of 39 selected navigational stars, for the 15th of each month, during the year 2000. Also given are annual correction factors by which the SHA and declination of the stars may be corrected for each succeeding year. The tables are on six pages, with two months for each page.

The GHA of a star can be obtained from:

GHA Star = GHA Aries + SHA Star

How to find the SHA and declination of a star.

1. Enter the tables listing star positions for the month in question. For the star in question, note the year 2000 SHA and declination which are tabulated for the 15th of that month. If 0.1' precision is necessary, use interpolation to adjust these values for the date in question.

2. Subtract 2000 from the year in question and multiply the annual correction factors by this number. Add these corrections to the SHA and the declination noted in step one to obtain the final corrected SHA and declination.

Example. Find the GHA and declination of the star Dubhe for 19h 13m 6s on May 12th, 2036

1. Entering the tables for the month of May, note that the SHA is listed as 194° 04.1' and the declination is listed as N 61° 45.2'.

2. Subtracting 2000 from 2036 leaves 36. Multiply the annual correction factors by 36. The annual correction factor for the SHA of Dubhe is −0.920', multiplying by 36 gives a value of −33.1'.

The corrected value for the SHA is then 193° 31.0'

From the example for the GHA of Aries on page 62, the GHA of Aries for this date and time is 159° 24.8'.

The GHA of Dubhe is then:

159° 24.8'	GHA of Aries
+193° 31.0'	SHA of Dubhe
352° 55.8'	GHA of Dubhe

For the declination, the annual correction factor is given as −0.325'. Multiplying by 36 gives −11.7'.

The corrected value for the declination is then 61° 45.2' − 11.7' leaving a corrected declination of   N 61° 33.5'.

The GHA of Dubhe is then 352° 55.8'
The declination for Dubhe is N 61° 33.5'

WORKFORM FOR GHA, DEC AND OBSERVED ALTITUDE

DATE: Day _____ Month _____ Year _____

TIME OF SIGHT (GMT): hrs _____ mins _____ secs _____

For the year in question: **a**_____ **b** _____

SUN GHA

	deg.	mins.
GHA for the day		
Total hourly accn		
Quad corr		
Hours increment		
Mins. increment		
Secs. increment		
Final GHA		
−360° if needed		

STAR GHA for _____

	deg.	mins.
GHA Aries for the day		
a increment		
Hours increment		
Mins. increment		
Secs. increment		
Final GHA Aries		
−360° if needed		
SHA Star +		
GHA Star		
−360° if needed		

DECLINATION

		deg.	mins.
Dec for the day	N S		
Total hrly rate (sun)			
Ann/Quad corr			
Final Dec	N S		

OBSERVED ALTITUDE Ho

	deg.	mins.
Sextant alt.		
Index error		
Dip corr		
Refraction corr		
Ho		

WORKFORM FOR GHA, DEC AND OBSERVED ALTITUDE

DATE: Day _18_ Month _JULY_ Year _2014_

TIME OF SIGHT (GMT): hrs _11_ mins _27_ secs _39_

For the year in question: a _3_ b _2_

SUN GHA

	deg.	mins.
GHA for the day	178	27·4
Total hourly accn		− 0·6
Quad corr		− 0·5
Hours increment	165	
Mins. increment	6	45·0
Secs. increment		9·8
Final GHA	**350**	**21·1**
−360° if needed		

STAR GHA for _____

	deg.	mins.
GHA Aries for the day		
a increment		
Hours increment		
Mins. increment		
Secs. increment		
Final GHA Aries		
−360° if needed		
SHA Star +		
GHA Star		
−360° if needed		

DECLINATION

		deg.	mins.
Dec for the day	Ⓝ S	21	5·3
Total hrly rate (sun)			− 5·1
Ann/Quad corr			− 1·1
Final Dec	Ⓝ S	**20**	**59·1**

OBSERVED ALTITUDE Ho

	deg.	mins.
Sextant alt.		
Index error		
Dip corr		
Refraction corr		
Ho		

Example workform for GHA, dec and observed altitude

Above is a workform filled in for the example calculation of the GHA and declination of the sun given on pages 60 and 61.

The time and date for the example was 11hrs 27mins 39 secs on the 18th of July 2014

EXPLANATION OF ALTITUDE CORRECTION TABLES

Overview

Assuming that **hs,** the sextant altitude, has been corrected for index error and other instrument errors, then **ha**, the apparent altitude, is obtained by correcting for dip. The tables on page 67 give dip corrections for height of eye in both feet and metres. Corrections are given to the nearest 0.1' for heights up to 100 feet or 30 metres, and to the nearest whole minute for heights up to 2,400 feet or 800 metres. Mental interpolation should be used for heights in between those tabulated.

The observed altitude, **Ho**, is obtained by correcting **ha** for refraction of the light from the celestial body in the earth's atmosphere. Correction for refraction is given in two tables on page 67, one for apparent altitudes from 9° to 90° and one for apparent altitudes below 9°.

Refraction corrections are given for observations of the lower and upper limbs of the sun and for the stars. The corrections for the lower and upper limbs of the sun include an adjustment to give the altitude of the centre of the sun. The corrections listed for stars assume that the centre of the body is being observed.

The adjustment to give the altitude of the centre of the sun when observing its lower or upper limb assumes an apparent semi-diameter for the sun of 16.1'. But this is only true for the months of March and October. For other months of the year, a further correction must be made to account for the change in the apparent semi-diameter. These are listed in the table of *Monthly corrections for the sun's limbs* below.

MONTHLY CORRECTIONS FOR THE SUN'S LIMBS

LIMB	JAN	FEB	MAR	APR	MAY	JUN	JUL	AUG	SEP	OCT	NOV	DEC
lower	+0.2'	+0.1'	0.0'	−0.1'	−0.2'	−0.3'	−0.3'	−0.3'	−0.2'	0.0'	+0.1'	+0.2'
upper	−0.2'	−0.1'	0.0'	+0.1'	+0.2'	+0.3'	+0.3'	+0.3'	+0.2'	0.0'	+0.1'	−0.2'

Example. It is January and a marine sextant is used to make an observation of the lower limb of the sun at a height of 10 feet above the water. The sextant altitude, corrected for index error, is 23° 42.6'. What is **Ho**, the observed altitude?

For a height of eye of 10 feet, the correction is −3.1'. So **ha**, the apparent altitude, will be 23° 39.5'

The refraction correction for an **ha** of 24° is given as +14.0' for an observation of the sun's lower limb. As the observation was made in January, a further correction of +0.2' must be made, so yielding a total refraction correction of +14.2'

Ho, the observed altitude, is then 23° 53.7'

Workform for GHA, dec and observed altitude

A workform to facilitate calculation of the final GHA, declination and observed altitude for the sun and stars is given on page 65.

ALTITUDE CORRECTION TABLES 9° – 90°

Apparent Altitude	SUN limb lower	SUN limb upper	STARS	Ht.of eye FEET	Corr.	Ht.of eye METRES	Corr.
	REFRACTION AND PARALLAX			DIP			
9°	+10.3′	−21.9	−5.9′	2	−1.4′	1.0	−1.8′
10	+10.8	−21.4	−5.3	4	−1.9	1.5	−2.1
11	+11.3	−20.9	−4.8	6	−2.4	2.0	−2.5
12	+11.7	−20.5	−4.5	8	−2.7	2.5	−2.8
13	+12.0	−20.2	−4.1	10	−3.1	3.0	−3.0
14	+12.3	−19.9	−3.8	12	−3.4	3.5	−3.3
15	+12.6	−19.6	−3.6	14	−3.6	4.0	−3.5
16	+12.8	−19.4	−3.3	16	−3.9	4.5	−3.7
17	+13.0	−19.2	−3.1	18	−4.1	5.0	−3.9
18	+13.2	−19.0	−3.0	20	−4.3	6.0	−4.3
19	+13.4	−18.8	−2.8	25	−4.9	7.0	−4.7
20	+13.5	−18.7	−2.6	30	−5.3	8.0	−5.0
21	+13.7	−18.5	−2.5	40	−6.1	10	−5.6
22	+13.8	−18.4	−2.4	50	−6.9	12	−6.1
23	+13.9	−18.3	−2.3	60	−7.5	15	−6.8
24	+14.0	−18.2	−2.2	70	−8.1	20	−7.9
25	+14.1	−18.1	−2.1	80	−8.7	25	−8.8
26	+14.2	−18.0	−2.0	100	−9.7	30	−9.6
27	+14.3	−17.9	−1.9	125	−11	40	−11
28	+14.4	−17.8	−1.8	150	−12	50	−12
30	+14.5	−17.7	−1.7	175	−13	60	−14
32	+14.6	−17.6	−1.6	200	−14	70	−15
34	+14.7	−17.5	−1.4	250	−15	80	−16
36	+14.8	−17.4	−1.3	300	−17	90	−17
38	+14.9	−17.3	−1.2	350	−18	100	−18
40	+15.0	−17.2	−1.1	400	−19	125	−20
42	+15.1	−17.1	−1.1	500	−22	150	−22
44	+15.2	−17.0	−1.0	600	−24	175	−23
46	+15.2	−17.0	−0.9	700	−26	200	−25
48	+15.3	−16.9	−0.9	800	−27	225	−26
50	+15.4	−16.8	−0.8	900	−29	250	−28
52	+15.4	−16.8	−0.8	1000	−31	275	−29
54	+15.5	−16.7	−0.7	1250	−34	300	−30
56	+15.5	−16.7	−0.7	1500	−38	400	−35
58	+15.6	−16.6	−0.6	1750	−41	500	−39
60	+15.6	−16.6	−0.6	2000	−43	600	−43
62	+15.6	−16.6	−0.5	2500	−49	800	−50
64	+15.7	−16.5	−0.5				
66	+15.8	−16.5	−0.4				
70	+15.8	−16.4	−0.3				
80	+15.9	−16.3	−0.2				
90	+16.1	−16.1	0.0				

ALTITUDE CORRECTION TABLES 0° – 9°

Apparent Altitude	SUN limb lower	SUN limb upper	STARS	Apparent Altitude	SUN limb lower	SUN limb upper	STARS
0° 00′	−18.3	−50.5	−34.5	3° 00′	+1.9	−30.3	−14.4
0° 03′	−17.7	−49.9	−33.9	3° 15′	+2.6	−29.6	−13.6
0° 06′	−17.0	−49.2	−33.3	3° 30′	+3.3	−28.9	−13.0
0° 10′	−16.2	−48.4	−32.5	3° 45′	+3.9	−28.3	−12.3
0° 14′	−15.4	−47.6	−31.7	4° 00′	+4.5	−27.7	−11.8
0° 18′	−14.7	−46.9	−30.9	4° 15′	+5.0	−27.2	−11.2
0° 22′	−14.0	−46.3	−30.2	4° 30′	+5.5	−26.7	−10.8
0° 26′	−13.3	−45.5	−29.5	4° 45′	+5.9	−26.3	−10.3
0° 30′	−12.6	−44.8	−28.8	5° 00′	+6.3	−25.9	− 9.9
0° 35′	−11.7	−43.9	−28.0	5° 15′	+6.7	−25.5	− 9.5
0° 40′	−11.0	−43.2	−27.2	5° 30′	+7.1	−25.1	− 9.2
0° 45′	−10.2	−42.4	−26.5	5° 45′	+7.4	−24.8	− 8.8
0° 50′	− 9.5	−41.7	−25.7	6° 00′	+7.7	−24.5	− 8.5
0° 55′	− 8.8	−41.0	−25.0	6° 15′	+8.0	−24.2	− 8.2
1° 00′	− 8.1	−40.3	−24.4	6° 30′	+8.3	−23.9	− 8.0
1° 10′	− 6.9	−39.1	−23.1	6° 45′	+8.5	−23.7	− 7.7
1° 20′	− 5.8	−38.0	−22.0	7° 00′	+8.8	−23.4	− 7.5
1° 30′	− 4.7	−36.9	−20.9	7° 15′	+9.0	−23.2	− 7.2
1° 40′	− 3.7	−35.9	−20.0	7° 30′	+9.2	−23.0	− 7.0
1° 50′	− 2.8	−35.0	−19.1	7° 45′	+9.4	−22.8	− 6.8
2° 00′	− 2.0	−34.2	−18.3	8° 00′	+9.6	−22.6	− 6.6
2° 15′	− 0.9	−33.1	−17.1	8° 15′	+9.8	−22.4	− 6.5
2° 30′	+ 0.1	−32.0	−16.1	8° 30′	+10.0	−22.2	− 6.3
2° 45′	+ 1.0	−31.2	−15.2	8° 45′	+10.1	−22.1	− 6.1

SIGHT REDUCTION USING A CALCULATOR

Overview

Calculators with trigonometric functions are readily available and they can be used as a quick and convenient means of reducing sights to a position line on a map or chart.

The formulae given here were chosen as the most suitable for use with a calculator, taking into account ease of use and required accuracy. The same formulae are given in the *Nautical Almanac*.

The sight reduction method assumed here is the standard Marcq St.- Hilaire altitude intercept method, in which the altitude intercept distance from an estimated position to a position line is determined. The altitude intercept distance **a** is derived from the difference between the observed altitude **Ho** and the calculated altitude **Hc**. The azimuth **Zn** is also required to give a bearing to the intercept from the estimated position.

Three inputs are required: the Local Hour Angle (LHA) between the observer's estimated longitude and the Greenwich Hour Angle (GHA) of the celestial body, the observer's estimated latitude (Lat) and the declination of the celestial body (Dec).

The outputs are the calculated altitude **Hc** and azimuth **Zn** for the celestial body, as would be observed from the estimated position.

The Local Hour Angle is calculated using the GHA of the celestial body and the longitude of the estimated or assumed position as follows:

> LHA = GHA – longitude, if the longitude is West
> LHA = GHA + longitude, if the longitude is East

Formulae for calculated altitude and azimuth

$$\mathbf{Hc} = Sin^{-1}\left(Sin\,Dec\;Sin\,\text{Lat} + Cos\,Dec\;Cos\,\text{Lat}\;Cos\,\text{LHA}\right)$$

$$Z = Cos^{-1}\left(\frac{Sin\,Dec\;Cos\,\text{Lat} - Cos\,Dec\;Sin\,\text{Lat}\;Cos\,\text{LHA}}{Cos\,\mathbf{Hc}}\right)$$

Use the convention that the angles for Lat and Dec are plus for Northern hemisphere positions and minus for Southern hemisphere positions.

If a minus value is returned for **Hc**, this indicates the celestial object is below the celestial horizon. (Due to the effects of refraction and height of eye, objects on or close to the visual horizon are usually below the celestial horizon.)

If the LHA is greater than 180°, the azimuth **Zn** = Z
If the LHA is less than 180°, the azimuth **Zn** = 360° – Z

Notes

Though a calculator may have trigonometric functions, it is usually much easier to enter angles into the calculator in decimal degree form rather than as degrees and minutes. The table *Minutes and seconds as decimal parts of an hour or degree* on page 62 gives approximate conversions.

EXPLANATION OF THE SIGHT REDUCTION TABLES

Overview

The tables used here are a form of the "NAO Sight Reduction Tables" as used in the *Nautical Almanac*.

The sight reduction method assumed here is the standard Marcq St.- Hilaire altitude intercept method, in which the altitude intercept distance from an assumed position to a position line is determined. The altitude intercept distance **a** is derived from the difference between the observed altitude **Ho** and the calculated altitude **Hc**. The azimuth **Zn** is also required to give a bearing to the intercept from the assumed position.

The tables have three inputs: the Local Hour Angle (LHA) between the observer's assumed longitude and the Greenwich Hour Angle (GHA) of the celestial body, the observer's assumed latitude (Lat) and the declination of the celestial body.

The outputs of the tables are the calculated altitude **Hc** and azimuth **Zn** for the celestial body, as would be observed from the assumed position.

The LHA and Lat must be entered in the tables as whole degrees. So an assumed position is used for the sight reduction rather than the position as estimated by deduced reckoning.

A workform (page 76) is provided which greatly facilitates the use of these tables. The workform was developed by the Starpath School of Navigation (www.starpath.com) and its use is recommended with these tables.

Obtaining the calculated altitude and azimuth

1. Select an assumed latitude having integral degrees (that is, whole degrees with zero minutes) nearest the estimated latitude.

Having determined the Greenwich Hour Angle (GHA) for the body of interest, choose a longitude near the estimated longitude such that the Local Hour Angle (LHA) has integral degrees, where:
LHA = GHA + longitude, if the longitude is East.
LHA = GHA − longitude, if the longitude is West.

2. Open the tables at the pages appropriate for the assumed latitude (Lat). For the assumed latitude and LHA, record the quantities A, B and Z_1.
>   RULES
>   B is minus if the LHA is between 90° and 270°.
Z_1 has the same sign as B.

Let A′ = the minutes part of A.
Let $\overline{A}$ = the value of A rounded to the nearest whole degree.
>   RULES
>   Round A up for values of A′ greater than 29. Otherwise, round down.

3. Let F = B + Declination.
>   RULES
>   Declination is minus if the latitude and declination have contrary names.

If F is negative, the body is below the celestial horizon. (Bodies on or near the visible horizon will generally be below the celestial horizon.) Regard F as positive until step 7.

Let F' = the minutes part of F.
Let $\overline{F}$ = the value of F rounded to the nearest whole degree.
> RULES
> Round F up for values of F' greater than 29. Otherwise round down.

4.   Open the tables at the pages appropriate for $\overline{A}$. For the values $\overline{A}$ and $\overline{F}$, record the quantities H, P and Z_2 .

Let P' = the minutes part of P.
Let $\overline{P}$ = the value of P rounded to the nearest whole degree.
> RULES
> Round P up for values of P' greater than 29.

Let $\overline{Z}_2$ = the value of Z_2 rounded to the nearest whole degree.
> RULES
> Round up when the decimal part of Z_2 is 0.5 or greater. Otherwise, round down.

5.   Open the auxiliary tables and for the values of F' and $\overline{P}$, record the value of corr1.
> RULES
> corr1 is minus if F is less than 90° **and** F' is greater than 29.
> corr1 is minus if F is greater than 90° **and** F' is less than 30.

6.   Open the auxiliary tables and for the values of A' and $\overline{Z}_2$, record the value of corr2.
> RULES
> corr2 is minus if A' is less than 30.

7.   **Hc**, the calculated altitude, is found from: **Hc** = H + corr1 + corr2.
RULES
If F is negative, let **Hc** be negative.

8.   Let Z be the absolute value (discounting any resulting minus sign) of (Z_1 + Z_2).
RULES
> Z_2 is minus if F is greater than 90°.
If F is negative, replace Z_2 with 180° – Z_2 .

9.   To obtain **Zn**, the azimuth.

For latitudes in the Northern hemisphere:
>   If the LHA is greater than 180°, let **Zn** = Z.
>   If the LHA is less than 180°, let **Zn** = 360°– Z.

For latitudes in the Southern hemisphere:
>   If the LHA is greater than 180°, let **Zn** = 180°– Z.
>   If the LHA is less than 180°, let **Zn** = 180°+ Z.

Example 1. The star Dubhe is observed from an estimated position of 55° 15′ N and 2° 43′ W. The GHA of Dubhe is 118° 47′ and the declination is N 61° 33′. Find **Hc** and **Zn**.

1. Calculating the LHA from the estimated position yields:

The GHA of Dubhe	118° 47′	As the longitude is West,
The longitude of the estimated position	− 2° 43′	longitude is taken from
Final LHA	= 116° 04′	GHA to give the LHA.

For an assumed longitude of 2° 47′, the LHA will have an integral value of 116°. Let the assumed latitude be 55° N.

2. Entering the tables for an assumed latitude (Lat) of 55° and an LHA of 116° yields:
A = 31° 02′, B = − 17° 04′ and Z_1 = − 30.8.
(As the LHA lies between 90° and 270°, B and so Z_1 are minus.)
From A, A′= 02 and $\overline{A}$ = 31.

3. F = B + Declination. So:

$$\begin{array}{rl} B & - \ 17°\ 04′ \\ \text{Declination} & + \ 61°\ 33′ \\ \hline F & = \ 44°\ 29′ \end{array}$$

From F, F′ = 29 and $\overline{F}$ = 44.

4. Entering the tables for the values $\overline{A}$ = 31 and $\overline{F}$ = 44 yields:
H = 36° 33′, P = 50° 08′ and Z_2 = 63.6
From P, P′= 08 and $\overline{P}$ = 50. Z_2 is rounded up so that $\overline{Z}_2$ = 64.

5. Entering the Auxiliary Tables for F′ = 29 and $\overline{P}$ = 50 yields corr1 = +22.

6. Entering the Auxiliary Tables for A′= 02 and $\overline{Z}_2$ = 64 yields corr2 = −1
(corr2 is minus as A′ is less than 30.)

7. The calculated altitude **Hc** = H + corr1 + corr2, so:

$$\begin{array}{rl} H & 36°\ 33′ \\ \text{corr1} \ + & 22′ \\ \text{corr2} \ - & \underline{\ \ 01′} \\ \textbf{Hc} \ = & 36°\ 54′ \end{array}$$

8. Z is the absolute value of ($Z_1 + Z_2$). So for Z_1 = − 30.8 and Z_2 = 63.6, Z will be 32.8°.

9. Applying the rule for Northern hemisphere latitudes where the LHA is less than 180°:
The azimuth **Zn** = 360° − Z, or 327.2°.

Example 1 as worked out using the workform on page 76,

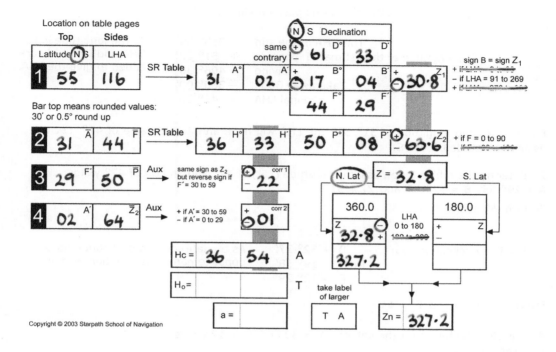

Copyright © 2003 Starpath School of Navigation

Example 2. The sun is observed from an estimated position 46° 38' S, 51° 22' E. The GHA of the sun is 355° 08' and the declination is N 19° 59'. Find **Hc** and **Zn**.

1. Calculating the LHA from the estimated position yields:

The GHA of the sun	355° 08'	As the longitude is East, GHA and longitude are added to give the LHA.
The longitude of the estimated position	+ 51° 22'	
Giving	= 406° 30'	
Take away 360°	− 360° 00'	
Final LHA	= 46° 30'	

For an assumed longitude of 51° 52', the LHA will have an integral value of 47°. Let the assumed latitude be 47° S.

2. Entering the tables for an assumed latitude (Lat) of 47° and an LHA of 47° yields:
A = 29° 55', B = 32° 27' and Z_1 = 51.9

From A, A'= 55 and $\overline{A}$ = 30.

3. F = B + declination. So:

B	+ 32° 27'	As the latitude and declination have opposite names, declination is minus.
Dec.	− 19° 58'	
F	= 12° 29'	

From F, F' = 29 and $\overline{F}$ = 12.

4. Entering the tables for the values $\overline{A}$ = 30 and $\overline{F}$ = 12 yields:
H = 10° 22', P = 59° 27' and Z_2 = 83.9.
From P, P'= 27 and $\overline{P}$ = 59. Z_2 is rounded up so that $\overline{Z}_2$ = 84.

5. Entering the Auxiliary Tables for F' = 29 and $\overline{P}$ = 59 yields corr1 = +25.

6. Entering the Auxiliary Tables for A'= 55 and $\overline{Z}_2$ = 84 yields corr2 = +1.

7. The calculated altitude **Hc** = H + corr1 + corr2, so:

H	10° 22'
corr1 +	25'
corr2 +	01'
Hc =	10° 48'

8. Z is the absolute value of ($Z_1 + Z_2$). So for Z_1 = 51.9 and Z_2 = 83.9, Z will be 135.8°.

9. Applying the rule for Southern hemisphere latitudes where the LHA is less than 180°, the azimuth **Zn** = 180° + Z, or 315.8°.

Example 2 as worked out using the workform on page 76.

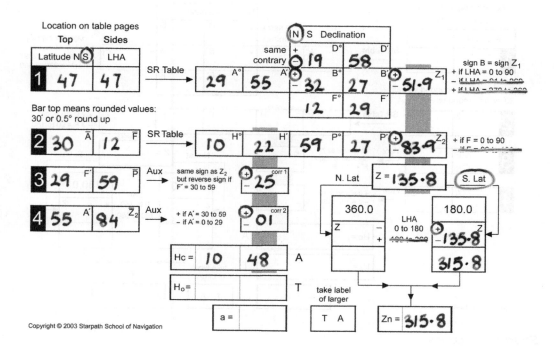

Copyright © 2003 Starpath School of Navigation

WORKFORM FOR THE SIGHT REDUCTION TABLES

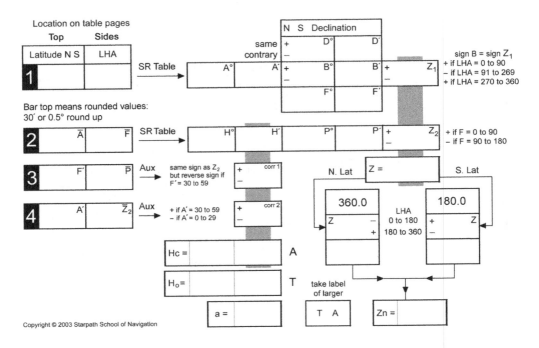

Copyright © 2003 Starpath School of Navigation

Short instructions

1. In row 1, record the assumed Lat, LHA and declination (D). Circle the names of Lat and Dec and using the rules, mark the signs of D, B and Z_1.

2. In row 1, with Lat and LHA, enter the sight reduction (SR) tables and record A, B and Z_1.

3. Add D and B to get F.

4. Copy A' into row 4 and mark the sign of corr2.

5. Round off A to the nearest whole degree and record it as $\overline{A}$ in row 2.

6. Mark the signs of Z_2 and corr1 in rows 2 and 3.

7. Round off F to the nearest whole degree and record it as $\overline{F}$ in row 2.

8. With $\overline{A}$ and $\overline{F}$ enter the SR tables and record H, P and Z_2 in row 2.

9. Round off P and Z_2 to the nearest whole degree and record them as $\overline{P}$ and $\overline{Z}_2$ in rows 3 and 4.

10. With F' and $\overline{P}$ enter the Auxiliary Table (Aux) and record corr1 in row 3.

11. With A' and $\overline{Z}_2$ enter the Aux table and record corr2 in row 4.

12. Add corr1 and corr2 to H to get **Hc**, the calculated altitude.

13. Add Z_1 to Z_2 to get Z. Record Z in the box below appropriate to the latitude hemisphere.

14. Convert Z to **Zn**, the azimuth, by choosing the appropriate Z sign for the LHA.

15. Record **Ho** below **Hc**. Take their difference and record it as **a** with the proper label. (T is *towards* the celestial body and A is *away* from it.)

GREAT CIRCLE ROUTE – COURSE AND DISTANCE

Overview

It is also possible to use the sight reduction tables to calculate a Great Circle Route course and distance from an assumed position to another geographical location, called here the destination. The principle is exactly the same as calculating azimuth and altitude from an assumed position to the geographical position of a celestial body.

The tables will have three inputs: the Local Hour Angle (LHA) between the observer's assumed longitude and the longitude of the destination; the observer's assumed latitude (Lat); and the latitude of the destination.

The instructions *Obtaining the calculated altitude and azimuth* on page 70 may be used directly by letting:
GHA = longitude of the destination, and
Declination = latitude of the destination

The outputs of the tables will, of course, be a calculated altitude **Hc** and azimuth **Zn**. However, the initial course for the Great Circle Route will just be **Zn** and the distance will be 60(90 – **Hc**) nautical miles, where **Hc** is in degrees.

Example. From an estimated position at 53° 26′ N, 3° 34′ W, what is the Great Circle Route course and distance to destination 40° 32′ N, 74° 07′ W ?

For the purposes of calculation, let the Declination = N 40° 32′, from the latitude of the destination; and let GHA = 74° 07′, from the longitude of the destination.

1. Calculating the LHA from the estimated position yields:

GHA	74° 07′	As the longitude is West,
The longitude of the estimated position −	3° 34′	longitude is taken from
Final LHA =	70° 33′	GHA to give the LHA.

For an assumed longitude of 3° 07′ W, the LHA will have an integral value of 71°. Let the assumed latitude be 53° N.

2. Entering the tables for an assumed latitude (Lat) of 53° and an LHA of 71° yields:
$A = 34° 41′$, $B = 13° 47′$ and $Z_1 = 23.3$

From A, $A′ = 41$ and $\overline{A} = 35$.

3. F = B + Declination. So:

$$\begin{array}{rr} B & 13° 47′ \\ \text{Declination} + & 40° 32′ \\ \hline F = & 54° 19′ \end{array}$$

From F, $F′ = 19$ and $\overline{F} = 54$.

4. Entering the tables for the values $\overline{A} = 35$ and $\overline{F} = 54$ yields:
$H = 41° 30′$, $P = 40° 01′$ and $Z_2 = 51.7$

From P, $P′ = 01$ and $\overline{P} = 40$. Z_2 is rounded up so that $\overline{Z}_2 = 52$.

5. Entering the Auxiliary Tables for F' = 19 and $\overline{P}$ = 40 yields corr1 = +12.

6. Entering the Auxiliary Tables for A'= 41 and $\overline{Z}_2$ = 52 yields corr2 = +12

7. The calculated altitude **Hc** = H + corr1 + corr2, so:

$$
\begin{aligned}
\text{H} &\quad 41°\ 30' \\
\text{corr1}\ + &\quad 12' \\
\text{corr2}\ + &\quad \underline{\quad 12'} \\
\textbf{Hc}\ = &\quad 41°\ 54'
\end{aligned}
$$

8. Z is the absolute value of ($Z_1 + Z_2$). So for Z_1 = 23.3 and Z_2 = 51.7, Z will be 74.0°.

9. Applying the rule for Northern hemisphere latitudes where the LHA is less than 180°: The azimuth **Zn** = 360° – Z, or 286.0°.

The initial course for the Great Circle Route from the assumed position to the destination will be **Zn**, which is 286.0°.

The distance from the assumed position to the destination will be 60(90 – **Hc**), where **Hc** is 41.9°, giving 2886 nautical miles.

A small correction needs to be made to obtain the Great Circle Route distance from the estimated position, rather than the assumed position. This is easiest done graphically, plotting the assumed and estimated positions on a Mercator grid plotting sheet suitable for the latitude.

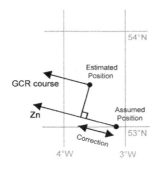

The azimuth drawn from the assumed position is repeated from the estimated position as the Great Circle Route initial course.

A perpendicular is dropped from the estimated position to the azimuth line from the assumed position. (If the assumed position is ahead of the estimated position, a perpendicular would be dropped from the assumed position to the GCR course line from the estimated position.)

The distance from the intercept to (in this case) the assumed position, is the correction for the distance from the estimated position to the destination.

The correction distance measured off the plot can be compared to the distance between latitude degree lines, which will always be 60 nautical miles. From this, the correction can be judged to be about 22 nautical miles.

The final distance from the estimated position and the destination is thus 2886 – 22, giving 2864 nautical miles.

SIGHT REDUCTION TABLES

LATITUDE/Ā: 0° – 5°

B: (–) for 90° < LHA < 270°
Dec: (–) for Lat. contrary name

Z₁: same sign as B
Z₂: (–)for F > 90°

LHA/F̄	0° A/H	0° B/P	0° Z₁/Z₂	1° A/H	1° B/P	1° Z₁/Z₂	2° A/H	2° B/P	2° Z₁/Z₂	3° A/H	3° B/P	3° Z₁/Z₂	4° A/H	4° B/P	4° Z₁/Z₂	5° A/H	5° B/P	5° Z₁/Z₂	LHA
180	0 00	90 00	90.0	0 00	89 00	90.0	0 00	88 00	90.0	0 00	87 00	90.0	0 00	86 00	90.0	0 00	85 00	90.0	180
179	1 00	90 00	90.0	1 00	89 00	90.0	1 00	88 00	90.0	1 00	87 00	89.9	1 00	86 00	89.9	1 00	85 00	89.9	181
178	2 00	90 00	90.0	2 00	89 00	90.0	2 00	88 00	90.0	2 00	87 00	89.8	2 00	86 00	89.9	2 59	85 00	89.8	182
177	3 00	90 00	90.0	3 00	89 00	90.0	3 00	88 00	89.9	3 00	87 00	89.8	3 59	86 00	89.8	3 59	85 00	89.7	183
176	4 00	90 00	90.0	4 00	89 00	90.0	4 00	88 00	89.9	4 00	87 00	89.7	4 59	85 59	89.7	4 59	84 59	89.7	184
175	5 00	90 00	90.0	5 00	89 00	89.9	5 00	88 00	89.8	5 00	86 59	89.7	5 59	85 59	89.7	5 59	84 59	89.6	185
174	6 00	90 00	90.0	6 00	89 00	89.9	6 00	87 59	89.8	6 00	86 59	89.6	6 59	85 59	89.6	6 58	84 58	89.5	186
173	7 00	90 00	90.0	7 00	89 00	89.9	7 00	87 59	89.7	7 59	86 59	89.6	7 59	85 59	89.5	7 58	84 58	89.4	187
172	8 00	90 00	90.0	8 00	88 59	89.9	8 00	87 59	89.7	8 59	86 58	89.6	8 59	85 58	89.5	8 58	84 57	89.3	188
171	9 00	90 00	90.0	9 00	88 59	89.9	9 00	87 59	89.7	9 59	86 58	89.5	9 59	85 57	89.4	9 58	84 56	89.2	189
170	10 00	90 00	90.0	10 00	88 59	89.8	10 00	87 59	89.6	10 59	86 58	89.5	10 58	85 56	89.4	10 57	84 56	89.1	190
169	11 00	90 00	90.0	11 00	88 59	89.8	11 00	87 58	89.6	11 59	86 56	89.4	11 58	85 56	89.3	11 57	84 55	89.0	191
168	12 00	90 00	90.0	12 00	88 59	89.8	12 00	87 57	89.6	12 59	86 55	89.3	12 58	85 54	89.2	12 57	84 54	88.9	192
167	13 00	90 00	90.0	13 00	88 58	89.8	13 00	87 57	89.5	13 59	86 54	89.3	13 58	85 53	89.1	13 57	84 53	88.8	193
166	14 00	90 00	90.0	14 00	88 58	89.8	14 59	87 56	89.5	14 59	86 54	89.2	14 58	85 52	89.0	14 56	84 51	88.7	194
165	15 00	90 00	90.0	15 00	88 58	89.8	15 59	87 56	89.4	15 59	86 53	89.2	15 58	85 52	89.0	15 56	84 49	88.6	195
164	16 00	90 00	90.0	16 00	88 58	89.7	16 59	87 55	89.4	16 59	86 52	89.1	16 57	85 50	88.9	16 56	84 48	88.5	196
163	17 00	90 00	90.0	17 00	88 57	89.7	17 59	87 55	89.4	17 58	86 51	89.0	17 57	85 49	88.8	17 56	84 46	88.4	197
162	18 00	90 00	90.0	18 00	88 57	89.7	18 59	87 54	89.3	18 58	86 50	89.0	18 57	85 48	88.7	18 55	84 45	88.3	198
161	19 00	90 00	90.0	19 00	88 57	89.7	19 59	87 53	89.3	19 58	86 48	89.0	19 57	85 46	88.6	19 55	84 43	88.2	199
160	20 00	90 00	90.0	20 00	88 56	89.6	20 59	87 52	89.2	20 58	86 48	88.9	20 57	85 45	88.5	20 55	84 41	88.1	200
159	21 00	90 00	90.0	21 00	88 56	89.6	21 59	87 51	89.2	21 58	86 47	88.8	21 57	85 43	88.5	21 55	84 39	88.0	201
158	22 00	90 00	90.0	22 00	88 55	89.6	22 59	87 51	89.2	22 58	86 46	88.8	22 56	85 41	88.4	22 54	84 37	87.9	202
157	23 00	90 00	90.0	23 00	88 55	89.6	23 59	87 50	89.1	23 58	86 44	88.7	23 56	85 39	88.3	23 54	84 34	87.8	203
156	24 00	90 00	90.0	24 00	88 54	89.6	24 59	87 49	89.1	24 58	86 43	88.7	24 56	85 37	88.2	24 54	84 32	87.7	204
155	25 00	90 00	90.0	25 00	88 54	89.5	25 59	87 48	89.1	25 58	86 41	88.6	25 56	85 35	88.1	25 54	84 29	87.6	205
154	26 00	90 00	90.0	26 00	88 53	89.5	26 59	87 46	89.0	26 58	86 40	88.5	26 56	85 33	88.1	26 53	84 26	87.5	206
153	27 00	90 00	90.0	27 00	88 53	89.5	27 59	87 45	89.0	27 57	86 38	88.5	27 56	85 31	88.0	27 53	84 24	87.3	207
152	28 00	90 00	90.0	28 00	88 52	89.5	28 59	87 44	88.9	28 57	86 36	88.4	28 55	85 28	87.9	28 53	84 20	87.2	208
151	29 00	90 00	90.0	29 00	88 51	89.4	29 59	87 43	88.9	29 57	86 34	88.3	29 55	85 26	87.8	29 52	84 17	87.1	209
150	30 00	90 00	90.0	30 00	88 51	89.4	30 59	87 41	88.8	30 57	86 32	88.3	30 55	85 23	87.7	30 52	84 14	87.0	210
149	31 00	90 00	90.0	31 00	88 50	89.4	31 59	87 40	88.8	31 57	86 30	88.1	31 55	85 20	87.6	31 52	84 10	86.9	211
148	32 00	90 00	90.0	32 00	88 49	89.4	32 59	87 39	88.8	32 57	86 28	88.1	32 55	85 17	87.5	32 52	84 07	86.8	212
147	33 00	90 00	90.0	33 00	88 48	89.3	33 59	87 37	88.7	33 57	86 25	88.1	33 54	85 14	87.4	33 51	84 03	86.6	213
146	34 00	90 00	90.0	34 00	88 48	89.3	34 59	87 35	88.7	34 57	86 23	87.9	34 54	85 11	87.3	34 51	83 59	86.5	214
145	35 00	90 00	90.0	35 00	88 47	89.3	35 58	87 34	88.6	35 57	86 20	87.8	35 54	85 07	87.2	35 51	83 54	86.4	215
144	36 00	90 00	90.0	36 00	88 46	89.2	36 58	87 30	88.5	36 56	86 18	87.7	36 54	85 04	87.1	36 50	83 50	86.2	216
143	37 00	90 00	90.0	37 00	88 45	89.2	37 58	87 28	88.5	37 56	86 15	87.7	37 53	85 00	87.0	37 50	83 45	86.1	217
142	38 00	90 00	90.0	38 00	88 44	89.2	38 58	87 26	88.4	38 56	86 12	87.6	38 53	84 56	86.9	38 49	83 40	86.0	218
141	39 00	90 00	90.0	39 00	88 43	89.2	39 58	87 23	88.3	39 56	86 05	87.6	39 53	84 52	86.8	39 49	83 35	85.8	219
140	40 00	90 00	90.0	40 00	88 42	89.1	40 58	87 21	88.3	40 56	86 02	87.4	40 53	84 47	86.7	40 49	83 29	85.7	220
139	41 00	90 00	90.0	41 00	88 40	89.1	41 58	87 19	88.2	41 56	85 58	87.3	41 52	84 42	86.6	41 48	83 23	85.5	221
138	42 00	90 00	90.0	42 00	88 39	89.1	42 58	87 16	88.1	42 56	85 55	87.2	42 52	84 37	86.5	42 48	83 17	85.4	222
137	43 00	90 00	90.0	43 00	88 38	89.1	43 58	87 13	88.1	43 55	85 50	87.1	43 52	84 32	86.4	43 47	83 11	85.2	223
136	44 00	90 00	90.0	43 59	88 37	89.0	44 58	87 10	88.0	44 55	85 46	87.0	44 52	84 27	86.1	44 48	83 04	85.0	224
135	45 00	90 00	90.0	44 59	88 35	89.0	45 58	87 06	88.0	45 55	85 41	86.9	45 52	84 21	86.0	44 47	82 57	85.0	225

Lat./F̄ LHA/F	Lat.	0° A/H	0° B/P	0° Z₁/Z₂	1° A/H	1° B/P	1° Z₁/Z₂	2° A/H	2° B/P	2° Z₁/Z₂	3° A/H	3° B/P	3° Z₁/Z₂	4° A/H	4° B/P	4° Z₁/Z₂	5° A/H	5° B/P	5° Z₁/Z₂	Lat./Ā	LHA
135	45	45 00	90 00	90.0	44 59	88 35	89.0	44 58	87 10	88.0	44 55	85 46	87.0	44 52	84 21	86.0	44 47	82 57	85.0	225	315
134	46	46 00	90 00	90.0	45 59	88 34	89.0	45 58	87 07	87.9	45 55	85 41	86.9	45 51	84 15	85.9	45 46	82 49	84.8	226	314
133	47	47 00	90 00	90.0	46 59	88 32	88.9	46 58	87 04	87.9	46 55	85 36	86.8	46 51	84 09	85.8	46 46	82 41	84.7	227	313
132	48	48 00	90 00	90.0	47 59	88 30	88.9	47 58	87 01	87.8	47 55	85 31	86.7	47 51	84 02	85.6	47 46	82 33	84.5	228	312
131	49	49 00	90 00	90.0	48 59	88 29	88.8	48 58	86 57	87.7	48 55	85 25	86.6	48 51	83 55	85.4	48 45	82 24	84.3	229	311
130	50	50 00	90 00	90.0	49 59	88 27	88.8	49 58	86 53	87.6	49 54	85 20	86.4	49 50	83 47	85.2	49 44	82 15	84.1	230	310
129	51	51 00	90 00	90.0	50 59	88 25	88.8	50 57	86 49	87.5	50 54	85 14	86.3	50 50	83 40	85.1	50 44	82 05	83.9	231	309
128	52	52 00	90 00	90.0	51 59	88 23	88.7	51 57	86 45	87.4	51 54	85 08	86.2	51 49	83 31	84.9	51 43	81 55	83.6	232	308
127	53	53 00	90 00	90.0	52 59	88 20	88.7	52 57	86 41	87.3	52 54	85 01	86.0	52 49	83 22	84.7	52 43	81 44	83.4	233	307
126	54	54 00	90 00	90.0	53 59	88 18	88.6	53 57	86 36	87.2	53 54	84 54	85.9	53 49	83 13	84.5	53 42	81 32	83.2	234	306
125	55	55 00	90 00	90.0	54 59	88 15	88.6	54 57	86 31	87.1	54 53	84 47	85.7	54 48	83 03	84.3	54 41	81 20	82.9	235	305
124	56	56 00	90 00	90.0	55 59	88 13	88.5	55 57	86 26	87.0	55 53	84 39	85.6	55 48	82 52	84.1	55 41	81 06	82.6	236	304
123	57	57 00	90 00	90.0	56 59	88 10	88.5	56 57	86 20	86.9	56 53	84 30	85.4	56 47	82 41	83.9	56 40	80 52	82.4	237	303
122	58	58 00	90 00	90.0	57 59	88 07	88.4	57 57	86 14	86.8	57 53	84 22	85.2	57 47	82 29	83.6	57 39	80 38	82.1	238	302
121	59	59 00	90 00	90.0	58 59	88 04	88.3	58 57	86 07	86.7	58 52	84 11	85.0	58 46	82 16	83.4	58 38	80 22	81.7	239	301
120	60	60 00	90 00	90.0	59 59	88 00	88.3	59 56	86 00	86.5	59 52	84 01	84.8	59 46	82 02	83.1	59 37	80 04	81.4	240	300
119	61	61 00	90 00	90.0	60 59	87 56	88.2	60 56	85 53	86.4	60 52	83 50	84.6	60 45	81 48	82.8	60 37	79 46	81.1	241	299
118	62	62 00	90 00	90.0	61 59	87 52	88.1	61 56	85 45	86.2	61 51	83 38	84.4	61 44	81 32	82.5	61 36	79 27	80.7	242	298
117	63	63 00	90 00	90.0	62 59	87 48	88.0	62 56	85 36	86.1	62 51	83 25	84.1	62 44	81 15	82.2	62 35	79 06	80.3	243	297
116	64	64 00	90 00	90.0	63 59	87 43	88.0	63 56	85 27	85.9	63 50	83 11	83.9	63 43	80 56	81.9	63 33	78 43	79.9	244	296
115	65	65 00	90 00	90.0	64 59	87 38	87.9	64 56	85 17	85.7	64 50	82 56	83.6	64 42	80 36	81.5	64 32	78 18	79.4	245	295
114	66	66 00	90 00	90.0	65 59	87 33	87.8	65 55	85 06	85.5	65 49	82 39	83.3	65 41	80 15	81.1	65 31	77 52	78.9	246	294
113	67	67 00	90 00	90.0	66 59	87 26	87.6	66 55	84 54	85.3	66 49	82 22	83.0	66 40	79 51	80.7	66 29	77 23	78.4	247	293
112	68	68 00	90 00	90.0	67 59	87 20	87.5	67 55	84 40	85.1	67 48	82 02	82.6	67 39	79 26	80.2	67 28	76 51	77.8	248	292
111	69	69 00	90 00	90.0	68 59	87 13	87.4	68 55	84 26	84.8	68 48	81 41	82.2	68 38	78 57	79.7	68 26	76 17	77.2	249	291
110	70	70 00	90 00	90.0	69 59	87 05	87.3	69 54	84 10	84.5	69 47	81 17	81.8	69 37	78 27	79.2	69 25	75 39	76.5	250	290
109	71	71 00	90 00	90.0	70 58	86 56	87.1	70 54	83 53	84.2	70 46	80 51	81.4	70 36	77 53	78.5	70 23	74 57	75.8	251	289
108	72	72 00	90 00	90.0	71 58	86 46	86.9	71 54	83 33	83.9	71 46	80 22	80.8	71 35	77 15	77.9	71 20	74 12	75.0	252	288
107	73	73 00	90 00	90.0	72 58	86 35	86.7	72 53	83 11	83.5	72 45	79 50	80.3	72 33	76 33	77.1	72 18	73 20	74.1	253	287
106	74	74 00	90 00	90.0	73 58	86 22	86.5	73 53	82 47	83.1	73 44	79 14	79.7	73 31	75 46	76.3	73 15	72 23	73.1	254	286
105	75	75 00	90 00	90.0	74 58	86 08	86.3	74 52	82 19	82.6	74 43	78 33	78.9	74 29	74 53	75.4	74 12	71 19	72.0	255	285
104	76	76 00	90 00	90.0	75 58	85 52	86.0	75 52	81 47	82.0	75 41	77 47	78.1	75 27	73 53	74.4	75 09	70 07	70.7	256	284
103	77	77 00	90 00	90.0	76 58	85 34	85.7	76 51	81 11	81.4	76 40	76 53	77.2	76 25	72 44	73.2	76 05	68 45	69.3	257	283
102	78	78 00	90 00	90.0	77 58	85 12	85.3	77 50	80 28	80.7	77 38	75 51	76.2	77 22	71 25	71.8	77 01	67 11	67.7	258	282
101	79	79 00	90 00	90.0	78 57	84 46	84.9	78 49	79 38	79.8	78 36	74 38	74.9	78 18	69 52	70.3	77 56	65 22	65.8	259	281
100	80	80 00	90 00	90.0	79 57	84 16	84.3	79 48	78 38	78.8	79 34	73 12	73.5	79 14	68 04	68.4	78 50	63 16	63.7	260	280
99	81	81 00	90 00	90.0	80 57	83 38	83.7	80 47	77 25	77.6	80 31	71 29	71.7	80 09	65 55	66.2	79 43	60 47	61.2	261	279
98	82	82 00	90 00	90.0	81 56	82 51	82.9	81 45	75 55	76.1	81 28	69 19	69.6	81 04	63 19	63.6	80 34	57 51	58.2	262	278
97	83	83 00	90 00	90.0	82 56	81 51	81.9	82 43	74 01	74.1	82 23	66 44	66.9	81 57	60 09	60.4	81 24	54 20	54.6	263	277
96	84	84 00	90 00	90.0	83 55	80 31	80.6	83 41	71 32	71.6	83 18	63 22	63.5	82 48	56 13	56.4	82 12	50 04	50.3	264	276
95	85	85 00	90 00	90.0	84 54	78 40	78.7	84 37	68 10	68.3	84 10	59 05	59.1	83 36	51 16	51.4	82 56	44 53	45.1	265	275
94	86	86 00	90 00	90.0	85 53	75 57	76.0	85 32	63 24	63.5	85 00	53 05	53.2	84 21	45 11	45.1	83 36	38 34	38.7	266	274
93	87	87 00	90 00	90.0	86 50	71 33	71.6	86 24	56 17	56.3	85 45	44 58	45.0	85 00	36 49	36.9	84 10	30 53	31.0	267	273
92	88	88 00	90 00	90.0	87 46	63 26	63.4	87 10	44 59	45.0	86 24	33 40	33.7	85 32	26 31	26.6	84 37	21 45	21.8	268	272
91	89	89 00	90 00	90.0	88 35	45 00	45.0	87 46	26 33	26.6	86 50	18 25	18.4	85 53	14 01	14.0	84 54	11 17	11.3	269	271
90	90	90 00	0 00	0.0	89 00	0 00	0.0	88 00	0 00	0.0	87 00	0 00	0.0	86 00	0 00	0.0	85 00	0 00	0.0	270	270

N. Lat.: for LHA>180°... Zn = Z
for LHA<180°... Zn =360° − Z

S. Lat.: for LHA > 180°... Zn =180° − Z
for LHA < 180°... Zn =180° + Z

LATITUDE/Ā : 6° − 11°

Lat./Ā	LHA/F̄	6° A/H	6° B/P	6° Z₁/Z₂	7° A/H	7° B/P	7° Z₁/Z₂	8° A/H	8° B/P	8° Z₁/Z₂	9° A/H	9° B/P	9° Z₁/Z₂	10° A/H	10° B/P	10° Z₁/Z₂	11° A/H	11° B/P	11° Z₁/Z₂	LHA	LHA
0	180	0 00	84 00	90.0	0 00	83 00	90.0	0 00	82 00	90.0	0 00	81 00	90.0	0 00	80 00	90.0	0 00	79 00	90.0	360	180
1	179	1 00	84 00	89.9	1 00	83 00	89.9	0 59	82 00	89.9	0 59	81 00	89.8	0 59	80 00	89.8	0 59	79 00	89.8	359	181
2	178	1 59	84 00	89.8	1 59	83 00	89.8	1 59	82 00	89.7	1 59	81 00	89.7	1 58	80 00	89.6	1 58	79 00	89.6	358	182
3	177	2 59	84 00	89.7	2 59	82 59	89.6	2 58	81 59	89.6	2 58	80 59	89.5	2 57	80 00	89.5	2 57	78 59	89.4	357	183
4	176	3 59	83 59	89.6	3 58	82 59	89.5	3 58	81 59	89.4	3 57	80 59	89.4	3 56	79 59	89.3	3 56	78 58	89.2	356	184
5	175	4 58	83 59	89.5	4 58	82 58	89.4	4 57	81 58	89.3	4 56	80 58	89.2	4 55	79 58	89.1	4 54	78 58	89.0	355	185
6	174	5 58	83 58	89.4	5 57	82 58	89.3	5 56	81 57	89.2	5 56	80 57	89.1	5 55	79 57	89.0	5 53	78 56	88.9	354	186
7	173	6 58	83 57	89.3	6 57	82 57	89.1	6 56	81 56	89.0	6 55	80 56	88.9	6 54	79 56	88.8	6 52	78 55	88.7	353	187
8	172	7 57	83 57	89.2	7 56	82 56	89.0	7 55	81 55	88.9	7 54	80 55	88.7	7 53	79 54	88.6	7 51	78 54	88.5	352	188
9	171	8 57	83 56	89.1	8 56	82 55	88.9	8 55	81 54	88.7	8 53	80 53	88.6	8 52	79 53	88.4	8 50	78 52	88.3	351	189
10	170	9 57	83 54	88.9	9 55	82 54	88.8	9 54	81 53	88.6	9 53	80 52	88.4	9 51	79 51	88.2	9 49	78 50	88.1	350	190
11	169	10 56	83 53	88.8	10 55	82 52	88.6	10 53	81 51	88.5	10 52	80 50	88.3	10 50	79 49	88.0	10 48	78 48	87.9	349	191
12	168	11 56	83 52	88.7	11 54	82 51	88.5	11 53	81 49	88.3	11 51	80 48	88.1	11 49	79 47	87.9	11 46	78 46	87.7	348	192
13	167	12 56	83 51	88.6	12 54	82 49	88.4	12 52	81 48	88.2	12 50	80 46	87.9	12 48	79 45	87.7	12 45	78 43	87.5	347	193
14	166	13 55	83 49	88.5	13 54	82 47	88.3	13 51	81 46	88.0	13 49	80 44	87.8	13 47	79 42	87.5	13 44	78 40	87.3	346	194
15	165	14 55	83 47	88.4	14 53	82 45	88.1	14 51	81 43	87.9	14 49	80 41	87.6	14 46	79 39	87.3	14 43	78 37	87.1	345	195
16	164	15 55	83 46	88.3	15 53	82 43	88.0	15 50	81 41	87.7	15 48	80 39	87.4	15 45	79 36	87.1	15 42	78 34	86.9	344	196
17	163	16 54	83 44	88.2	16 52	82 41	87.9	16 50	81 38	87.6	16 47	80 36	87.3	16 44	79 33	87.0	16 40	78 31	86.7	343	197
18	162	17 54	83 42	88.1	17 52	82 39	87.7	17 49	81 36	87.4	17 46	80 33	87.1	17 43	79 30	86.8	17 38	78 27	86.5	342	198
19	161	18 54	83 39	87.9	18 51	82 36	87.6	18 48	81 33	87.3	18 45	80 29	86.9	18 42	79 26	86.6	18 37	78 23	86.2	341	199
20	160	19 53	83 37	87.8	19 51	82 33	87.5	19 48	81 30	87.1	19 45	80 26	86.7	19 41	79 22	86.4	19 36	78 19	86.0	340	200
21	159	20 53	83 35	87.7	20 50	82 30	87.3	20 47	81 26	86.9	20 44	80 22	86.6	20 40	79 18	86.2	20 34	78 14	85.8	339	201
22	158	21 52	83 32	87.6	21 50	82 27	87.2	21 46	81 23	86.8	21 43	80 18	86.4	21 39	79 14	86.0	21 33	78 10	85.6	338	202
23	157	22 52	83 29	87.5	22 49	82 24	87.0	22 46	81 19	86.6	22 42	80 14	86.2	22 38	79 09	85.8	22 32	78 05	85.4	337	203
24	156	23 52	83 26	87.3	23 49	82 21	86.9	23 45	81 15	86.5	23 41	80 10	86.0	23 37	79 05	85.6	23 30	77 59	85.2	336	204
25	155	24 51	83 23	87.2	24 48	82 17	86.7	24 44	81 11	86.3	24 40	80 05	85.8	24 36	79 00	85.4	24 29	77 54	84.9	335	205
26	154	25 51	83 20	87.1	25 48	82 13	86.6	25 44	81 07	86.1	25 39	80 00	85.6	25 35	78 54	85.2	25 28	77 48	84.7	334	206
27	153	26 50	83 16	87.0	26 47	82 09	86.4	26 43	81 02	85.9	26 38	79 55	85.4	26 33	78 48	85.0	26 26	77 42	84.4	333	207
28	152	27 50	83 13	86.8	27 46	82 05	86.3	27 42	80 57	85.8	27 38	79 50	85.2	27 32	78 42	84.8	27 25	77 35	84.2	332	208
29	151	28 50	83 09	86.7	28 46	82 01	86.1	28 41	80 52	85.6	28 37	79 44	85.0	28 31	78 36	84.6	28 23	77 28	84.0	331	209
30	150	29 49	83 05	86.5	29 45	81 56	86.0	29 41	80 47	85.4	29 36	79 38	84.8	29 30	78 29	84.3	29 22	77 21	83.7	330	210
31	149	30 49	83 01	86.4	30 45	81 51	85.8	30 40	80 41	85.2	30 35	79 32	84.6	30 29	78 22	84.0	30 20	77 13	83.5	329	211
32	148	31 48	82 56	86.3	31 44	81 46	85.6	31 39	80 35	85.0	31 34	79 25	84.4	31 27	78 15	83.8	31 19	77 05	83.2	328	212
33	147	32 48	82 51	86.1	32 43	81 40	85.5	32 38	80 29	84.8	32 33	79 18	84.2	32 26	78 08	83.6	32 17	76 57	82.9	327	213
34	146	33 47	82 46	86.0	33 43	81 35	85.3	33 37	80 23	84.6	33 32	79 11	84.0	33 25	78 00	83.3	33 16	76 48	82.7	326	214
35	145	34 47	82 41	85.8	34 42	81 29	85.1	34 37	80 16	84.4	34 30	79 03	83.7	34 24	77 51	83.1	34 14	76 39	82.4	325	215
36	144	35 46	82 36	85.7	35 41	81 22	84.9	35 35	80 09	84.2	35 28	78 55	83.5	35 22	77 42	82.9	35 13	76 29	82.1	324	216
37	143	36 46	82 30	85.5	36 41	81 16	84.8	36 35	80 01	84.0	36 27	78 47	83.3	36 21	77 33	82.7	36 11	76 19	81.8	323	217
38	142	37 45	82 24	85.3	37 40	81 09	84.6	37 34	79 53	83.8	37 27	78 38	83.0	37 19	77 23	82.5	37 10	76 09	81.5	322	218
39	141	38 45	82 18	85.2	38 39	81 01	84.4	38 33	79 45	83.6	38 26	78 29	82.8	38 18	77 13	82.1	38 08	75 57	81.2	321	219
40	140	39 44	82 11	85.0	39 39	80 54	84.2	39 32	79 36	83.3	39 25	78 19	82.5	39 16	77 02	81.7	39 07	75 46	80.9	320	220
41	139	40 44	82 04	84.8	40 38	80 46	84.0	40 31	79 27	83.1	40 23	78 09	82.3	40 15	76 51	81.4	40 05	75 33	80.6	319	221
42	138	41 43	81 57	84.6	41 37	80 37	83.7	41 30	79 17	82.9	41 22	77 58	82.0	41 13	76 39	81.1	41 04	75 21	80.3	318	222
43	137	42 42	81 49	84.4	42 36	80 29	83.5	42 29	79 07	82.6	42 21	77 47	81.7	42 12	76 27	80.8	42 02	75 07	79.9	317	223
44	136	43 42	81 41	84.2	43 35	80 19	83.3	43 28	78 57	82.3	43 20	77 35	81.4	43 10	76 14	80.5	43 00	74 53	79.6	316	224
45	135	44 41	81 33	84.0	44 34	80 09	83.1	44 27	78 46	82.1	44 18	77 22	81.1	44 08	76 00	80.1	43 57	74 38	79.2	315	225

Lat./A̅		6°			7°			8°			9°			10°			11°			Lat./A̅	
	LHA/F̅	A/H	B/P	Z_1/Z_2	A/H	B/P	Z_1/Z_2	A/H	B/P	Z_1/Z_2	A/H	B/P	Z_1/Z_2	A/H	B/P	Z_1/Z_2	A/H	B/P	Z_1/Z_2		LHA
45	135	44 41	81 33	84.0	44 34	80 09	83.1	44 27	78 46	82.1	44 18	77 22	81.1	44 08	76 00	80.1	43 57	74 38	79.2	225	315
46	134	45 41	81 24	83.8	45 34	79 59	82.8	45 26	78 34	81.8	45 16	77 09	80.8	45 06	75 45	79.8	44 55	74 22	78.8	226	314
47	133	46 40	81 14	83.6	46 33	79 48	82.6	46 24	78 21	81.5	46 15	76 56	80.5	46 04	75 30	79.5	45 53	74 05	78.4	227	313
48	132	47 39	81 04	83.4	47 32	79 36	82.3	47 23	78 08	81.2	47 13	76 41	80.1	47 03	75 14	79.1	46 51	73 48	78.0	228	312
49	131	48 38	80 54	83.1	48 31	79 24	82.0	48 22	77 55	80.9	48 12	76 26	79.8	48 01	74 57	78.7	47 48	73 30	77.6	229	311
50	130	49 38	80 43	82.9	49 30	79 11	81.7	49 20	77 40	80.6	49 10	76 09	79.4	48 58	74 40	78.3	48 46	73 10	77.2	230	310
51	129	50 37	80 31	82.6	50 29	78 58	81.4	50 19	77 25	80.2	50 08	75 52	79.1	49 56	74 21	77.9	49 43	72 50	76.7	231	309
52	128	51 36	80 19	82.4	51 27	78 43	81.1	51 18	77 08	79.9	51 06	75 34	78.7	50 54	74 01	77.5	50 40	72 29	76.3	232	308
53	127	52 35	80 06	82.1	52 26	78 28	80.8	52 16	76 51	79.5	52 04	75 15	78.3	51 52	73 40	77.1	51 37	72 06	75.8	233	307
54	126	53 34	79 52	81.8	53 25	78 12	80.5	53 14	76 33	79.2	53 02	74 55	77.8	52 49	73 18	76.6	52 35	71 42	75.3	234	306
55	125	54 33	79 37	81.5	54 24	77 55	80.1	54 13	76 14	78.8	54 00	74 34	77.4	53 47	72 55	76.1	53 31	71 17	74.8	235	305
56	124	55 32	79 21	81.2	55 22	77 37	79.9	55 11	75 54	78.3	54 58	74 11	76.9	54 44	72 30	75.6	54 28	70 50	74.2	236	304
57	123	56 31	79 05	80.9	56 21	77 18	79.4	56 09	75 32	77.9	55 56	73 47	76.5	55 41	72 04	75.0	55 25	70 22	73.6	237	303
58	122	57 30	78 47	80.5	57 19	76 57	79.0	57 07	75 09	77.4	56 53	73 22	75.9	56 38	71 36	74.5	56 21	69 51	73.0	238	302
59	121	58 29	78 28	80.1	58 18	76 35	78.5	58 05	74 44	77.0	57 51	72 54	75.4	57 35	71 06	73.9	57 17	69 19	72.4	239	301
60	120	59 28	78 08	79.7	59 16	76 12	78.1	59 03	74 18	76.4	58 48	72 25	74.8	58 32	70 34	73.3	58 13	68 45	71.7	240	300
61	119	60 26	77 46	79.3	60 14	75 47	77.6	60 01	73 50	75.9	59 45	71 54	74.2	59 28	70 01	72.6	59 09	68 09	71.0	241	299
62	118	61 25	77 23	78.9	61 12	75 21	77.1	60 58	73 20	75.3	60 42	71 21	73.6	60 24	69 25	71.9	60 05	67 30	70.3	242	298
63	117	62 23	76 58	78.4	62 10	74 52	76.5	61 56	72 48	74.7	61 39	70 46	72.9	61 20	68 46	71.2	61 00	66 49	69.5	243	297
64	116	63 22	76 31	77.9	63 08	74 21	76.0	62 53	72 13	74.1	62 35	70 08	72.2	62 16	68 05	70.4	61 55	66 05	68.6	244	296
65	115	64 20	76 02	77.4	64 06	73 48	75.4	63 50	71 36	73.4	63 32	69 27	71.5	63 12	67 21	69.6	62 50	65 18	67.8	245	295
66	114	65 18	75 31	76.8	65 03	73 12	74.7	64 47	70 56	72.6	64 28	68 43	70.8	64 07	66 34	68.7	63 44	64 27	66.8	246	294
67	113	66 16	74 57	76.2	66 01	72 33	74.0	65 43	70 13	71.8	65 23	67 56	69.8	65 02	65 43	67.8	64 38	63 33	65.8	247	293
68	112	67 14	74 20	75.5	66 58	71 51	73.2	66 40	69 26	71.0	66 19	67 05	68.8	65 56	64 48	66.7	65 32	62 35	64.7	248	292
69	111	68 12	73 39	74.8	67 55	71 05	72.4	67 36	68 35	70.1	67 14	66 09	67.8	66 50	63 48	65.7	66 25	61 31	63.6	249	291
70	110	69 09	72 55	74.0	68 51	70 15	71.5	68 31	67 40	69.1	68 09	65 09	66.7	67 44	62 44	64.5	67 17	60 23	62.3	250	290
71	109	70 07	72 06	73.1	69 48	69 20	70.5	69 27	66 39	68.0	69 03	64 03	65.6	68 37	61 34	63.2	68 09	59 10	61.0	251	289
72	108	71 03	71 13	72.2	70 44	68 20	69.4	70 21	65 33	66.8	69 57	62 52	64.3	69 29	60 17	61.9	69 00	57 55	59.6	252	288
73	107	72 00	70 14	71.1	71 39	67 13	68.3	71 16	64 20	65.5	70 50	61 33	62.9	70 21	58 54	60.4	69 50	56 23	58.0	253	287
74	106	72 56	69 08	70.0	72 34	65 59	67.0	72 09	62 59	64.1	71 42	60 07	61.4	71 12	57 24	58.8	70 40	54 48	56.4	254	286
75	105	73 52	67 54	68.7	73 29	64 37	65.5	73 03	61 30	62.6	72 34	58 32	59.7	72 02	55 44	57.1	71 28	53 06	54.5	255	285
76	104	74 48	66 31	67.3	74 23	63 05	64.0	73 56	59 51	60.8	73 24	56 47	57.9	72 51	53 55	55.1	72 16	51 13	52.6	256	284
77	103	75 42	64 57	65.6	75 16	61 22	62.2	74 46	58 00	58.9	74 14	54 52	55.9	73 39	51 55	53.1	73 02	49 10	50.4	257	283
78	102	76 36	63 11	63.8	76 08	59 26	60.2	75 37	55 57	56.8	75 02	52 42	53.6	74 26	49 42	50.8	73 47	46 56	48.1	258	282
79	101	77 29	61 09	61.7	76 59	57 14	57.9	76 26	53 38	54.4	75 49	50 18	51.2	75 11	47 16	48.2	74 30	44 28	45.5	259	281
80	100	78 21	58 49	59.3	77 49	54 44	55.3	77 13	51 01	51.7	76 35	47 38	48.4	75 54	44 34	45.4	75 11	41 47	42.7	260	280
81	99	79 12	56 06	56.6	78 37	51 52	52.4	77 59	48 04	48.7	77 18	44 39	45.4	76 35	41 35	42.4	75 49	38 50	39.7	261	279
82	98	80 01	52 56	53.4	79 23	48 35	49.1	78 42	44 43	45.3	77 59	41 18	41.9	77 13	38 17	39.0	76 26	35 36	36.4	262	278
83	97	80 47	49 13	49.6	80 07	44 47	45.2	79 23	40 56	41.4	78 37	37 35	38.1	77 49	34 39	35.3	76 59	32 05	32.8	263	277
84	96	81 31	44 51	45.2	80 47	40 24	40.8	80 01	36 38	37.2	79 12	33 25	33.9	78 21	30 40	31.2	77 29	28 16	28.8	264	276
85	95	82 12	39 40	39.9	81 24	35 22	35.7	80 34	31 48	32.2	79 43	28 49	29.2	78 50	26 18	26.7	77 56	24 09	24.6	265	275
86	94	82 48	33 34	33.8	81 57	29 36	29.8	81 04	26 24	26.7	80 09	23 46	24.1	79 14	21 35	21.9	78 18	19 44	20.1	266	274
87	93	83 18	26 28	26.6	82 23	23 05	23.3	81 28	20 25	20.6	80 31	18 17	18.5	79 34	16 32	16.8	78 36	15 04	15.4	267	273
88	92	83 41	18 22	18.5	82 43	15 52	16.0	81 48	13 57	14.1	80 47	12 26	12.6	79 48	11 12	11.4	78 49	10 11	10.4	268	272
89	91	83 55	9 26	9.5	82 56	8 05	8.2	81 56	7 05	7.1	80 57	6 17	6.4	79 57	5 39	5.7	78 57	5 08	5.2	269	271
90	90	84 00	0 00	0.0	83 00	0 00	0.0	82 00	0 00	0.0	81 00	0 00	0.0	80 00	0 00	0.0	79 00	0 00	0.0	270	270

N. Lat.: for LHA>180° ...: Zn = Z
for LHA<180° ...: Zn = 360° − Z

S. Lat.: for LHA > 180° ...: Zn = 180° − Z
for LHA < 180° ...: Zn = 180° + Z

B: (−) for 90° < LHA < 270°
Dec: (−) for Lat. contrary name

Z₁: same sign as B
Z₂: (−)for F > 90°

LATITUDE / Ā : 12° − 17°

Lat./Ā	12°			13°			14°			15°			16°			17°			Lat./Ā
LHA/F	A/H	B/P	Z₁/Z₂	A/H	B/P	Z₁/Z₂	A/H	B/P	Z₁/Z₂	A/H	B/P	Z₁/Z₂	A/H	B/P	Z₁/Z₂	A/H	B/P	Z₁/Z₂	LHA
0	0 00	78 00	90.0	0 00	77 00	90.0	0 00	76 00	90.0	0 00	75 00	90.0	0 00	74 00	90.0	0 00	73 00	90.0	180
1	0 59	78 00	89.8	0 58	77 00	89.8	0 58	76 00	89.8	0 58	75 00	89.7	0 58	74 00	89.7	0 57	73 00	89.7	179
2	1 57	78 00	89.6	1 57	77 00	89.6	1 56	76 00	89.5	1 56	74 59	89.5	1 55	73 59	89.4	1 55	72 59	89.4	178
3	2 56	77 59	89.4	2 55	76 59	89.4	2 55	75 59	89.3	2 54	74 59	89.2	2 53	73 59	89.2	2 52	72 59	89.1	177
4	3 55	77 58	89.2	3 54	76 58	89.2	3 53	75 58	89.1	3 52	74 58	89.0	3 51	73 58	89.0	3 49	72 58	88.8	176
5	4 53	77 57	89.0	4 52	76 57	88.9	4 51	75 57	88.8	4 50	74 57	88.7	4 48	73 57	88.6	4 47	72 56	88.5	175
6	5 52	77 56	88.7	5 51	76 56	88.6	5 49	75 56	88.5	5 48	74 55	88.4	5 46	73 55	88.3	5 44	72 55	88.2	174
7	6 51	77 55	88.5	6 49	76 54	88.4	6 47	75 54	88.3	6 46	74 54	88.2	6 44	73 53	88.1	6 42	72 53	87.9	173
8	7 49	77 53	88.3	7 48	76 53	88.2	7 46	75 52	88.1	7 44	74 52	87.9	7 41	73 51	87.8	7 39	72 51	87.6	172
9	8 48	77 51	88.1	8 46	76 51	88.0	8 44	75 50	87.8	8 41	74 49	87.7	8 39	73 49	87.5	8 36	72 48	87.3	171
10	9 47	77 49	87.9	9 44	76 48	87.7	9 42	75 48	87.6	9 39	74 47	87.4	9 37	73 46	87.2	9 34	72 45	87.0	170
11	10 45	77 47	87.7	10 43	76 46	87.5	10 40	75 45	87.3	10 37	74 44	87.1	10 34	73 43	86.9	10 31	72 42	86.7	169
12	11 44	77 44	87.5	11 41	76 43	87.3	11 38	75 42	87.1	11 35	74 41	86.9	11 32	73 40	86.6	11 28	72 39	86.4	168
13	12 43	77 42	87.3	12 40	76 40	87.0	12 37	75 39	86.8	12 33	74 37	86.6	12 29	73 36	86.4	12 25	72 35	86.1	167
14	13 41	77 39	87.0	13 38	76 37	86.8	13 35	75 35	86.5	13 31	74 34	86.3	13 27	73 32	86.1	13 23	72 31	85.8	166
15	14 40	77 35	86.8	14 36	76 33	86.6	14 33	75 32	86.3	14 29	74 30	86.0	14 24	73 28	85.8	14 20	72 26	85.5	165
16	15 38	77 32	86.6	15 35	76 30	86.4	15 31	75 28	86.1	15 26	74 25	85.8	15 22	73 23	85.5	15 17	72 21	85.2	164
17	16 37	77 28	86.4	16 33	76 26	86.1	16 29	75 23	85.8	16 24	74 21	85.5	16 19	73 19	85.2	16 14	72 16	84.9	163
18	17 36	77 24	86.1	17 31	76 21	85.8	17 27	75 19	85.5	17 22	74 16	85.2	17 17	73 13	84.9	17 11	72 11	84.6	162
19	18 34	77 20	85.9	18 30	76 17	85.6	18 25	75 14	85.2	18 20	74 11	84.9	18 14	73 08	84.6	18 08	72 05	84.3	161
20	19 33	77 15	85.7	19 28	76 12	85.4	19 23	75 08	85.1	19 17	74 05	84.7	19 12	73 02	84.3	19 05	71 59	83.9	160
21	20 31	77 10	85.4	20 26	76 07	85.1	20 21	75 03	84.7	20 15	73 59	84.3	20 09	72 56	84.0	20 03	71 52	83.6	159
22	21 30	77 05	85.2	21 24	76 01	84.8	21 19	74 57	84.4	21 13	73 53	84.0	21 06	72 49	83.6	21 00	71 45	83.3	158
23	22 28	77 00	85.0	22 23	75 55	84.5	22 17	74 51	84.1	22 10	73 46	83.7	22 04	72 42	83.3	21 56	71 38	82.9	157
24	23 27	76 54	84.7	23 21	75 49	84.3	23 15	74 44	83.9	23 08	73 39	83.4	23 01	72 34	83.0	22 53	71 30	82.6	156
25	24 25	76 48	84.5	24 19	75 43	84.0	24 13	74 37	83.6	24 06	73 32	83.1	23 58	72 27	82.7	23 50	71 22	82.2	155
26	25 23	76 42	84.2	25 17	75 36	83.7	25 10	74 30	83.3	25 03	73 24	82.8	24 55	72 18	82.3	24 47	71 13	81.9	154
27	26 22	76 35	84.0	26 15	75 28	83.5	26 08	74 22	83.0	26 01	73 16	82.5	25 52	72 10	82.0	25 44	71 04	81.5	153
28	27 20	76 28	83.7	27 13	75 21	83.2	27 06	74 14	82.7	26 58	73 08	82.2	26 50	72 00	81.7	26 41	70 54	81.2	152
29	28 18	76 20	83.4	28 11	75 13	82.9	28 04	74 05	82.4	27 55	72 58	81.8	27 47	71 51	81.3	27 37	70 44	80.8	151
30	29 17	76 13	83.2	29 09	75 04	82.6	29 01	73 56	82.0	28 53	72 48	81.5	28 44	71 41	81.0	28 34	70 33	80.4	150
31	30 15	76 04	82.9	30 07	74 56	82.3	29 59	73 47	81.7	29 50	72 38	81.2	29 41	71 30	80.6	29 30	70 22	80.0	149
32	31 13	75 56	82.6	31 05	74 46	82.0	30 57	73 37	81.4	30 47	72 28	80.8	30 37	71 19	80.2	30 27	70 11	79.6	148
33	32 11	75 47	82.3	32 03	74 37	81.7	31 54	73 27	81.1	31 44	72 17	80.5	31 34	71 07	79.9	31 23	69 58	79.2	147
34	33 10	75 37	82.0	33 01	74 26	81.4	32 52	73 16	80.7	32 42	72 05	80.1	32 31	70 55	79.5	32 20	69 45	78.8	146
35	34 08	75 27	81.7	33 59	74 16	81.0	33 49	73 04	80.4	33 39	71 53	79.7	33 28	70 42	79.1	33 16	69 32	78.4	145
36	35 06	75 17	81.4	34 56	74 04	80.7	34 46	72 52	80.0	34 36	71 40	79.4	34 24	70 29	78.7	34 12	69 18	78.0	144
37	36 04	75 06	81.1	35 54	73 53	80.4	35 44	72 40	79.7	35 33	71 28	79.0	35 21	70 15	78.3	35 08	69 03	77.6	143
38	37 02	74 54	80.8	36 52	73 40	80.0	36 41	72 27	79.3	36 29	71 13	78.6	36 17	70 00	77.8	36 04	68 48	77.1	142
39	38 00	74 42	80.4	37 49	73 27	79.7	37 38	72 13	78.9	37 26	70 59	78.2	37 13	69 45	77.4	37 00	68 32	76.7	141
40	38 57	74 30	80.1	38 47	73 14	79.3	38 35	71 58	78.5	38 23	70 43	77.7	38 10	69 29	77.0	37 56	68 15	76.2	140
41	39 55	74 16	79.8	39 44	72 59	78.9	39 32	71 43	78.1	39 19	70 27	77.3	39 06	69 12	76.5	38 51	67 57	75.7	139
42	40 53	74 02	79.4	40 41	72 45	78.5	40 29	71 27	77.7	40 16	70 10	76.9	40 02	68 54	76.1	39 47	67 38	75.3	138
43	41 51	73 48	79.0	41 39	72 29	78.2	41 26	71 11	77.3	41 12	69 53	76.4	40 58	68 35	75.6	40 42	67 19	74.7	137
44	42 48	73 32	78.6	42 36	72 12	77.7	42 23	70 53	76.9	42 09	69 34	76.0	41 54	68 16	75.1	41 38	66 58	74.2	136
45	43 46	73 16	78.3	43 33	71 55	77.3	43 19	70 35	76.4	43 05	69 15	75.5	42 49	67 56	74.6	42 33	66 37	73.7	135

Lat. / Ā		LHA
		180
		181
		182
		183
		184
		185
		186
		187
		188
		189
		190
		191
		192
		193
		194
		195
		196
		197
		198
		199
		200
		201
		202
		203
		204
		205
		206
		207
		208
		209
		210
		211
		212
		213
		214
		215
		216
		217
		218
		219
		220
		221
		222
		223
		224
		225

Z₁: same sign as B
Z₂: (−)for F > 90°

Lat. / Ā LHA/F̄	12° A/H	12° B/P	12° Z_1/Z_2	13° A/H	13° B/P	13° Z_1/Z_2	14° A/H	14° B/P	14° Z_1/Z_2	15° A/H	15° B/P	15° Z_1/Z_2	16° A/H	16° B/P	16° Z_1/Z_2	17° A/H	17° B/P	17° Z_1/Z_2	Lat. / Ā LHA
45 / 135	43 46	73 16	78.3	43 33	71 55	77.3	43 19	70 35	76.4	43 05	69 15	75.5	42 49	67 56	74.6	42 33	66 37	73.7	225 / 315
46 / 134	44 43	72 59	77.8	44 30	71 37	76.9	44 16	70 15	75.9	44 01	68 54	75.0	43 45	67 34	74.1	43 28	66 15	73.2	226 / 314
47 / 133	45 40	72 41	77.4	45 27	71 18	76.4	45 12	69 55	75.5	44 57	68 33	74.5	44 40	67 12	73.5	44 23	65 51	72.6	227 / 313
48 / 132	46 38	72 23	77.0	46 24	70 58	76.0	46 09	69 34	75.0	45 53	68 11	74.0	45 35	66 48	73.0	45 17	65 27	72.0	228 / 312
49 / 131	47 35	72 03	76.5	47 20	70 37	75.5	47 05	69 11	74.4	46 48	67 47	73.4	46 30	66 23	72.4	46 12	65 01	71.4	229 / 311
50 / 130	48 32	71 42	76.1	48 17	70 15	75.0	48 01	68 48	73.9	47 44	67 22	72.9	47 25	65 58	71.8	47 06	64 34	70.8	230 / 310
51 / 129	49 29	71 20	75.6	49 13	69 51	74.5	48 57	68 23	73.4	48 39	66 56	72.3	48 20	65 30	71.2	48 00	64 05	70.1	231 / 309
52 / 128	50 25	70 57	75.1	50 09	69 27	73.9	49 52	67 57	72.8	49 34	66 29	71.7	49 15	65 02	70.6	48 54	63 35	69.5	232 / 308
53 / 127	51 22	70 33	74.6	51 06	69 01	73.4	50 48	67 30	72.2	50 29	66 00	71.0	50 09	64 31	69.9	49 48	63 04	68.8	233 / 307
54 / 126	52 19	70 07	74.0	52 02	68 33	72.8	51 43	67 01	71.6	51 24	65 30	70.4	51 03	64 00	69.2	50 41	62 31	68.1	234 / 306
55 / 125	53 15	69 40	73.5	52 57	68 04	72.2	52 38	66 30	70.9	52 18	64 58	69.7	51 57	63 26	68.5	51 34	61 56	67.3	235 / 305
56 / 124	54 11	69 11	72.9	53 53	67 34	71.6	53 33	65 58	70.3	53 12	64 24	69.0	52 50	62 51	67.8	52 27	61 20	66.6	236 / 304
57 / 123	55 07	68 41	72.2	54 48	67 02	70.9	54 28	65 24	69.6	54 06	63 48	68.3	53 43	62 14	67.0	53 19	60 42	65.8	237 / 303
58 / 122	56 03	68 09	71.6	55 43	66 28	70.2	55 22	64 48	68.8	55 00	63 11	67.5	54 36	61 35	66.3	54 12	60 01	64.9	238 / 302
59 / 121	56 59	67 34	70.9	56 38	65 51	69.5	56 16	64 10	68.1	55 53	62 31	66.7	55 29	60 54	65.4	55 03	59 18	64.1	239 / 301
60 / 120	57 54	66 58	70.2	57 33	65 13	68.7	57 10	63 30	67.3	56 46	61 49	65.9	56 21	60 10	64.5	55 55	58 33	63.1	240 / 300
61 / 119	58 49	66 20	69.4	58 27	64 32	67.9	58 04	62 47	66.4	57 39	61 04	65.0	57 13	59 24	63.6	56 46	57 46	62.2	241 / 299
62 / 118	59 44	65 38	68.6	59 21	63 49	67.1	58 57	62 02	65.5	58 31	60 17	64.0	58 05	58 35	62.6	57 36	56 56	61.2	242 / 298
63 / 117	60 38	64 55	67.8	60 15	63 03	66.2	59 50	61 13	64.6	59 23	59 27	63.1	58 55	57 43	61.6	58 26	56 03	60.2	243 / 297
64 / 116	61 32	64 08	67.0	61 08	62 14	65.2	60 42	60 22	63.6	60 15	58 34	62.0	59 46	56 49	60.5	59 16	55 06	59.1	244 / 296
65 / 115	62 26	63 18	66.0	62 01	61 21	64.2	61 34	59 28	62.6	61 06	57 37	61.0	60 36	55 51	59.4	60 05	54 07	57.9	245 / 295
66 / 114	63 20	62 25	65.0	62 53	60 25	63.2	62 26	58 30	61.5	61 56	56 37	59.8	61 25	54 49	58.2	60 53	53 04	56.7	246 / 294
67 / 113	64 13	61 27	63.9	63 45	59 25	62.1	63 16	57 27	60.3	62 46	55 34	58.6	62 14	53 44	57.0	61 41	51 57	55.4	247 / 293
68 / 112	65 05	60 26	62.8	64 37	58 21	60.9	64 07	56 21	59.1	63 35	54 25	57.4	63 02	52 34	55.7	62 27	50 47	54.1	248 / 292
69 / 111	65 57	59 20	61.6	65 27	57 13	59.6	64 56	55 10	57.8	64 23	53 13	56.0	63 49	51 20	54.3	63 14	49 32	52.7	249 / 291
70 / 110	66 48	58 08	60.3	66 18	55 59	58.3	65 45	53 55	56.4	65 11	51 55	54.6	64 36	50 01	52.9	63 59	48 12	51.2	250 / 290
71 / 109	67 39	56 52	58.9	67 07	54 40	56.8	66 33	52 33	54.9	65 58	50 33	53.1	65 21	48 38	51.3	64 43	46 48	49.7	251 / 289
72 / 108	68 29	55 29	57.4	67 55	53 14	55.3	67 20	51 06	53.3	66 44	49 04	51.5	66 06	47 08	49.7	65 26	45 18	48.0	252 / 288
73 / 107	69 18	53 59	55.8	68 43	51 42	53.7	68 07	49 33	51.6	67 29	47 30	49.8	66 49	45 33	48.0	66 08	43 43	46.3	253 / 287
74 / 106	70 06	52 22	54.1	69 30	50 03	51.9	68 52	47 52	49.8	68 12	45 49	47.9	67 31	43 52	46.1	66 49	42 02	44.4	254 / 286
75 / 105	70 53	50 36	52.2	70 15	48 16	50.0	69 36	46 04	47.9	68 55	44 00	46.0	68 12	42 04	44.2	67 29	40 15	42.5	255 / 285
76 / 104	71 38	48 42	50.2	70 59	46 20	47.9	70 19	44 08	45.9	69 36	42 05	43.9	68 52	40 09	42.1	68 07	38 21	40.5	256 / 284
77 / 103	72 23	46 37	48.0	71 42	44 15	45.7	71 00	42 03	43.7	70 15	40 01	41.7	69 30	38 07	39.9	68 43	36 21	38.3	257 / 283
78 / 102	73 06	44 22	45.6	72 23	42 00	43.4	71 38	39 49	41.3	70 53	37 49	39.4	70 06	35 57	37.6	69 18	34 13	36.0	258 / 282
79 / 101	73 47	41 55	43.1	73 02	39 34	40.8	72 16	37 26	38.8	71 28	35 27	36.9	70 40	33 38	35.2	69 50	31 58	33.6	259 / 281
80 / 100	74 26	39 15	40.3	73 39	36 57	38.1	72 51	34 51	36.1	72 02	32 57	34.3	71 12	31 12	32.6	70 21	29 36	31.1	260 / 280
81 / 99	75 02	36 21	37.3	74 14	34 07	35.1	73 24	32 06	33.2	72 34	30 17	31.5	71 42	28 37	29.9	70 50	27 06	28.4	261 / 279
82 / 98	75 37	33 13	34.1	74 46	31 05	32.0	73 55	29 10	30.2	73 03	27 27	28.5	72 09	25 53	27.0	71 16	24 29	25.7	262 / 278
83 / 97	76 08	29 50	30.6	75 16	27 50	28.6	74 23	26 03	26.9	73 29	24 27	25.4	72 34	23 02	24.0	71 39	21 44	22.8	263 / 277
84 / 96	76 36	26 11	26.8	75 42	24 22	25.0	74 48	22 45	23.5	73 52	21 19	22.1	72 56	20 04	20.9	72 00	18 53	19.8	264 / 276
85 / 95	77 01	22 18	22.8	76 05	20 41	21.3	75 09	19 16	19.9	74 12	18 01	18.7	73 15	16 54	17.6	72 18	15 55	16.7	265 / 275
86 / 94	77 22	18 10	18.6	76 25	16 49	17.3	75 27	15 38	16.1	74 29	14 36	15.1	73 31	13 40	14.2	72 33	12 51	13.5	266 / 274
87 / 93	77 38	13 50	14.1	76 40	12 46	13.1	75 41	11 51	12.2	74 43	11 03	11.4	73 44	10 21	10.8	72 45	9 43	10.2	267 / 273
88 / 92	77 50	9 19	9.5	76 51	8 36	8.8	75 52	7 58	8.2	74 52	7 25	7.7	73 53	6 56	7.2	72 53	6 31	6.8	268 / 272
89 / 91	77 58	4 42	4.8	76 58	4 19	4.4	75 58	4 00	4.1	74 58	3 44	3.9	73 58	3 29	3.6	72 58	3 16	3.4	269 / 271
90 / 90	78 00	0 00	0.0	77 00	0 00	0.0	76 00	0 00	0.0	75 00	0 00	0.0	74 00	0 00	0.0	73 00	0 00	0.0	270 / 270

N. Lat.: for LHA>180°.... Zn = Z
for LHA<180°.... Zn = 360° − Z

S. Lat.: for LHA > 180°.... Zn = 180° − Z
for LHA < 180°.... Zn = 180° + Z

B: (−) for 90° < LHA < 270°
Dec: (−) for Lat. contrary name

LATITUDE/Ā : 18° – 23°

Z1: same sign as B
Z2: (−) for F > 90°

LHA/F	18° A/H	18° B/P	18° Z1/Z2	19° A/H	19° B/P	19° Z1/Z2	20° A/H	20° B/P	20° Z1/Z2	21° A/H	21° B/P	21° Z1/Z2	22° A/H	22° B/P	22° Z1/Z2	23° A/H	23° B/P	23° Z1/Z2	LHA
0	0 00	72 00	90.0	0 00	71 00	90.0	0 00	70 00	90.0	0 00	69 00	90.0	0 00	68 00	90.0	0 00	67 00	90.0	180
1	0 57	72 00	89.7	0 57	71 00	89.7	0 56	70 00	89.7	0 56	69 00	89.6	0 56	68 00	89.6	0 55	67 00	89.6	181
2	1 54	71 59	89.4	1 53	70 59	89.3	1 53	69 59	89.3	1 52	68 59	89.3	1 51	67 59	89.3	1 50	66 59	89.2	182
3	2 51	71 59	89.1	2 50	70 59	89.0	2 49	69 58	89.0	2 48	68 58	88.9	2 47	67 58	88.9	2 46	66 58	88.8	183
4	3 48	71 58	88.8	3 47	70 57	88.7	3 46	69 57	88.6	3 44	68 57	88.6	3 42	67 57	88.5	3 41	66 57	88.4	184
5	4 45	71 56	88.5	4 44	70 56	88.4	4 42	69 56	88.3	4 40	68 56	88.2	4 38	67 55	88.1	4 36	66 55	88.0	185
6	5 42	71 54	88.1	5 40	70 54	88.0	5 38	69 54	87.9	5 36	68 54	87.8	5 34	67 53	87.7	5 31	66 53	87.6	186
7	6 39	71 52	87.8	6 37	70 52	87.7	6 35	69 52	87.6	6 32	68 51	87.5	6 29	67 51	87.4	6 26	66 51	87.3	187
8	7 36	71 49	87.5	7 34	70 50	87.4	7 31	69 49	87.2	7 28	68 49	87.1	7 25	67 48	87.0	7 22	66 48	86.9	188
9	8 33	71 47	87.2	8 30	70 47	87.0	8 27	69 46	86.9	8 24	68 46	86.8	8 20	67 45	86.6	8 17	66 45	86.5	189
10	9 30	71 44	86.9	9 27	70 44	86.7	9 23	69 43	86.5	9 20	68 42	86.4	9 16	67 42	86.2	9 12	66 41	86.1	190
11	10 27	71 41	86.6	10 24	70 40	86.4	10 20	69 39	86.2	10 16	68 39	86.0	10 11	67 38	85.8	10 07	66 37	85.7	191
12	11 24	71 37	86.2	11 20	70 36	86.0	11 16	69 35	85.8	11 12	68 34	85.6	11 07	67 33	85.4	11 02	66 32	85.3	192
13	12 21	71 33	85.9	12 17	70 32	85.6	12 12	69 31	85.5	12 07	68 30	85.3	12 02	67 29	85.1	11 57	66 28	84.9	193
14	13 18	71 29	85.6	13 13	70 28	85.3	13 08	69 26	85.1	13 03	68 25	84.9	12 58	67 24	84.7	12 52	66 22	84.4	194
15	14 15	71 24	85.3	14 10	70 23	85.0	14 05	69 21	84.8	13 59	68 20	84.5	13 53	67 18	84.3	13 47	66 17	84.0	195
16	15 12	71 19	84.9	15 06	70 18	84.7	15 01	69 16	84.4	14 55	68 14	84.1	14 48	67 12	83.9	14 42	66 11	83.6	196
17	16 09	71 14	84.6	16 03	70 12	84.3	15 57	69 10	84.0	15 50	68 08	83.7	15 44	67 06	83.5	15 37	66 04	83.2	197
18	17 05	71 08	84.3	16 59	70 06	84.0	16 53	69 03	83.7	16 46	68 01	83.4	16 39	66 59	83.1	16 32	65 57	82.8	198
19	18 02	71 02	83.9	17 56	69 59	83.6	17 49	68 57	83.3	17 42	67 54	83.0	17 34	66 52	82.7	17 26	65 49	82.3	199
20	18 59	70 56	83.6	18 52	69 53	83.2	18 45	68 50	82.9	18 37	67 47	82.6	18 29	66 44	82.2	18 21	65 41	81.9	200
21	19 56	70 49	83.2	19 48	69 45	82.9	19 41	68 42	82.5	19 33	67 39	82.2	19 24	66 36	81.8	19 16	65 33	81.5	201
22	20 52	70 41	82.9	20 45	69 38	82.5	20 37	68 34	82.1	20 28	67 31	81.8	20 19	66 27	81.4	20 10	65 24	81.0	202
23	21 49	70 33	82.5	21 41	69 29	82.1	21 32	68 26	81.7	21 24	67 22	81.4	21 14	66 18	81.0	21 05	65 15	80.6	203
24	22 45	70 25	82.2	22 37	69 21	81.8	22 28	68 17	81.3	22 19	67 12	80.9	22 09	66 09	80.5	21 59	65 05	80.1	204
25	23 42	70 17	81.8	23 33	69 12	81.4	23 24	68 07	80.9	23 14	67 02	80.5	23 04	65 58	80.1	22 54	64 54	79.7	205
26	24 38	70 07	81.4	24 29	69 02	81.0	24 20	67 57	80.5	24 09	66 52	80.1	23 59	65 48	79.6	23 48	64 43	79.2	206
27	25 35	69 58	81.1	25 25	68 52	80.6	25 15	67 47	80.1	25 05	66 42	79.7	24 54	65 36	79.2	24 42	64 32	78.7	207
28	26 31	69 48	80.7	26 21	68 42	80.2	26 11	67 37	79.7	26 00	66 30	79.2	25 48	65 25	78.7	25 36	64 19	78.3	208
29	27 27	69 37	80.3	27 17	68 31	79.8	27 06	67 24	79.3	26 55	66 18	78.8	26 43	65 12	78.3	26 30	64 07	77.8	209
30	28 24	69 26	79.9	28 13	68 19	79.4	28 01	67 12	78.8	27 50	66 06	78.3	27 37	64 59	77.8	27 24	63 53	77.3	210
31	29 20	69 14	79.5	29 09	68 07	78.9	28 57	67 00	78.4	28 44	65 53	77.9	28 31	64 46	77.3	28 18	63 39	76.8	211
32	30 16	69 02	79.1	30 04	67 54	78.5	29 52	66 46	77.9	29 39	65 39	77.4	29 26	64 32	76.8	29 12	63 25	76.3	212
33	31 12	68 49	78.7	31 00	67 41	78.1	30 47	66 32	77.5	30 34	65 24	76.9	30 20	64 17	76.3	30 05	63 09	75.8	213
34	32 08	68 36	78.2	31 55	67 27	77.6	31 42	66 18	77.0	31 28	65 09	76.4	31 14	64 01	75.8	30 59	62 53	75.2	214
35	33 04	68 22	77.8	32 51	67 12	77.2	32 37	66 03	76.5	32 23	64 54	75.9	32 08	63 45	75.3	31 52	62 36	74.7	215
36	33 59	68 07	77.3	33 46	66 57	76.7	33 32	65 47	76.0	33 17	64 37	75.4	33 01	63 28	74.8	32 45	62 19	74.2	216
37	34 55	67 52	76.9	34 41	66 41	76.2	34 26	65 30	75.5	34 11	64 20	74.9	33 55	63 10	74.2	33 38	62 01	73.6	217
38	35 50	67 36	76.4	35 36	66 24	75.7	35 21	65 13	75.0	35 05	64 02	74.4	34 48	62 51	73.7	34 31	61 41	73.0	218
39	36 46	67 19	75.9	36 31	66 06	75.2	36 15	64 54	74.5	35 59	63 43	73.8	35 42	62 32	73.1	35 24	61 21	72.4	219
40	37 41	67 01	75.5	37 26	65 48	74.7	37 10	64 35	74.0	36 53	63 23	73.3	36 35	62 12	72.6	36 17	61 01	71.8	220
41	38 36	66 42	75.0	38 20	65 29	74.2	38 04	64 15	73.4	37 46	63 02	72.7	37 28	61 50	72.0	37 09	60 39	71.2	221
42	39 31	66 23	74.5	39 15	65 08	73.7	38 58	63 54	72.9	38 40	62 41	72.1	38 21	61 28	71.4	38 01	60 16	70.6	222
43	40 26	66 03	73.9	40 09	64 47	73.1	39 51	63 33	72.3	39 33	62 18	71.5	39 13	61 05	70.7	38 53	59 52	70.0	223
44	41 21	65 42	73.4	41 03	64 25	72.5	40 45	63 10	71.7	40 26	61 55	70.9	40 06	60 41	70.1	39 45	59 27	69.3	224
45	42 16	65 19	72.8	41 57	64 02	72.0	41 38	62 46	71.1	41 19	61 30	70.3	40 58	60 15	69.5	40 37	59 01	68.7	225

LHA/F	Ā	18° A/H	18° B/P	18° Z_1/Z_2	19° A/H	19° B/P	19° Z_1/Z_2	20° A/H	20° B/P	20° Z_1/Z_2	21° A/H	21° B/P	21° Z_1/Z_2	22° A/H	22° B/P	22° Z_1/Z_2	23° A/H	23° B/P	23° Z_1/Z_2	Ā	LHA
45	135	42 16	65 19	72.8	41 57	64 02	72.0	41 38	62 46	71.1	41 19	61 30	70.3	40 58	60 15	69.5	40 37	59 01	68.7	315	225
46	134	43 10	64 56	72.3	42 51	63 38	71.4	42 32	62 21	70.5	42 11	61 05	69.6	41 50	59 49	68.8	41 28	58 34	68.0	314	226
47	133	44 04	64 32	71.7	43 45	63 13	70.8	43 25	61 55	69.9	43 04	60 38	69.0	42 42	59 21	68.1	42 19	58 06	67.3	313	227
48	132	44 58	64 06	71.1	44 38	62 46	70.1	44 18	61 27	69.2	43 56	60 09	68.3	43 33	58 53	67.4	43 10	57 37	66.5	312	228
49	131	45 52	63 39	70.4	45 32	62 18	69.5	45 10	60 59	68.5	44 48	59 40	67.6	44 24	58 22	66.7	44 00	57 06	65.8	311	229
50	130	46 46	63 11	69.8	46 25	61 49	68.8	46 03	60 29	67.8	45 39	59 09	66.9	45 15	57 51	65.9	44 50	56 34	65.0	310	230
51	129	47 39	62 42	69.1	47 17	61 19	68.1	46 55	59 57	67.1	46 31	58 37	66.1	46 06	57 18	65.2	45 40	56 00	64.2	309	231
52	128	48 33	62 11	68.4	48 10	60 47	67.4	47 46	59 25	66.4	47 22	58 03	65.4	46 56	56 44	64.4	46 30	55 25	63.4	308	232
53	127	49 25	61 38	67.7	49 02	60 13	66.6	48 38	58 50	65.6	48 13	57 28	64.6	47 46	56 07	63.6	47 19	54 48	62.6	307	233
54	126	50 18	61 04	67.0	49 54	59 38	65.9	49 29	58 14	64.8	49 03	56 51	63.7	48 36	55 30	62.7	48 08	54 10	61.7	306	234
55	125	51 10	60 28	66.2	50 46	59 01	65.1	50 20	57 36	64.0	49 53	56 12	62.9	49 25	54 50	61.9	48 56	53 30	60.8	305	235
56	124	52 03	59 50	65.4	51 37	58 23	64.2	51 10	56 56	63.1	50 43	55 32	62.0	50 14	54 09	61.0	49 44	52 48	59.9	304	236
57	123	52 54	59 11	64.6	52 28	57 42	63.4	52 00	56 15	62.2	51 32	54 49	61.1	51 02	53 26	60.0	50 32	52 04	59.0	303	237
58	122	53 46	58 29	63.7	53 18	56 59	62.5	52 50	55 31	61.3	52 21	54 05	60.2	51 50	52 41	59.1	51 19	51 18	58.0	302	238
59	121	54 37	57 45	62.8	54 08	56 14	61.5	53 39	54 45	60.4	53 09	53 18	59.2	52 38	51 53	58.1	52 06	50 30	57.0	301	239
60	120	55 27	56 59	61.8	54 57	55 27	60.6	54 28	53 57	59.4	53 57	52 29	58.2	53 25	51 04	57.0	52 52	49 40	55.9	300	240
61	119	56 17	56 10	60.9	55 47	54 37	59.6	55 16	53 06	58.3	54 44	51 38	57.1	54 11	50 12	55.9	53 37	48 48	54.8	299	241
62	118	57 07	55 19	59.8	56 36	53 45	58.5	56 04	52 13	57.2	55 31	50 44	56.0	54 57	49 17	54.8	54 22	47 53	53.7	298	242
63	117	57 56	54 25	58.8	57 24	52 49	57.4	56 51	51 17	56.1	56 17	49 47	54.9	55 42	48 20	53.7	55 06	46 55	52.5	297	243
64	116	58 44	53 27	57.6	58 12	51 51	56.3	57 38	50 18	55.0	57 03	48 48	53.7	56 27	47 20	52.5	55 50	45 55	51.3	296	244
65	115	59 32	52 27	56.5	58 59	50 50	55.1	58 23	49 16	53.7	57 47	47 45	52.5	57 10	46 17	51.3	56 32	44 52	50.0	295	245
66	114	60 19	51 23	55.2	59 45	49 45	53.8	59 09	48 11	52.5	58 32	46 39	51.2	57 53	45 11	50.0	57 14	43 47	48.7	294	246
67	113	61 06	50 15	53.9	60 30	48 37	52.5	59 53	47 02	51.1	59 15	45 30	49.8	58 36	44 02	48.6	57 55	42 38	47.4	293	247
68	112	61 52	49 04	52.6	61 15	47 25	51.1	60 36	45 50	49.7	59 57	44 18	48.4	59 17	42 50	47.2	58 36	41 26	46.0	292	248
69	111	62 37	47 48	51.2	61 58	46 09	49.7	61 19	44 33	48.3	60 39	43 02	47.0	59 57	41 34	45.7	59 15	40 10	44.5	291	249
70	110	63 21	46 28	49.7	62 41	44 48	48.2	62 01	43 13	46.8	61 19	41 42	45.4	60 36	40 15	44.2	59 53	38 52	43.0	290	250
71	109	64 04	45 03	48.1	63 23	43 24	46.6	62 41	41 49	45.2	61 58	40 18	43.9	61 15	38 52	42.6	60 30	37 29	41.4	289	251
72	108	64 45	43 34	46.4	64 04	41 54	44.9	63 21	40 20	43.5	62 37	38 50	42.2	61 52	37 25	40.9	61 06	36 03	39.7	288	252
73	107	65 26	41 59	44.7	64 43	40 20	43.2	63 59	38 46	41.8	63 14	37 18	40.5	62 27	35 53	39.2	61 41	34 34	38.0	287	253
74	106	66 06	40 19	42.9	65 21	38 41	41.4	64 36	37 08	40.0	63 49	35 41	38.7	63 02	34 18	37.4	62 14	33 00	36.3	286	254
75	105	66 44	38 32	40.9	65 58	36 56	39.5	65 11	35 25	38.1	64 23	33 59	36.8	63 35	32 39	35.6	62 46	31 22	34.4	285	255
76	104	67 20	36 40	38.9	66 33	35 07	37.4	65 45	33 37	36.1	64 56	32 13	34.8	64 07	30 55	33.6	63 16	29 41	32.5	284	256
77	103	67 55	34 42	36.8	67 07	33 09	35.3	66 18	31 43	34.0	65 27	30 22	32.8	64 37	29 06	31.6	63 45	27 55	30.6	283	257
78	102	68 29	32 37	34.5	67 39	31 07	33.1	66 48	29 44	31.9	65 57	28 26	30.7	65 05	27 14	29.6	64 13	26 06	28.5	282	258
79	101	69 00	30 25	32.2	68 09	28 59	30.8	67 17	27 40	29.6	66 25	26 26	28.5	65 32	25 17	27.4	64 38	24 12	26.4	281	259
80	100	69 29	28 07	29.7	68 37	26 46	28.4	67 44	25 30	27.3	66 50	24 22	26.2	65 56	23 15	25.2	65 02	22 15	24.3	280	260
81	99	69 57	25 43	27.1	69 03	24 26	25.9	68 09	23 15	24.8	67 14	22 10	23.8	66 18	21 10	22.9	65 23	20 14	22.1	279	261
82	98	70 21	23 11	24.5	69 27	22 00	23.3	68 31	20 56	22.3	67 36	19 56	21.4	66 40	19 00	20.6	65 43	18 09	19.8	278	262
83	97	70 44	20 34	21.7	69 48	19 29	20.7	68 51	18 31	19.7	67 55	17 37	18.9	66 58	16 47	18.1	66 01	16 01	17.4	277	263
84	96	71 03	17 50	18.8	70 07	16 53	17.9	69 09	16 01	17.0	68 11	15 14	16.3	67 14	14 30	15.7	66 16	13 50	15.1	276	264
85	95	71 20	15 01	15.8	70 23	14 12	15.0	69 25	13 28	14.3	68 26	12 48	13.7	67 28	12 10	13.1	66 29	11 36	12.6	275	265
86	94	71 35	12 07	12.8	70 36	11 27	12.1	69 37	10 51	11.6	68 38	10 18	11.0	67 39	9 48	10.6	66 40	9 20	10.1	274	266
87	93	71 46	9 09	9.6	70 46	8 39	9.1	69 47	8 11	8.7	68 48	7 46	8.3	67 48	7 23	8.0	66 49	7 02	7.6	273	267
88	92	71 54	6 08	6.4	70 54	5 47	6.1	69 54	5 29	5.8	68 55	5 12	5.6	67 55	4 56	5.3	66 55	4 42	5.1	272	268
89	91	71 58	3 04	3.2	70 58	2 54	3.1	69 59	2 45	2.9	68 59	2 36	2.8	67 59	2 28	2.7	66 59	2 21	2.6	271	269
90	90	72 00	0 00	0.0	71 00	0 00	0.0	70 00	0 00	0.0	69 00	0 00	0.0	68 00	0 00	0.0	67 00	0 00	0.0	270	270

N. Lat.: for LHA>180°.....Zn=Z
for LHA<180°.....Zn=360°−Z

S. Lat.: for LHA>180°.....Zn=180°−Z
for LHA<180°.....Zn=180°+Z

B: (−) for 90° < LHA < 270°
Dec: (−) for Lat. contrary name

LATITUDE / Ā : 24° − 29°

Z₁ : same sign as B
Z₂ : (−)for F > 90°

Lat./Ā LHA/F	24°			25°			26°			27°			28°			29°			Lat./Ā LHA
LHA/F	A/H	B/P	Z_1/Z_2	A/H	B/P	Z_1/Z_2	A/H	B/P	Z_1/Z_2	A/H	B/P	Z_1/Z_2	A/H	B/P	Z_1/Z_2	A/H	B/P	Z_1/Z_2	LHA
0 180	0 00	66 00	90.0	0 00	65 00	90.0	0 00	64 00	90.0	0 00	63 00	90.0	0 00	62 00	90.0	0 00	61 00	90.0	180 360
1 179	0 55	66 00	89.6	0 54	65 00	89.6	0 54	64 00	89.6	0 53	63 00	89.5	0 53	62 00	89.5	0 52	61 00	89.5	181 359
2 178	1 50	65 59	89.2	1 49	64 59	89.1	1 48	63 59	89.1	1 47	62 59	89.1	1 46	61 59	89.1	1 45	60 59	89.0	182 358
3 177	2 44	65 58	88.8	2 43	64 58	88.7	2 42	63 58	88.7	2 40	62 58	88.6	2 39	61 58	88.6	2 37	60 58	88.5	183 357
4 176	3 39	65 57	88.4	3 37	64 57	88.3	3 36	63 57	88.2	3 34	62 57	88.2	3 32	61 57	88.1	3 30	60 56	88.1	184 356
5 175	4 34	65 55	88.0	4 32	64 55	87.9	4 30	63 55	87.8	4 27	62 55	87.7	4 25	61 55	87.6	4 22	60 54	87.6	185 355
6 174	5 29	65 53	87.6	5 26	64 53	87.5	5 23	63 53	87.4	5 21	62 52	87.3	5 18	61 52	87.2	5 15	60 52	87.1	186 354
7 173	6 24	65 50	87.1	6 20	64 50	87.0	6 17	63 50	86.9	6 14	62 50	86.8	6 11	61 49	86.7	6 07	60 49	86.6	187 353
8 172	7 18	65 47	86.7	7 15	64 47	86.6	7 11	63 47	86.5	7 07	62 46	86.4	7 04	61 46	86.2	6 59	60 46	86.1	188 352
9 171	8 13	65 44	86.3	8 09	64 44	86.2	8 05	63 43	86.0	8 01	62 43	85.9	7 56	61 42	85.7	7 52	60 42	85.6	189 351
10 170	9 08	65 40	85.9	9 03	64 40	85.7	8 59	63 39	85.6	8 54	62 39	85.4	8 49	61 38	85.3	8 44	60 38	85.1	190 350
11 169	10 02	65 36	85.5	9 57	64 35	85.3	9 52	63 35	85.1	9 47	62 34	85.0	9 42	61 33	84.8	9 36	60 33	84.6	191 349
12 168	10 57	65 32	85.1	10 52	64 31	84.9	10 46	63 30	84.7	10 41	62 29	84.5	10 35	61 28	84.3	10 29	60 28	84.1	192 348
13 167	11 52	65 27	84.6	11 46	64 26	84.4	11 40	63 25	84.2	11 34	62 24	84.0	11 27	61 23	83.8	11 21	60 22	83.6	193 347
14 166	12 46	65 21	84.2	12 40	64 20	84.0	12 34	63 19	83.8	12 27	62 18	83.5	12 20	61 17	83.3	12 13	60 16	83.1	194 346
15 165	13 41	65 15	83.8	13 34	64 14	83.5	13 27	63 13	83.3	13 20	62 11	83.1	13 13	61 10	82.8	13 05	60 09	82.6	195 345
16 164	14 35	65 09	83.3	14 28	64 07	83.1	14 21	63 06	82.8	14 13	62 04	82.6	14 05	61 03	82.3	13 57	60 02	82.1	196 344
17 163	15 29	65 02	82.9	15 22	64 00	82.6	15 14	62 59	82.4	15 06	61 57	82.1	14 58	60 56	81.8	14 49	59 54	81.6	197 343
18 162	16 24	64 55	82.5	16 16	63 53	82.2	16 08	62 51	81.9	15 59	61 49	81.6	15 50	60 47	81.3	15 41	59 46	81.0	198 342
19 161	17 18	64 47	82.0	17 10	63 45	81.7	17 01	62 43	81.4	16 52	61 41	81.1	16 42	60 39	80.8	16 33	59 37	80.5	199 341
20 160	18 12	64 39	81.6	18 03	63 36	81.3	17 54	62 34	80.9	17 45	61 32	80.6	17 35	60 30	80.3	17 24	59 28	80.0	200 340
21 159	19 07	64 30	81.1	18 57	63 28	80.8	18 47	62 25	80.4	18 37	61 23	80.1	18 27	60 20	79.8	18 16	59 18	79.5	201 339
22 158	20 01	64 21	80.7	19 51	63 18	80.3	19 41	62 15	80.0	19 30	61 13	79.6	19 19	60 10	79.3	19 08	59 08	78.9	202 338
23 157	20 55	64 11	80.2	20 44	63 08	79.8	20 34	62 05	79.5	20 22	61 02	79.1	20 11	59 59	78.7	19 59	58 57	78.4	203 337
24 156	21 49	64 01	79.7	21 38	62 58	79.3	21 27	61 54	79.0	21 15	60 51	78.6	21 03	59 48	78.2	20 50	58 45	77.8	204 336
25 155	22 43	63 50	79.3	22 31	62 46	78.8	22 19	61 43	78.5	22 07	60 39	78.0	21 55	59 36	77.7	21 42	58 33	77.3	205 335
26 154	23 36	63 39	78.8	23 25	62 35	78.3	23 12	61 31	77.9	22 59	60 27	77.5	22 46	59 24	77.1	22 33	58 20	76.7	206 334
27 153	24 30	63 27	78.3	24 18	62 22	77.8	24 05	61 18	77.4	23 52	60 14	77.0	23 38	59 10	76.5	23 24	58 07	76.1	207 333
28 152	25 24	63 14	77.8	25 11	62 10	77.3	24 57	61 05	76.9	24 44	60 01	76.4	24 29	58 57	76.0	24 15	57 53	75.5	208 332
29 151	26 17	63 01	77.3	26 04	61 56	76.8	25 50	60 51	76.3	25 36	59 47	75.9	25 21	58 42	75.4	25 05	57 38	75.0	209 331
30 150	27 11	62 48	76.8	26 57	61 42	76.3	26 42	60 37	75.8	26 27	59 32	75.3	26 12	58 27	74.8	25 56	57 23	74.4	210 330
31 149	28 04	62 33	76.3	27 50	61 27	75.8	27 35	60 22	75.2	27 19	59 16	74.7	27 03	58 11	74.2	26 46	57 07	73.8	211 329
32 148	28 57	62 18	75.7	28 42	61 12	75.2	28 27	60 06	74.7	28 10	59 00	74.2	27 54	57 55	73.7	27 37	56 50	73.1	212 328
33 147	29 50	62 02	75.2	29 35	60 56	74.7	29 19	59 49	74.1	29 02	58 43	73.6	28 45	57 38	73.0	28 27	56 33	72.5	213 327
34 146	30 43	61 46	74.7	30 27	60 39	74.1	30 10	59 32	73.5	29 53	58 26	73.0	29 35	57 20	72.4	29 17	56 14	71.9	214 326
35 145	31 36	61 28	74.1	31 19	60 21	73.5	31 02	59 14	72.9	30 44	58 07	72.4	30 26	57 01	71.8	30 07	55 55	71.2	215 325
36 144	32 29	61 10	73.5	32 11	60 02	72.9	31 53	58 55	72.3	31 35	57 48	71.7	31 16	56 41	71.2	30 56	55 35	70.6	216 324
37 143	33 21	60 52	73.0	33 03	59 43	72.3	32 45	58 35	71.7	32 26	57 28	71.1	32 06	56 21	70.5	31 46	55 14	69.9	217 323
38 142	34 13	60 32	72.4	33 55	59 23	71.7	33 36	58 15	71.1	33 16	57 07	70.5	32 56	55 59	69.9	32 35	54 53	69.3	218 322
39 141	35 06	60 11	71.8	34 47	59 02	71.1	34 27	57 53	70.5	34 06	56 45	69.8	33 45	55 37	69.2	33 24	54 30	68.6	219 321
40 140	35 58	59 50	71.2	35 38	58 41	70.5	35 17	57 31	69.8	34 56	56 22	69.2	34 35	55 14	68.5	34 12	54 07	67.9	220 320
41 139	36 49	59 28	70.5	36 29	58 17	69.8	36 08	57 08	69.1	35 46	55 59	68.5	35 24	54 50	67.8	35 01	53 42	67.1	221 319
42 138	37 41	59 04	69.9	37 20	57 54	69.2	36 58	56 43	68.5	36 36	55 34	67.8	36 13	54 25	67.1	35 49	53 17	66.4	222 318
43 137	38 32	58 40	69.2	38 11	57 29	68.5	37 48	56 18	67.8	37 25	55 08	67.1	37 02	53 59	66.4	36 37	52 50	65.7	223 317
44 136	39 23	58 15	68.6	39 01	57 03	67.8	38 38	55 52	67.1	38 14	54 41	66.3	37 50	53 32	65.6	37 25	52 23	64.9	224 316
45 135	40 14	57 48	67.9	39 51	56 36	67.1	39 28	55 24	66.3	39 03	54 13	65.6	38 38	53 04	64.9	38 12	51 54	64.1	225 315

Lat. / F̄		24°			25°			26°			27°			28°			29°			Lat. / Ā	
	LHA/F̄	A/H	B/P	Z_1/Z_2	A/H	B/P	Z_1/Z_2	A/H	B/P	Z_1/Z_2	A/H	B/P	Z_1/Z_2	A/H	B/P	Z_1/Z_2	A/H	B/P	Z_1/Z_2		LHA
45	135	40 14	57 48	67.9	39 51	56 36	67.1	39 28	55 24	66.3	39 03	54 13	65.6	38 38	53 04	64.9	38 12	51 54	64.1	225	315
46	134	41 05	57 21	67.2	40 41	56 08	66.4	40 17	54 56	65.6	39 52	53 44	64.8	39 26	52 34	64.1	38 59	51 25	63.3	226	314
47	133	41 55	56 52	66.4	41 31	55 38	65.6	41 06	54 26	64.8	40 40	53 14	64.0	40 13	52 04	63.3	39 46	50 54	62.5	227	313
48	132	42 45	56 22	65.7	42 20	55 08	64.9	41 54	53 55	64.0	41 28	52 43	63.2	41 00	51 32	62.5	40 32	50 22	61.7	228	312
49	131	43 35	55 50	64.9	43 09	54 36	64.1	42 43	53 22	63.2	42 15	52 10	62.4	41 47	50 59	61.6	41 18	49 48	60.9	229	311
50	130	44 25	55 17	64.1	43 58	54 02	63.3	43 31	52 49	62.4	43 03	51 36	61.6	42 34	50 24	60.8	42 04	49 14	60.0	230	310
51	129	45 14	54 43	63.3	44 47	53 28	62.4	44 18	52 13	61.6	43 49	51 00	60.7	43 20	49 48	59.9	42 49	48 38	59.1	231	309
52	128	46 03	54 08	62.5	45 35	52 52	61.6	45 06	51 37	60.7	44 36	50 23	59.8	44 05	49 11	59.0	43 34	48 00	58.2	232	308
53	127	46 51	53 30	61.6	46 22	52 14	60.7	45 52	50 59	59.8	45 22	49 45	58.9	44 51	48 32	58.1	44 18	47 21	57.2	233	307
54	126	47 39	52 51	60.8	47 09	51 34	59.8	46 39	50 19	58.9	46 07	49 05	58.0	45 35	47 52	57.1	45 02	46 41	56.3	234	306
55	125	48 27	52 11	59.8	47 56	50 53	58.9	47 25	49 37	58.0	46 53	48 23	57.0	46 19	47 10	56.2	45 46	45 59	55.3	235	305
56	124	49 14	51 28	58.9	48 43	50 11	57.9	48 10	48 54	57.0	47 37	47 40	56.1	47 03	46 27	55.2	46 29	45 15	54.3	236	304
57	123	50 01	50 44	57.9	49 28	49 26	56.9	48 55	48 09	56.0	48 21	46 54	55.0	47 46	45 41	54.1	47 11	44 30	53.3	237	303
58	122	50 47	49 58	56.9	50 14	48 39	55.9	49 40	47 22	54.9	49 05	46 07	54.0	48 29	44 54	53.1	47 53	43 43	52.2	238	302
59	121	51 33	49 09	55.9	50 58	47 51	54.9	50 23	46 33	53.9	49 48	45 18	52.9	49 11	44 05	52.0	48 34	42 54	51.1	239	301
60	120	52 18	48 19	54.8	51 43	47 00	53.8	51 07	45 43	52.8	50 30	44 28	51.8	49 53	43 14	50.9	49 14	42 03	50.0	240	300
61	119	53 02	47 26	53.7	52 26	46 07	52.7	51 49	44 50	51.7	51 12	43 35	50.7	50 33	42 22	49.7	49 54	41 10	48.8	241	299
62	118	53 46	46 31	52.6	53 09	45 12	51.5	52 31	43 54	50.5	51 53	42 39	49.5	51 13	41 27	48.6	50 33	40 16	47.6	242	298
63	117	54 29	45 33	51.4	53 51	44 14	50.3	53 13	42 57	49.3	52 33	41 42	48.3	51 53	40 30	47.3	51 12	39 19	46.4	243	297
64	116	55 12	44 33	50.2	54 33	43 14	49.1	53 53	41 57	48.1	53 13	40 42	47.1	52 31	39 30	46.1	51 49	38 20	45.2	244	296
65	115	55 53	43 30	48.9	55 13	42 11	47.8	54 33	40 55	46.8	53 51	39 40	45.8	53 09	38 29	44.8	52 26	37 19	43.9	245	295
66	114	56 34	42 25	47.6	55 53	41 06	46.5	55 12	39 50	45.4	54 29	38 36	44.4	53 46	37 25	43.5	53 02	36 16	42.6	246	294
67	113	57 14	41 16	46.2	56 32	39 58	45.1	55 50	38 42	44.1	55 06	37 29	43.1	54 22	36 19	42.1	53 37	35 11	41.2	247	293
68	112	57 53	40 05	44.8	57 10	38 47	43.7	56 27	37 29	42.7	55 42	36 19	41.7	54 57	35 10	40.7	54 11	34 03	39.8	248	292
69	111	58 32	38 50	43.3	57 47	37 33	42.2	57 03	36 18	41.2	56 17	35 07	40.2	55 31	33 59	39.3	54 44	32 53	38.4	249	291
70	110	59 09	37 32	41.8	58 23	36 16	40.7	57 38	35 02	39.7	56 51	33 52	38.7	56 04	32 45	37.8	55 16	31 41	36.9	250	290
71	109	59 45	36 11	40.2	58 58	34 55	39.2	58 12	33 43	38.1	57 24	32 35	37.2	56 36	31 29	36.3	55 47	30 26	35.4	251	289
72	108	60 19	34 46	38.6	59 32	33 32	37.6	58 44	32 21	36.5	57 56	31 14	35.6	57 07	30 10	34.7	56 17	29 08	33.8	252	288
73	107	60 53	33 18	36.9	60 05	32 05	35.9	59 16	30 56	34.9	58 26	29 51	34.0	57 36	28 48	33.1	56 46	27 49	32.2	253	287
74	106	61 25	31 46	35.2	60 36	30 35	34.2	59 46	29 28	33.2	58 55	28 25	32.3	58 05	27 24	31.4	57 13	26 26	30.6	254	286
75	105	61 56	30 10	33.4	61 06	29 02	32.4	60 15	27 57	31.4	59 23	26 56	30.5	58 31	25 57	29.7	57 39	25 02	28.9	255	285
76	104	62 26	28 31	31.5	61 34	27 25	30.5	60 42	26 23	29.6	59 50	25 24	28.8	58 57	24 28	28.0	58 04	23 35	27.2	256	284
77	103	62 53	26 48	29.6	62 01	25 45	28.6	61 08	24 47	27.8	60 15	23 49	27.0	59 21	22 56	26.2	58 27	22 05	25.5	257	283
78	102	63 20	25 02	27.6	62 26	24 02	26.7	61 32	23 05	25.9	60 38	22 12	25.1	59 44	21 21	24.4	58 49	20 34	23.7	258	282
79	101	63 44	23 12	25.5	62 50	22 15	24.7	61 55	21 22	23.9	61 00	20 32	23.2	60 05	19 44	22.5	59 09	19 00	21.8	259	281
80	100	64 07	21 18	23.4	63 12	20 25	22.6	62 16	19 36	21.9	61 20	18 49	21.2	60 24	18 05	20.6	59 28	17 24	20.0	260	280
81	99	64 28	19 22	21.3	63 32	18 33	20.5	62 35	17 47	19.9	61 39	17 04	19.2	60 42	16 24	18.6	59 45	15 46	18.1	261	279
82	98	64 47	17 22	19.1	63 50	16 37	18.4	62 53	15 56	17.8	61 56	15 17	17.2	60 58	14 40	16.7	60 01	14 06	16.2	262	278
83	97	65 03	15 18	16.8	64 06	14 39	16.2	63 08	14 02	15.6	62 10	13 27	15.1	61 12	12 55	14.7	60 14	12 24	14.2	263	277
84	96	65 18	13 13	14.5	64 20	12 38	14.0	63 23	12 06	13.5	62 23	11 36	13.0	61 25	11 07	12.6	60 26	10 41	12.2	264	276
85	95	65 31	11 05	12.1	64 32	10 35	11.7	63 33	10 08	11.3	62 35	9 42	10.9	61 36	9 19	10.6	60 37	8 56	10.2	265	275
86	94	65 41	8 54	9.8	64 42	8 30	9.4	63 43	8 08	9.1	62 44	7 48	8.8	61 44	7 28	8.5	60 45	7 10	8.2	266	274
87	93	65 49	6 42	7.3	64 50	6 24	7.1	63 50	6 07	6.8	62 51	5 52	6.6	61 51	5 37	6.4	60 52	5 24	6.2	267	273
88	92	65 55	4 29	4.9	64 56	4 17	4.7	63 56	4 06	4.6	62 56	3 55	4.4	61 56	3 45	4.3	60 56	3 36	4.1	268	272
89	91	65 59	2 15	2.5	64 59	2 09	2.4	63 59	2 03	2.3	62 59	1 58	2.2	61 59	1 53	2.1	60 59	1 48	2.1	269	271
90	90	66 00	0 00	0.0	65 00	0 00	0.0	64 00	0 00	0.0	63 00	0 00	0.0	62 00	0 00	0.0	61 00	0 00	0.0	270	270

N. Lat.: for LHA>180°.... Zn = Z
for LHA<180°.... Zn =360° − Z

S. Lat.: for LHA > 180°.... Zn =180° − Z
for LHA < 180°.... Zn =180° + Z

LATITUDE / Ā : 30° – 35°

B: (−) for 90° < LHA < 270°
Dec: (−) for Lat. contrary name

Z_1: same sign as B
Z_2: (−) for F > 90°

LHA/F	F̄	30° A/H	30° B/P	30° Z_1/Z_2	31° A/H	31° B/P	31° Z_1/Z_2	32° A/H	32° B/P	32° Z_1/Z_2	33° A/H	33° B/P	33° Z_1/Z_2	34° A/H	34° B/P	34° Z_1/Z_2	35° A/H	35° B/P	35° Z_1/Z_2	LHA
0	180	0 00	60 00	90.0	0 00	59 00	90.0	0 00	58 00	90.0	0 00	57 00	90.0	0 00	56 00	90.0	0 00	55 00	90.0	180
1	179	0 52	60 00	89.5	0 51	59 00	89.5	0 51	58 00	89.5	0 50	57 00	89.5	0 50	56 00	89.4	0 49	55 00	89.4	181
2	178	1 44	59 59	89.0	1 43	58 59	89.0	1 42	57 59	88.9	1 41	56 59	88.9	1 39	55 59	88.9	1 38	54 59	88.9	182
3	177	2 36	59 58	88.5	2 34	58 58	88.5	2 33	57 58	88.4	2 31	56 58	88.4	2 29	55 58	88.3	2 27	54 58	88.3	183
4	176	3 28	59 56	88.0	3 26	58 56	87.9	3 23	57 56	87.9	3 21	56 56	87.8	3 19	55 56	87.8	3 17	54 56	87.7	184
5	175	4 20	59 54	87.5	4 17	58 54	87.4	4 14	57 54	87.3	4 12	56 54	87.3	4 09	55 54	87.2	4 06	54 54	87.1	185
6	174	5 12	59 52	87.0	5 08	58 52	86.9	5 05	57 52	86.8	5 02	56 51	86.7	4 58	55 51	86.6	4 55	54 51	86.6	186
7	173	6 04	59 49	86.5	6 00	58 49	86.4	5 56	57 48	86.3	5 52	56 48	86.2	5 48	55 48	86.1	5 44	54 48	86.0	187
8	172	6 55	59 45	86.0	6 51	58 45	85.9	6 47	57 45	85.7	6 42	56 44	85.6	6 38	55 44	85.5	6 33	54 44	85.4	188
9	171	7 47	59 42	85.5	7 42	58 41	85.3	7 37	57 41	85.2	7 32	56 40	85.1	7 27	55 40	84.9	7 22	54 40	84.8	189
10	170	8 39	59 37	85.0	8 34	58 37	84.8	8 28	57 36	84.7	8 22	56 36	84.5	8 17	55 36	84.4	8 11	54 35	84.2	190
11	169	9 31	59 32	84.4	9 25	58 32	84.3	9 19	57 31	84.1	9 13	56 31	84.0	9 06	55 30	83.8	9 00	54 30	83.6	191
12	168	10 22	59 27	83.9	10 16	58 26	83.8	10 09	57 26	83.6	10 03	56 25	83.4	9 56	55 25	83.2	9 48	54 24	83.0	192
13	167	11 14	59 21	83.4	11 07	58 21	83.3	11 00	57 20	83.0	10 52	56 19	82.8	10 45	55 18	82.6	10 37	54 18	82.5	193
14	166	12 06	59 15	82.9	11 58	58 14	82.7	11 50	57 13	82.5	11 42	56 12	82.3	11 34	55 12	82.1	11 26	54 11	81.9	194
15	165	12 57	59 08	82.4	12 49	58 07	82.1	12 41	57 06	81.9	12 32	56 05	81.7	12 23	55 04	81.5	12 14	54 04	81.3	195
16	164	13 49	59 01	81.8	13 40	57 59	81.6	13 31	56 58	81.4	13 22	55 57	81.1	13 13	54 57	80.9	13 03	53 56	80.7	196
17	163	14 40	58 53	81.3	14 31	57 51	81.1	14 21	56 50	80.8	14 12	55 49	80.5	14 02	54 48	80.3	13 51	53 47	80.1	197
18	162	15 31	58 44	80.8	15 22	57 43	80.5	15 12	56 42	80.2	15 01	55 40	80.0	14 51	54 39	79.7	14 40	53 38	79.4	198
19	161	16 23	58 35	80.2	16 12	57 34	79.9	16 02	56 32	79.7	15 51	55 31	79.4	15 40	54 30	79.1	15 28	53 29	78.8	199
20	160	17 14	58 26	79.7	17 03	57 24	79.4	16 52	56 23	79.1	16 40	55 21	78.8	16 28	54 20	78.5	16 16	53 19	78.2	200
21	159	18 05	58 16	79.1	17 53	57 14	78.8	17 42	56 12	78.5	17 29	55 11	78.2	17 17	54 09	77.9	17 04	53 08	77.6	201
22	158	18 56	58 05	78.6	18 44	57 03	78.2	18 31	56 01	77.9	18 19	55 00	77.6	18 06	53 58	77.3	17 52	52 56	77.0	202
23	157	19 47	57 54	78.0	19 34	56 52	77.7	19 21	55 50	77.3	19 08	54 48	77.0	18 54	53 46	76.6	18 40	52 44	76.3	203
24	156	20 37	57 42	77.4	20 24	56 40	77.1	20 11	55 38	76.7	19 57	54 36	76.4	19 42	53 34	76.0	19 28	52 32	75.7	204
25	155	21 28	57 30	76.9	21 14	56 27	76.5	21 00	55 25	76.1	20 46	54 23	75.8	20 31	53 21	75.4	20 15	52 19	75.0	205
26	154	22 19	57 17	76.3	22 04	56 14	75.9	21 49	55 12	75.5	21 34	54 09	75.1	21 19	53 07	74.7	21 03	52 05	74.4	206
27	153	23 09	57 03	75.7	22 54	56 00	75.3	22 39	54 57	74.9	22 23	53 55	74.5	22 07	52 52	74.1	21 50	51 50	73.7	207
28	152	23 59	56 49	75.1	23 44	55 46	74.7	23 28	54 43	74.3	23 11	53 40	73.8	22 54	52 37	73.4	22 37	51 35	73.0	208
29	151	24 50	56 34	74.5	24 33	55 31	74.1	24 17	54 27	73.6	23 59	53 24	73.2	23 42	52 22	72.8	23 24	51 19	72.4	209
30	150	25 40	56 19	73.9	25 23	55 15	73.4	25 05	54 11	73.0	24 48	53 08	72.5	24 29	52 05	72.1	24 11	51 03	71.7	210
31	149	26 29	56 02	73.3	26 12	54 58	72.8	25 54	53 54	72.3	25 35	52 51	71.9	25 17	51 48	71.4	24 57	50 45	71.0	211
32	148	27 19	55 45	72.6	27 01	54 41	72.2	26 42	53 37	71.7	26 23	52 33	71.2	26 04	51 30	70.7	25 44	50 27	70.3	212
33	147	28 09	55 27	72.0	27 50	54 23	71.5	27 31	53 19	71.0	27 11	52 15	70.5	26 50	51 12	70.0	26 30	50 08	69.6	213
34	146	28 58	55 09	71.4	28 38	54 04	70.8	28 19	53 00	70.3	27 58	51 56	69.8	27 37	50 52	69.3	27 16	49 49	68.8	214
35	145	29 47	54 49	70.7	29 27	53 44	70.2	29 06	52 40	69.6	28 45	51 36	69.1	28 24	50 32	68.6	28 01	49 29	68.1	215
36	144	30 36	54 29	70.0	30 15	53 24	69.5	29 54	52 19	68.9	29 32	51 15	68.4	29 10	50 11	67.9	28 47	49 07	67.4	216
37	143	31 25	54 08	69.4	31 03	53 03	68.8	30 41	51 58	68.2	30 19	50 53	67.7	29 56	49 49	67.2	29 32	48 45	66.6	217
38	142	32 13	53 46	68.7	31 51	52 40	68.1	31 28	51 35	67.5	31 05	50 30	66.9	30 41	49 26	66.4	30 17	48 23	65.9	218
39	141	33 02	53 23	68.0	32 39	52 17	67.4	32 15	51 12	66.8	31 51	50 07	66.2	31 27	49 03	65.6	31 02	47 59	65.1	219
40	140	33 50	53 00	67.2	33 26	51 53	66.6	33 02	50 48	66.0	32 37	49 43	65.4	32 12	48 38	64.9	31 46	47 34	64.3	220
41	139	34 37	52 35	66.5	34 13	51 29	65.9	33 48	50 23	65.3	33 23	49 17	64.7	32 57	48 13	64.1	32 30	47 09	63.5	221
42	138	35 25	52 09	65.8	35 00	51 03	65.1	34 34	49 56	64.5	34 08	48 51	63.9	33 42	47 46	63.3	33 14	46 42	62.7	222
43	137	36 12	51 43	65.0	35 46	50 36	64.3	35 20	49 29	63.7	34 53	48 24	63.1	34 26	47 19	62.5	33 58	46 15	61.9	223
44	136	36 59	51 15	64.2	36 33	50 08	63.6	36 06	49 01	62.9	35 38	47 55	62.3	35 10	46 51	61.6	34 41	45 46	61.0	224
45	135	37 46	50 46	63.4	37 19	49 39	62.7	36 51	48 32	62.1	36 22	47 26	61.4	35 53	46 21	60.8	35 24	45 17	60.2	225

Lat. / Ā
For 90° < LHA < 270°
LHA/F̄

Lat./Ā	LHA/F	30°			31°			32°			33°			34°			35°			LHA	Lat./Ā
		A/H	B/P	Z_1/Z_2	A/H	B/P	Z_1/Z_2	A/H	B/P	Z_1/Z_2	A/H	B/P	Z_1/Z_2	A/H	B/P	Z_1/Z_2	A/H	B/P	Z_1/Z_2		
45	135	37 46	50 46	63.4	37 19	49 39	62.7	36 51	48 32	62.1	36 22	47 26	61.4	35 53	46 21	60.8	35 24	45 17	60.2	315	225
46	134	38 32	50 16	62.6	38 04	49 08	61.9	37 36	48 02	61.2	37 06	46 56	60.6	36 37	45 51	59.9	36 06	44 46	59.3	314	226
47	133	39 18	49 45	61.8	38 49	48 37	61.1	38 20	47 30	60.4	37 50	46 24	59.7	37 19	45 19	59.1	36 48	44 15	58.4	313	227
48	132	40 04	49 13	61.0	39 34	48 05	60.2	39 04	46 58	59.5	38 33	45 51	58.8	38 02	44 46	58.2	37 30	43 42	57.5	312	228
49	131	40 49	48 39	60.1	40 19	47 31	59.4	39 48	46 24	58.6	39 16	45 18	57.9	38 44	44 12	57.2	38 11	43 08	56.6	311	229
50	130	41 34	48 04	59.2	41 03	46 56	58.5	40 31	45 49	57.7	39 59	44 42	57.0	39 26	43 37	56.3	38 52	42 33	55.6	310	230
51	129	42 18	47 28	58.3	41 46	46 20	57.5	41 14	45 12	56.8	40 41	44 06	56.1	40 07	43 01	55.4	39 32	41 57	54.7	309	231
52	128	43 02	46 50	57.4	42 29	45 42	56.6	41 56	44 34	55.9	41 23	43 28	55.1	40 47	42 23	54.4	40 12	41 19	53.7	308	232
53	127	43 46	46 11	56.4	43 12	45 03	55.6	42 38	43 55	54.9	42 03	42 49	54.1	41 28	41 44	53.4	40 52	40 41	52.7	307	233
54	126	44 29	45 31	55.5	43 54	44 22	54.7	43 19	43 15	53.9	42 44	42 09	53.1	42 07	41 04	52.4	41 30	40 01	51.7	306	234
55	125	45 11	44 49	54.5	44 36	43 40	53.7	44 00	42 33	52.9	43 24	41 27	52.1	42 46	40 23	51.4	42 09	39 19	50.7	305	235
56	124	45 53	44 05	53.5	45 17	42 57	52.6	44 40	41 50	51.8	44 03	40 44	51.1	43 25	39 40	50.3	42 46	38 37	49.6	304	236
57	123	46 35	43 20	52.4	45 58	42 11	51.6	45 20	41 05	50.8	44 42	39 59	50.0	44 03	38 55	49.3	43 24	37 53	48.5	303	237
58	122	47 16	42 33	51.3	46 38	41 25	50.5	45 59	40 18	49.7	45 20	39 13	48.9	44 40	38 09	48.2	44 00	37 07	47.5	302	238
59	121	47 56	41 44	50.2	47 17	40 36	49.4	46 38	39 30	48.6	45 58	38 25	47.8	45 17	37 22	47.1	44 36	36 20	46.3	301	239
60	120	48 35	40 54	49.1	47 56	39 46	48.3	47 16	38 40	47.4	46 35	37 36	46.7	45 53	36 33	45.9	45 11	35 32	45.2	300	240
61	119	49 14	40 01	47.9	48 34	38 54	47.1	47 53	37 48	46.3	47 11	36 45	45.5	46 29	35 42	44.7	45 46	34 42	44.0	299	241
62	118	49 53	39 07	46.8	49 11	38 00	45.9	48 29	36 55	45.1	47 46	35 52	44.3	47 03	34 50	43.6	46 19	33 50	42.8	298	242
63	117	50 30	38 11	45.5	49 48	37 04	44.7	49 05	36 00	43.9	48 21	34 57	43.1	47 37	33 57	42.3	46 53	32 57	41.6	297	243
64	116	51 07	37 13	44.3	50 23	36 07	43.4	49 40	35 03	42.6	48 55	34 01	41.8	48 10	33 01	41.1	47 25	32 03	40.4	296	244
65	115	51 43	36 12	43.0	50 58	35 07	42.2	50 14	34 04	41.3	49 28	33 03	40.6	48 43	32 04	39.8	47 56	31 07	39.1	295	245
66	114	52 18	35 10	41.7	51 33	34 06	40.8	50 47	33 04	40.0	50 01	32 04	39.3	49 14	31 05	38.5	48 27	30 09	37.8	294	246
67	113	52 52	34 05	40.3	52 06	33 01	39.5	51 19	32 01	38.7	50 32	31 02	37.9	49 44	30 05	37.2	48 56	29 10	36.5	293	247
68	112	53 25	32 59	38.9	52 38	31 56	38.1	51 50	30 57	37.3	51 02	30 00	36.6	50 14	29 03	35.8	49 25	28 09	35.2	292	248
69	111	53 57	31 50	37.5	53 09	30 49	36.7	52 21	29 50	35.9	51 32	28 53	35.2	50 43	27 59	34.5	49 53	27 06	33.8	291	249
70	110	54 28	30 39	36.1	53 39	29 39	35.2	52 50	28 42	34.5	52 00	27 46	33.8	51 10	26 53	33.1	50 20	26 02	32.4	290	250
71	109	54 58	29 25	34.6	54 08	28 27	33.8	53 18	27 31	33.0	52 28	26 38	32.3	51 37	25 46	31.6	50 46	24 56	31.0	289	251
72	108	55 27	28 09	33.0	54 37	27 13	32.2	53 46	26 19	31.5	52 54	25 28	30.8	52 03	24 37	30.2	51 11	23 49	29.5	288	252
73	107	55 55	26 51	31.4	55 03	25 57	30.7	54 12	25 04	30.0	53 19	24 14	29.3	52 27	23 26	28.7	51 34	22 40	28.1	287	253
74	106	56 21	25 31	29.8	55 29	24 39	29.1	54 36	23 48	28.4	53 43	23 00	27.8	52 50	22 14	27.1	51 57	21 29	26.6	286	254
75	105	56 46	24 09	28.2	55 53	23 18	27.5	55 00	22 30	26.8	54 06	21 44	26.2	53 12	21 00	25.6	52 18	20 17	25.0	285	255
76	104	57 10	22 44	26.5	56 16	21 56	25.8	55 22	21 10	25.3	54 28	20 26	24.6	53 33	19 44	24.0	52 38	19 04	23.5	284	256
77	103	57 33	21 17	24.8	56 38	20 31	24.1	55 43	19 48	23.5	54 48	19 06	23.0	53 53	18 27	22.4	52 57	17 49	21.9	283	257
78	102	57 54	19 48	23.0	56 59	19 05	22.4	56 03	18 24	21.9	55 07	17 45	21.3	54 11	17 08	20.8	53 15	16 32	20.3	282	258
79	101	58 13	18 17	21.2	57 17	17 37	20.7	56 21	16 59	20.1	55 25	16 22	19.6	54 28	15 48	19.2	53 31	15 15	18.7	281	259
80	100	58 32	16 44	19.4	57 35	16 07	18.9	56 38	15 32	18.4	55 41	14 58	17.9	54 44	14 26	17.5	53 47	13 56	17.1	280	260
81	99	58 48	15 10	17.6	57 51	14 36	17.1	56 53	14 03	16.6	55 56	13 33	16.2	54 58	13 03	15.8	54 00	12 36	15.4	279	261
82	98	59 03	13 33	15.7	58 05	13 02	15.3	57 07	12 33	14.9	56 09	12 06	14.5	55 11	11 40	14.1	54 13	11 14	13.8	278	262
83	97	59 16	11 55	13.8	58 18	11 28	13.4	57 19	11 02	13.0	56 21	10 38	12.7	55 22	10 14	12.4	54 24	9 52	12.1	277	263
84	96	59 28	10 16	11.9	58 29	9 52	11.5	57 30	9 30	11.2	56 31	9 09	10.9	55 32	8 49	10.6	54 33	8 29	10.4	276	264
85	95	59 37	8 35	9.9	58 38	8 15	9.6	57 39	7 56	9.4	56 40	7 39	9.1	55 41	7 22	8.9	54 41	7 06	8.7	275	265
86	94	59 46	6 53	8.0	58 46	6 37	7.7	57 46	6 22	7.5	56 47	6 08	7.3	55 48	5 54	7.1	54 48	5 41	7.0	274	266
87	93	59 52	5 11	6.0	58 52	4 59	5.8	57 52	4 47	5.6	56 53	4 36	5.5	55 53	4 26	5.4	54 53	4 16	5.2	273	267
88	92	59 57	3 28	4.0	58 57	3 19	3.9	57 57	3 12	3.8	56 57	3 05	3.7	55 57	2 58	3.6	54 57	2 51	3.5	272	268
89	91	59 59	1 44	2.0	58 59	1 40	1.9	57 59	1 36	1.9	56 59	1 32	1.8	55 59	1 29	1.8	54 59	1 26	1.7	271	269
90	90	60 00	0 00	0.0	59 00	0 00	0.0	58 00	0 00	0.0	57 00	0 00	0.0	56 00	0 00	0.0	55 00	0 00	0.0	270	270

N. Lat.: for LHA>180° ... Zn = Z
for LHA<180° ... Zn =360° − Z

S. Lat.: for LHA > 180° ... Zn =180° − Z
for LHA < 180° ... Zn =180° + Z

LATITUDE/Ā : 36° – 41°

Lat./Ā	36°			37°			38°			39°			40°			41°			Lat./Ā
LHA/F	A/H	B/P	Z₁/Z₂	A/H	B/P	Z₁/Z₂	A/H	B/P	Z₁/Z₂	A/H	B/P	Z₁/Z₂	A/H	B/P	Z₁/Z₂	A/H	B/P	Z₁/Z₂	LHA
0 180	0 00	54 00	90.0	0 00	53 00	90.0	0 00	52 00	90.0	0 00	51 00	90.0	0 00	50 00	90.0	0 00	49 00	90.0	180 360
1 179	0 49	54 00	89.4	0 48	53 00	89.4	0 47	52 00	89.4	0 47	51 00	89.4	0 46	50 00	89.4	0 45	49 00	89.3	181 359
2 178	1 37	53 59	88.8	1 36	52 59	88.8	1 35	51 59	88.8	1 33	50 59	88.7	1 32	49 59	88.7	1 31	48 59	88.7	182 358
3 177	2 26	53 58	88.2	2 24	52 58	88.2	2 22	51 58	88.2	2 20	50 58	88.1	2 18	49 58	88.1	2 16	48 58	88.0	183 357
4 176	3 14	53 56	87.6	3 12	52 56	87.6	3 09	51 56	87.5	3 06	50 56	87.5	3 04	49 56	87.4	3 01	48 56	87.4	184 356
5 175	4 03	53 54	87.1	3 59	52 54	87.0	3 56	51 54	86.9	3 53	50 54	86.8	3 50	49 54	86.8	3 46	48 54	86.7	185 355
6 174	4 51	53 51	86.5	4 47	52 51	86.4	4 43	51 51	86.3	4 40	50 51	86.2	4 36	49 51	86.1	4 31	48 51	86.1	186 354
7 173	5 39	53 48	85.9	5 35	52 48	85.8	5 31	51 48	85.7	5 26	50 47	85.6	5 21	49 47	85.5	5 17	48 47	85.4	187 353
8 172	6 28	53 44	85.3	6 23	52 44	85.2	6 18	51 44	85.1	6 13	50 44	84.9	6 07	49 43	84.8	6 02	48 43	84.7	188 352
9 171	7 16	53 40	84.7	7 11	52 39	84.6	7 05	51 39	84.5	6 59	50 39	84.3	6 53	49 39	84.2	6 47	48 39	84.1	189 351
10 170	8 05	53 35	84.1	7 58	52 35	83.9	7 52	51 34	83.8	7 45	50 34	83.7	7 39	49 34	83.5	7 32	48 34	83.4	190 350
11 169	8 53	53 30	83.5	8 46	52 29	83.3	8 39	51 29	83.2	8 32	50 29	83.0	8 24	49 29	82.9	8 17	48 28	82.7	191 349
12 168	9 41	53 24	82.9	9 33	52 23	82.7	9 26	51 23	82.5	9 18	50 23	82.4	9 10	49 23	82.2	9 02	48 22	82.1	192 348
13 167	10 29	53 17	82.3	10 21	52 17	82.1	10 13	51 17	81.9	10 04	50 16	81.7	9 55	49 16	81.6	9 46	48 16	81.4	193 347
14 166	11 17	53 10	81.7	11 08	52 10	81.5	10 59	51 10	81.3	10 50	50 09	81.1	10 41	49 09	80.9	10 31	48 09	80.7	194 346
15 165	12 05	53 03	81.0	11 56	52 02	80.8	11 46	51 02	80.6	11 36	50 02	80.4	11 26	49 01	80.2	11 16	48 01	80.0	195 345
16 164	12 53	52 55	80.4	12 43	51 54	80.2	12 33	50 54	80.0	12 22	49 53	79.8	12 11	48 53	79.6	12 00	47 53	79.3	196 344
17 163	13 41	52 46	79.8	13 30	51 46	79.6	13 19	50 45	79.3	13 08	49 45	79.1	12 57	48 44	78.9	12 45	47 44	78.7	197 343
18 162	14 29	52 37	79.2	14 17	51 37	78.9	14 06	50 36	78.7	13 54	49 35	78.4	13 42	48 35	78.2	13 29	47 34	78.0	198 342
19 161	15 16	52 28	78.6	15 04	51 27	78.3	14 52	50 26	78.0	14 39	49 25	77.8	14 27	48 25	77.5	14 13	47 24	77.3	199 341
20 160	16 04	52 17	77.9	15 51	51 16	77.6	15 38	50 16	77.4	15 25	49 15	77.1	15 11	48 14	76.8	14 58	47 14	76.6	200 340
21 159	16 51	52 07	77.3	16 38	51 05	77.0	16 24	50 05	76.7	16 10	49 04	76.4	15 56	48 03	76.1	15 42	47 03	75.9	201 339
22 158	17 39	51 55	76.6	17 24	50 54	76.3	17 10	49 53	76.0	16 56	48 52	75.7	16 41	47 51	75.5	16 25	46 51	75.2	202 338
23 157	18 26	51 43	76.0	18 11	50 42	75.7	17 56	49 41	75.4	17 41	48 40	75.0	17 25	47 39	74.7	17 09	46 38	74.4	203 337
24 156	19 13	51 30	75.3	18 57	50 29	75.0	18 42	49 28	74.7	18 26	48 27	74.3	18 09	47 26	74.0	17 53	46 25	73.7	204 336
25 155	20 00	51 17	74.7	19 44	50 15	74.3	19 27	49 14	74.0	19 10	48 12	73.6	18 53	47 12	73.3	18 36	46 12	73.0	205 335
26 154	20 46	51 03	74.0	20 30	50 01	73.6	20 13	49 00	73.3	19 55	47 59	72.9	19 37	46 58	72.6	19 19	45 57	72.3	206 334
27 153	21 33	50 48	73.3	21 15	49 47	73.0	20 58	48 45	72.6	20 40	47 44	72.2	20 21	46 43	71.9	20 02	45 42	71.5	207 333
28 152	22 19	50 33	72.6	22 01	49 31	72.3	21 43	48 30	71.9	21 24	47 28	71.5	21 05	46 28	71.1	20 45	45 27	70.8	208 332
29 151	23 06	50 17	72.0	22 47	49 15	71.6	22 28	48 14	71.2	22 08	47 12	70.8	21 48	46 11	70.4	21 28	45 11	70.0	209 331
30 150	23 52	50 00	71.3	23 32	48 58	70.8	23 12	47 57	70.4	22 52	46 55	70.0	22 31	45 54	69.6	22 10	44 54	69.3	210 330
31 149	24 37	49 43	70.5	24 17	48 41	70.1	23 57	47 39	69.7	23 36	46 38	69.3	23 14	45 37	68.9	22 52	44 36	68.5	211 329
32 148	25 23	49 25	69.8	25 02	48 23	69.4	24 41	47 21	69.0	24 19	46 19	68.5	23 57	45 18	68.1	23 34	44 17	67.7	212 328
33 147	26 09	49 06	69.1	25 47	48 04	68.7	25 25	47 02	68.2	25 02	46 00	67.8	24 40	44 59	67.3	24 16	43 58	66.9	213 327
34 146	26 54	48 46	68.4	26 32	47 44	67.9	26 09	46 42	67.4	25 45	45 40	67.0	25 22	44 39	66.6	24 58	43 39	66.1	214 326
35 145	27 39	48 26	67.6	27 16	47 23	67.1	26 52	46 21	66.7	26 28	45 20	66.2	26 04	44 19	65.8	25 39	43 18	65.3	215 325
36 144	28 24	48 04	66.9	28 00	47 02	66.4	27 36	46 00	65.9	27 11	44 58	65.4	26 46	43 57	65.0	26 20	42 57	64.5	216 324
37 143	29 08	47 42	66.1	28 44	46 40	65.6	28 19	45 38	65.1	27 53	44 36	64.6	27 27	43 35	64.2	27 01	42 34	63.7	217 323
38 142	29 52	47 19	65.3	29 27	46 17	64.8	29 01	45 15	64.3	28 35	44 13	63.8	28 08	43 12	63.3	27 41	42 12	62.9	218 322
39 141	30 36	46 56	64.5	30 10	45 53	64.0	29 44	44 51	63.5	29 17	43 49	63.0	28 49	42 48	62.5	28 21	41 48	62.0	219 321
40 140	31 20	46 31	63.7	30 53	45 28	63.2	30 26	44 26	62.7	29 58	43 25	62.2	29 30	42 24	61.7	29 01	41 23	61.2	220 320
41 139	32 03	46 05	62.9	31 36	45 03	62.4	31 08	44 01	61.8	30 39	42 59	61.3	30 10	41 58	60.8	29 41	40 58	60.3	221 319
42 138	32 46	45 39	62.1	32 18	44 36	61.5	31 49	43 34	61.0	31 20	42 33	60.5	30 50	41 32	59.9	30 20	40 32	59.4	222 318
43 137	33 29	45 11	61.3	33 00	44 09	60.7	32 30	43 07	60.1	32 00	42 05	59.6	31 30	41 05	59.1	30 59	40 04	58.5	223 317
44 136	34 12	44 43	60.4	33 42	43 40	59.8	33 11	42 38	59.3	32 40	41 37	58.7	32 09	40 36	58.2	31 37	39 36	57.6	224 316
45 135	34 54	44 13	59.6	34 23	43 11	59.0	33 52	42 09	58.4	33 20	41 08	57.8	32 48	40 07	57.3	32 15	39 08	56.7	225 315

LHA / F	36° A/H	B/P	Z_1/Z_2	37° A/H	B/P	Z_1/Z_2	38° A/H	B/P	Z_1/Z_2	39° A/H	B/P	Z_1/Z_2	40° A/H	B/P	Z_1/Z_2	41° A/H	B/P	Z_1/Z_2	LHA / Ā
45 135	34 54	44 13	59.6	34 23	43 11	59.0	33 52	42 09	58.4	33 20	41 08	57.8	32 48	40 07	57.3	32 15	39 08	56.7	225 315
46 134	35 35	43 43	58.7	35 04	42 40	58.1	34 32	41 38	57.5	33 59	40 37	56.9	33 26	39 37	56.4	32 53	38 38	55.8	226 314
47 133	36 17	43 11	57.8	35 44	42 09	57.2	35 12	41 07	56.6	34 38	40 06	56.0	34 04	39 06	55.4	33 30	38 07	54.9	227 313
48 132	36 57	42 39	56.9	36 24	41 36	56.2	35 51	40 35	55.6	35 17	39 34	55.0	34 42	38 34	54.5	34 07	37 35	53.9	228 312
49 131	37 38	42 05	55.9	37 04	41 03	55.3	36 30	40 01	54.7	35 55	39 01	54.1	35 19	38 01	53.5	34 43	37 03	53.0	229 311
50 130	38 18	41 30	55.0	37 43	40 28	54.4	37 08	39 27	53.7	36 32	38 27	53.1	35 56	37 27	52.5	35 19	36 29	52.0	230 310
51 129	38 57	40 54	54.0	38 22	39 52	53.4	37 46	38 51	52.8	37 09	37 51	52.1	36 32	36 52	51.6	35 54	35 54	51.0	231 309
52 128	39 36	40 17	53.0	39 00	39 15	52.4	38 23	38 14	51.8	37 46	37 15	51.1	37 08	36 16	50.6	36 30	35 18	50.0	232 308
53 127	40 15	39 38	52.0	39 38	38 37	51.4	39 00	37 36	50.8	38 22	36 37	50.1	37 43	35 39	49.5	37 04	34 42	49.0	233 307
54 126	40 53	38 58	51.0	40 15	37 57	50.4	39 36	36 57	49.7	38 57	35 58	49.1	38 18	35 01	48.5	37 38	34 04	47.9	234 306
55 125	41 30	38 17	50.0	40 52	37 17	49.3	40 12	36 17	48.7	39 32	35 19	48.1	38 52	34 21	47.4	38 11	33 25	46.9	235 305
56 124	42 07	37 35	48.9	41 28	36 35	48.3	40 47	35 36	47.6	40 07	34 38	47.0	39 26	33 41	46.4	38 44	32 45	45.8	236 304
57 123	42 44	36 51	47.9	42 03	35 51	47.2	41 22	34 53	46.5	40 41	33 59	45.9	39 59	32 59	45.3	39 16	32 04	44.7	237 303
58 122	43 19	36 06	46.8	42 38	35 07	46.1	41 56	34 09	45.4	41 14	33 12	44.8	40 31	32 16	44.2	39 48	31 22	43.6	238 302
59 121	43 54	35 20	45.6	43 12	34 21	45.0	42 29	33 24	44.3	41 46	32 27	43.7	41 03	31 32	43.1	40 19	30 39	42.5	239 301
60 120	44 29	34 32	44.5	43 46	33 34	43.8	43 02	32 37	43.2	42 18	31 42	42.5	41 34	30 47	41.9	40 49	29 54	41.3	240 300
61 119	45 02	33 43	43.3	44 18	32 45	42.6	43 34	31 49	42.0	42 49	30 55	41.4	42 04	30 01	40.8	41 18	29 09	40.2	241 299
62 118	45 35	32 52	42.1	44 51	31 55	41.5	44 05	31 00	40.8	43 20	30 06	40.2	42 34	29 14	39.6	41 47	28 22	39.0	242 298
63 117	46 07	32 00	40.9	45 22	31 04	40.3	44 36	30 10	39.6	43 49	29 17	39.0	43 03	28 25	38.4	42 15	27 35	37.8	243 297
64 116	46 39	31 06	39.7	45 52	30 11	39.0	45 06	29 18	38.4	44 18	28 26	37.8	43 31	27 35	37.2	42 43	26 46	36.6	244 296
65 115	47 09	30 11	38.4	46 22	29 17	37.8	45 35	28 25	37.1	44 47	27 34	36.5	43 58	26 44	36.0	43 09	25 56	35.4	245 295
66 114	47 39	29 14	37.1	46 51	28 21	36.5	46 03	27 30	35.9	45 14	26 40	35.3	44 25	25 52	34.7	43 35	25 04	34.2	246 294
67 113	48 08	28 16	35.8	47 19	27 24	35.2	46 30	26 34	34.6	45 41	25 45	34.0	44 50	24 58	33.4	44 00	24 12	32.9	247 293
68 112	48 36	27 17	34.5	47 46	26 26	33.9	46 56	25 37	33.3	46 06	24 50	32.7	45 15	24 03	32.2	44 24	23 19	31.6	248 292
69 111	49 03	26 15	33.1	48 13	25 26	32.5	47 22	24 38	31.9	46 31	23 52	31.4	45 39	23 08	30.8	44 48	22 24	30.3	249 291
70 110	49 29	25 13	31.8	48 38	24 25	31.2	47 46	23 39	30.6	46 55	22 54	30.0	46 03	22 11	29.5	45 10	21 29	29.0	250 290
71 109	49 54	24 08	30.4	49 02	23 22	29.8	48 10	22 37	29.2	47 17	21 54	28.7	46 25	21 12	28.2	45 32	20 32	27.7	251 289
72 108	50 18	23 02	28.9	49 25	22 18	28.4	48 33	21 35	27.8	47 39	20 53	27.3	46 46	20 13	26.8	45 52	19 34	26.3	252 288
73 107	50 41	21 55	27.5	49 48	21 12	26.9	48 54	20 31	26.4	48 00	19 51	25.9	47 06	19 13	25.4	46 12	18 35	24.9	253 287
74 106	51 03	20 47	26.0	50 09	20 06	25.5	49 15	19 26	25.0	48 20	18 48	24.5	47 25	18 11	24.0	46 30	17 36	23.6	254 286
75 105	51 24	19 36	24.5	50 29	18 57	24.0	49 34	18 20	23.5	48 39	17 43	23.1	47 44	17 09	22.6	46 48	16 35	22.2	255 285
76 104	51 43	18 25	23.0	50 48	17 48	22.5	49 52	17 12	22.0	48 57	16 38	21.6	48 01	16 05	21.2	47 05	15 33	20.8	256 284
77 103	52 02	17 12	21.4	51 06	16 37	21.0	50 09	16 04	20.6	49 13	15 31	20.1	48 17	15 00	19.8	47 20	14 31	19.4	257 283
78 102	52 19	15 58	19.9	51 22	15 25	19.5	50 25	14 54	19.0	49 29	14 24	18.7	48 32	13 55	18.3	47 35	13 27	18.0	258 282
79 101	52 35	14 43	18.3	51 37	14 13	17.9	50 40	13 43	17.5	49 43	13 16	17.2	48 46	12 49	16.8	47 48	12 23	16.5	259 281
80 100	52 49	13 27	16.7	51 52	12 59	16.3	50 54	12 32	15.9	49 56	12 06	15.7	48 58	11 42	15.3	48 01	11 18	15.0	260 280
81 99	53 02	12 09	15.1	52 04	11 44	14.7	51 06	11 19	14.4	50 08	10 56	14.1	49 10	10 34	13.8	48 12	10 12	13.6	261 279
82 98	53 14	10 51	13.4	52 16	10 28	13.1	51 18	10 06	12.9	50 19	9 45	12.6	49 20	9 25	12.3	48 22	9 06	12.1	262 278
83 97	53 25	9 31	11.8	52 26	9 11	11.5	51 27	8 52	11.3	50 29	8 34	11.0	49 30	8 16	10.8	48 31	7 59	10.6	263 277
84 96	53 34	8 11	10.1	52 35	7 54	9.9	51 36	7 37	9.7	50 37	7 21	9.5	49 38	7 06	9.3	48 38	6 51	9.1	264 276
85 95	53 42	6 50	8.5	52 43	6 36	8.3	51 43	6 22	8.1	50 44	6 09	7.9	49 44	5 56	7.8	48 45	5 44	7.6	265 275
86 94	53 49	5 29	6.8	52 49	5 17	6.6	51 49	5 06	6.5	50 50	4 55	6.3	49 50	4 45	6.2	48 50	4 35	6.1	266 274
87 93	53 54	4 07	5.1	52 54	3 58	5.0	51 54	3 50	4.9	50 54	3 42	4.8	49 54	3 34	4.7	48 55	3 27	4.6	267 273
88 92	53 57	2 45	3.4	52 57	2 39	3.3	51 57	2 33	3.2	50 57	2 28	3.2	49 58	2 23	3.1	48 58	2 18	3.0	268 272
89 91	53 59	1 23	1.7	52 59	1 20	1.7	51 59	1 17	1.6	50 59	1 14	1.6	49 59	1 11	1.6	48 59	1 09	1.5	269 271
90 90	54 00	0 00	0.0	53 00	0 00	0.0	52 00	0 00	0.0	51 00	0 00	0.0	50 00	0 00	0.0	49 00	0 00	0.0	270 270

N. Lat.: for LHA>180°.... Zn = Z
for LHA<180°.... Zn =360° − Z

S. Lat.: for LHA > 180°.... Zn =180° − Z
for LHA < 180°.... Zn = 180° + Z

LATITUDE/Ā: 42° – 47°

B: (−) for 90° < LHA < 270°
Dec: (−) for Lat. contrary name

Z₁: same sign as B
Z₂: (−)for F > 90°

LHA/F	Lat./Ā	42° A/H	42° B/P	42° Z₁/Z₂	43° A/H	43° B/P	43° Z₁/Z₂	44° A/H	44° B/P	44° Z₁/Z₂	45° A/H	45° B/P	45° Z₁/Z₂	46° A/H	46° B/P	46° Z₁/Z₂	47° A/H	47° B/P	47° Z₁/Z₂	Lat./Ā	LHA
0	180	0 00	48 00	90.0	0 00	47 00	90.0	0 00	46 00	90.0	0 00	45 00	90.0	0 00	44 00	90.0	0 00	43 00	90.0	180	360
1	179	0 45	48 00	89.3	0 44	47 00	89.3	0 43	46 00	89.3	0 42	45 00	89.3	0 42	44 00	89.3	0 41	43 00	89.3	181	359
2	178	1 29	47 59	88.7	1 28	46 59	88.6	1 26	45 59	88.6	1 25	44 59	88.6	1 23	43 59	88.6	1 22	42 59	88.5	182	358
3	177	2 14	47 58	88.0	2 12	46 58	88.0	2 09	45 58	87.9	2 07	44 58	87.9	2 05	43 58	87.9	2 03	42 58	87.8	183	357
4	176	2 58	47 56	87.3	2 55	46 56	87.3	2 53	45 56	87.2	2 50	44 56	87.2	2 47	43 56	87.2	2 44	42 56	87.1	184	356
5	175	3 43	47 53	86.6	3 39	46 53	86.6	3 36	45 53	86.5	3 32	44 53	86.5	3 28	43 53	86.4	3 24	42 53	86.3	185	355
6	174	4 27	47 51	86.0	4 23	46 51	85.9	4 19	45 51	85.8	4 14	44 51	85.7	4 10	43 51	85.7	4 05	42 51	85.6	186	354
7	173	5 12	47 47	85.3	5 07	46 47	85.2	5 02	45 47	85.1	4 57	44 47	85.0	4 51	43 47	85.0	4 46	42 47	84.9	187	353
8	172	5 56	47 43	84.6	5 51	46 43	84.5	5 45	45 43	84.4	5 39	44 43	84.3	5 33	43 43	84.2	5 27	42 43	84.1	188	352
9	171	6 41	47 39	84.0	6 34	46 39	83.8	6 28	45 39	83.7	6 21	44 39	83.6	6 14	43 39	83.5	6 07	42 39	83.4	189	351
10	170	7 25	47 34	83.3	7 18	46 34	83.1	7 11	45 34	83.0	7 03	44 34	82.9	6 56	43 34	82.8	6 48	42 34	82.7	190	350
11	169	8 09	47 28	82.6	8 01	46 28	82.4	7 53	45 28	82.3	7 45	44 28	82.2	7 37	43 28	82.0	7 29	42 28	81.9	191	349
12	168	8 53	47 22	81.9	8 45	46 22	81.8	8 36	45 22	81.6	8 27	44 22	81.5	8 18	43 22	81.3	8 09	42 22	81.2	192	348
13	167	9 37	47 16	81.2	9 28	46 15	81.1	9 19	45 15	80.9	9 09	44 15	80.7	8 59	43 15	80.6	8 49	42 16	80.4	193	347
14	166	10 21	47 08	80.5	10 11	46 08	80.3	10 01	45 08	80.2	9 51	44 08	80.0	9 40	43 08	79.8	9 30	42 08	79.7	194	346
15	165	11 05	47 01	79.8	10 55	46 00	79.6	10 44	45 00	79.5	10 33	44 00	79.3	10 21	43 00	79.1	10 10	42 01	78.9	195	345
16	164	11 49	46 52	79.1	11 38	45 52	78.9	11 26	44 52	78.7	11 14	43 52	78.5	11 02	42 52	78.3	10 50	41 52	78.2	196	344
17	163	12 33	46 43	78.4	12 21	45 43	78.2	12 08	44 43	78.0	11 56	43 43	77.8	11 43	42 43	77.6	11 30	41 44	77.4	197	343
18	162	13 17	46 34	77.7	13 04	45 34	77.5	12 51	44 34	77.3	12 37	43 34	77.1	12 24	42 34	76.8	12 10	41 34	76.6	198	342
19	161	14 00	46 24	77.0	13 46	45 24	76.8	13 33	44 24	76.5	13 19	43 24	76.3	13 04	42 24	76.1	12 50	41 24	75.9	199	341
20	160	14 44	46 13	76.3	14 29	45 13	76.1	14 15	44 13	75.8	14 00	43 13	75.6	13 45	42 13	75.3	13 29	41 14	75.1	200	340
21	159	15 27	46 02	75.6	15 12	45 02	75.3	14 56	44 02	75.1	14 41	43 02	74.8	14 25	42 02	74.6	14 09	41 03	74.3	201	339
22	158	16 10	45 50	74.9	15 54	44 50	74.6	15 38	43 50	74.3	15 22	42 50	74.1	15 05	41 50	73.8	14 48	40 51	73.5	202	338
23	157	16 53	45 38	74.1	16 36	44 38	73.9	16 19	43 38	73.6	16 02	42 38	73.3	15 45	41 38	73.0	15 27	40 39	72.8	203	337
24	156	17 36	45 25	73.4	17 18	44 25	73.1	17 01	43 25	72.8	16 43	42 25	72.5	16 25	41 25	72.2	16 06	40 26	72.0	204	336
25	155	18 18	45 11	72.7	18 00	44 11	72.4	17 42	44 11	72.1	17 23	42 11	71.8	17 04	41 12	71.5	16 45	40 12	71.2	205	335
26	154	19 01	44 57	71.9	18 42	43 57	71.6	18 23	42 57	71.3	18 03	41 57	71.0	17 44	40 57	70.7	17 24	39 58	70.4	206	334
27	153	19 43	44 42	71.2	19 24	43 42	70.8	19 04	42 42	70.5	18 43	41 42	70.2	18 23	40 43	69.9	18 02	39 43	69.6	207	333
28	152	20 25	44 26	70.4	20 05	43 26	70.1	19 44	42 26	69.7	19 23	41 26	69.4	19 02	40 27	69.1	18 40	39 28	68.8	208	332
29	151	21 07	44 10	69.6	20 46	43 10	69.3	20 25	42 10	68.9	20 03	41 10	68.6	19 41	40 11	68.3	19 18	39 12	67.9	209	331
30	150	21 49	43 53	68.9	21 27	42 53	68.5	21 05	41 53	68.1	20 42	40 54	67.8	20 19	39 54	67.4	19 56	38 55	67.1	210	330
31	149	22 30	43 35	68.1	22 08	42 35	67.7	21 45	41 36	67.3	21 21	40 36	67.0	20 58	39 37	66.6	20 34	38 38	66.3	211	329
32	148	23 11	43 17	67.3	22 48	42 17	66.9	22 24	41 17	66.5	22 00	40 18	66.2	21 36	39 19	65.8	21 11	38 20	65.4	212	328
33	147	23 53	42 58	66.5	23 28	41 58	66.1	23 04	40 58	65.7	22 39	39 59	65.3	22 14	39 00	65.0	21 48	38 02	64.6	213	327
34	146	24 33	42 38	65.7	24 08	41 38	65.3	23 43	40 39	64.9	23 17	39 40	64.5	22 51	38 41	64.1	22 25	37 42	63.7	214	326
35	145	25 14	42 18	64.9	24 48	41 18	64.5	24 22	40 18	64.1	23 56	39 19	63.7	23 29	38 21	63.3	23 02	37 23	62.9	215	325
36	144	25 54	41 56	64.1	25 28	40 57	63.6	25 01	39 57	63.2	24 34	38 58	62.8	24 06	38 00	62.4	23 38	37 02	62.0	216	324
37	143	26 33	41 34	63.2	26 07	40 35	62.8	25 40	39 35	62.4	25 11	38 37	62.0	24 43	37 38	61.5	24 14	36 41	61.1	217	323
38	142	27 14	41 11	62.4	26 46	40 12	61.9	26 17	39 13	61.5	25 48	38 14	61.1	25 19	37 16	60.7	24 50	36 19	60.3	218	322
39	141	27 53	40 48	61.5	27 24	39 48	61.1	26 55	38 50	60.6	26 25	37 51	60.2	25 55	36 53	59.8	25 25	35 56	59.4	219	321
40	140	28 32	40 23	60.7	28 02	39 25	60.2	27 33	38 25	59.8	27 02	37 27	59.4	26 31	36 30	58.9	26 00	35 32	58.5	220	320
41	139	29 11	39 58	59.8	28 40	38 59	59.3	28 10	38 01	58.9	27 38	37 03	58.5	27 07	36 05	58.0	26 35	35 08	57.6	221	319
42	138	29 49	39 32	58.9	29 18	38 33	58.4	28 46	37 35	58.0	28 14	36 37	57.5	27 42	35 40	57.1	27 09	34 43	56.6	222	318
43	137	30 27	39 05	58.0	29 55	38 06	57.5	29 23	37 08	57.1	28 50	36 11	56.6	28 17	35 14	56.1	27 43	34 18	55.7	223	317
44	136	31 05	38 37	57.1	30 32	37 39	56.6	29 59	36 41	56.1	29 25	35 44	55.7	28 51	34 47	55.2	28 17	33 51	54.8	224	316
45	135	31 42	38 09	56.2	31 08	37 11	55.7	30 34	36 13	55.2	30 00	35 16	54.7	29 25	34 20	54.3	28 50	33 24	53.8	225	315

94

Lat. / Ā	LHA/F	42° A/H	42° B/P	42° Z₁/Z₂	43° A/H	43° B/P	43° Z₁/Z₂	44° A/H	44° B/P	44° Z₁/Z₂	45° A/H	45° B/P	45° Z₁/Z₂	46° A/H	46° B/P	46° Z₁/Z₂	47° A/H	47° B/P	47° Z₁/Z₂	LHA	Lat. / Ā
45	135	31 42	38 09	56.2	31 08	37 10	55.7	30 34	36 13	55.2	30 00	35 16	54.7	29 25	34 20	54.3	28 50	33 24	53.8	225	315
46	134	32 19	37 39	55.3	31 45	36 41	54.8	31 10	35 44	54.3	30 34	34 47	53.8	29 59	33 51	53.3	29 23	32 56	52.9	226	314
47	133	32 55	37 08	54.3	32 20	36 11	53.8	31 45	35 14	53.3	31 08	34 18	52.8	30 32	33 22	52.4	29 55	32 27	51.9	227	313
48	132	33 31	36 37	53.4	32 55	35 40	52.9	32 19	34 43	52.3	31 42	33 47	51.9	31 05	32 52	51.4	30 27	31 58	50.9	228	312
49	131	34 07	36 05	52.4	33 30	35 08	51.9	32 53	34 11	51.4	32 15	33 16	50.9	31 37	32 21	50.4	30 59	31 27	49.9	229	311
50	130	34 42	35 31	51.4	34 04	34 35	50.9	33 26	33 39	50.4	32 48	32 44	49.9	32 09	31 50	49.4	31 30	30 56	48.9	230	310
51	129	35 17	34 57	50.4	34 38	34 01	49.9	33 59	33 05	49.4	33 20	32 11	48.9	32 40	31 17	48.4	32 00	30 24	47.9	231	309
52	128	35 51	34 22	49.4	35 12	33 26	48.9	34 32	32 31	48.4	33 52	31 37	47.9	33 11	30 44	47.4	32 30	29 52	46.9	232	308
53	127	36 24	33 45	48.4	35 44	32 50	47.9	35 04	31 56	47.3	34 23	31 02	46.8	33 42	30 10	46.3	33 00	29 18	45.9	233	307
54	126	36 57	33 08	47.4	36 17	32 13	46.8	35 35	31 20	46.3	34 54	30 27	45.8	34 12	29 35	45.3	33 29	28 44	44.8	234	306
55	125	37 30	32 30	46.3	36 48	31 36	45.8	36 06	30 43	45.2	35 24	29 50	44.7	34 41	28 59	44.2	33 58	28 08	43.8	235	305
56	124	38 02	31 51	45.2	37 19	30 57	44.7	36 37	30 04	44.2	35 53	29 13	43.6	35 10	28 22	43.2	34 26	27 32	42.7	236	304
57	123	38 33	31 10	44.1	37 50	30 17	43.6	37 06	29 25	43.1	36 22	28 34	42.6	35 38	27 45	42.1	34 53	26 56	41.6	237	303
58	122	39 04	30 29	43.0	38 20	29 36	42.5	37 36	28 45	42.0	36 51	27 55	41.5	36 06	27 06	41.0	35 20	26 18	40.5	238	302
59	121	39 34	29 46	41.9	38 49	28 55	41.4	38 04	28 04	40.9	37 19	27 15	40.4	36 33	26 27	39.9	35 46	25 39	39.4	239	301
60	120	40 04	29 03	40.8	39 18	28 12	40.2	38 32	27 22	39.7	37 46	26 34	39.2	36 59	25 46	38.8	36 12	25 00	38.3	240	300
61	119	40 32	28 18	39.6	39 46	27 28	39.1	38 59	26 39	38.6	38 12	25 52	38.1	37 25	25 05	37.6	36 37	24 20	37.2	241	299
62	118	41 00	27 32	38.5	40 13	26 43	37.9	39 26	25 56	37.4	38 38	25 09	36.9	37 50	24 23	36.5	37 02	23 39	36.0	242	298
63	117	41 28	26 45	37.3	40 40	25 58	36.8	39 52	25 11	36.3	39 03	24 25	35.8	38 14	23 40	35.3	37 25	22 57	34.9	243	297
64	116	41 54	25 58	36.1	41 06	25 11	35.6	40 17	24 25	35.1	39 28	23 40	34.6	38 38	22 57	34.1	37 48	22 14	33.7	244	296
65	115	42 20	25 09	34.9	41 31	24 23	34.4	40 41	23 38	33.9	39 51	22 55	33.4	39 01	22 12	32.8	38 11	21 31	32.5	245	295
66	114	42 45	24 19	33.6	41 55	23 34	33.1	41 05	22 50	32.7	40 14	22 08	32.2	39 23	21 27	31.8	38 32	20 46	31.3	246	294
67	113	43 10	23 28	32.4	42 19	22 44	31.9	41 28	22 02	31.4	40 37	21 21	31.0	39 45	20 40	30.5	38 53	20 01	30.1	247	293
68	112	43 33	22 35	31.1	42 42	21 53	30.6	41 50	21 12	30.2	40 58	20 32	29.7	40 06	19 53	29.3	39 13	19 15	28.9	248	292
69	111	43 56	21 42	29.8	43 04	21 01	29.4	42 11	20 22	28.9	41 19	19 43	28.5	40 26	19 05	28.1	39 33	18 29	27.7	249	291
70	110	44 18	20 48	28.5	43 25	20 08	28.1	42 32	19 30	27.7	41 38	18 53	27.2	40 45	18 17	26.8	39 51	17 41	26.5	250	290
71	109	44 38	19 53	27.2	43 45	19 15	26.8	42 51	18 38	26.4	41 57	18 02	26.0	41 03	17 27	25.6	40 09	16 53	25.2	251	289
72	108	44 58	18 57	25.9	44 04	18 21	25.5	43 10	17 45	25.1	42 16	17 10	24.7	41 21	16 37	24.3	40 26	16 05	24.0	252	288
73	107	45 17	17 59	24.6	44 23	17 24	24.1	43 28	16 51	23.8	42 33	16 18	23.4	41 38	15 46	23.0	40 42	15 15	22.7	253	287
74	106	45 35	17 01	23.2	44 40	16 28	22.8	43 45	15 56	22.4	42 49	15 25	22.1	41 54	14 54	21.7	40 58	14 25	21.4	254	286
75	105	45 53	16 02	21.8	44 57	15 31	21.4	44 01	15 00	21.1	43 05	14 31	20.8	42 09	14 02	20.4	41 12	13 34	20.1	255	285
76	104	46 09	15 02	20.4	45 12	14 33	20.1	44 16	14 04	19.7	43 19	13 36	19.4	42 23	13 09	19.1	41 26	12 43	18.8	256	284
77	103	46 24	14 02	19.0	45 27	13 34	18.7	44 30	13 07	18.4	43 33	12 41	18.1	42 36	12 15	17.8	41 39	11 51	17.5	257	283
78	102	46 38	13 00	17.6	45 40	12 34	17.3	44 43	12 09	17.0	43 46	11 45	16.7	42 48	11 21	16.5	41 51	10 58	16.2	258	282
79	101	46 51	11 58	16.2	45 53	11 34	15.9	44 55	11 11	15.6	43 57	10 48	15.4	43 00	10 26	15.1	42 02	10 05	14.9	259	281
80	100	47 03	10 55	14.8	46 04	10 33	14.5	45 06	10 12	14.2	44 08	9 51	14.0	43 10	9 31	13.8	42 12	9 12	13.6	260	280
81	99	47 13	9 51	13.3	46 15	9 31	13.1	45 16	9 11	12.8	44 18	8 53	12.6	43 19	8 35	12.4	42 21	8 18	12.2	261	279
82	98	47 23	8 47	11.9	46 24	8 29	11.6	45 26	8 12	11.4	44 27	7 55	11.2	43 28	7 39	11.1	42 29	7 24	10.9	262	278
83	97	47 32	7 42	10.5	46 33	7 27	10.2	45 34	7 12	10.0	44 34	6 57	9.9	43 35	6 43	9.5	42 36	6 29	9.5	263	277
84	96	47 39	6 37	8.9	46 40	6 24	8.8	45 41	6 11	8.6	44 41	5 58	8.5	43 43	5 46	8.3	42 42	5 34	8.2	264	276
85	95	47 46	5 32	7.4	46 46	5 20	7.3	45 46	5 09	7.2	44 47	4 59	7.1	43 47	4 49	6.9	42 48	4 39	6.8	265	275
86	94	47 51	4 26	6.0	46 51	4 17	5.9	45 51	4 08	5.7	44 52	3 59	5.6	43 52	3 51	5.6	42 52	3 43	5.5	266	274
87	93	47 55	3 20	4.5	46 55	3 13	4.4	45 55	3 06	4.3	44 55	3 00	4.3	43 55	2 54	4.2	42 56	2 48	4.1	267	273
88	92	47 58	2 13	3.0	46 58	2 09	2.9	45 58	2 04	2.9	44 58	2 00	2.8	43 58	1 56	2.8	42 58	1 52	2.7	268	272
89	91	47 59	1 07	1.5	46 59	1 04	1.5	45 59	1 02	1.4	44 59	1 00	1.4	43 59	0 58	1.4	42 59	0 56	1.4	269	271
90	90	48 00	0 00	0.0	47 00	0 00	0.0	46 00	0 00	0.0	45 00	0 00	0.0	44 00	0 00	0.0	43 00	0 00	0.0	270	270

N. Lat.: for LHA>180°... Zn = Z
for LHA<180°... Zn = 360° − Z

S. Lat.: for LHA > 180°... Zn = 180° − Z
for LHA < 180°... Zn = 180° + Z

B: (−) for 90° < LHA < 270°
Dec: (−) for Lat. contrary name

Z_1 : same sign as B
Z_2 : (−) for F > 90°

LATITUDE / Ā : 48° – 53°

Lat./Ā LHA/F	48° A/H	48° B/P	48° Z_1/Z_2	49° A/H	49° B/P	49° Z_1/Z_2	50° A/H	50° B/P	50° Z_1/Z_2	51° A/H	51° B/P	51° Z_1/Z_2	52° A/H	52° B/P	52° Z_1/Z_2	53° A/H	53° B/P	53° Z_1/Z_2	Lat./Ā LHA
0 180	0 00	42 00	90.0	0 00	41 00	90.0	0 00	40 00	90.0	0 00	39 00	90.0	0 00	38 00	90.0	0 00	37 00	90.0	180 360
1 179	0 40	42 00	89.3	0 39	41 00	89.2	0 39	40 00	89.2	0 38	39 00	89.2	0 37	38 00	89.2	0 36	37 00	89.2	181 359
2 178	1 20	41 59	88.5	1 19	40 59	88.5	1 17	39 59	88.5	1 16	38 59	88.4	1 14	37 59	88.4	1 12	36 59	88.4	182 358
3 177	2 00	41 58	87.8	1 58	40 58	87.7	1 56	39 58	87.7	1 53	38 58	87.7	1 51	37 58	87.6	1 48	36 58	87.6	183 357
4 176	2 41	41 56	87.0	2 37	40 56	87.0	2 34	39 56	86.9	2 31	38 56	86.9	2 28	37 56	86.8	2 24	36 56	86.8	184 356
5 175	3 21	41 53	86.3	3 17	40 54	86.2	3 13	39 54	86.2	3 09	38 54	86.1	3 05	37 54	86.1	3 00	36 54	86.0	185 355
6 174	4 01	41 51	85.5	3 56	40 51	85.5	3 51	39 51	85.4	3 46	38 51	85.3	3 41	37 51	85.3	3 36	36 51	85.2	186 354
7 173	4 41	41 47	84.8	4 35	40 47	84.7	4 30	39 47	84.6	4 24	38 47	84.5	4 18	37 48	84.5	4 12	36 48	84.4	187 353
8 172	5 21	41 43	84.0	5 14	40 43	83.9	5 08	39 43	83.9	5 01	38 44	83.8	4 55	37 44	83.7	4 48	36 44	83.6	188 352
9 171	6 01	41 39	83.3	5 53	40 39	83.2	5 46	39 39	83.1	5 38	38 39	83.0	5 32	37 39	83.0	5 24	36 40	82.8	189 351
10 170	6 40	41 34	82.5	6 32	40 34	82.4	6 25	39 34	82.3	6 16	38 34	82.2	6 08	37 35	82.1	6 00	36 35	82.0	190 350
11 169	7 20	41 28	81.8	7 11	40 28	81.7	7 03	39 29	81.5	6 54	38 29	81.4	6 45	37 29	81.3	6 36	36 29	81.2	191 349
12 168	8 00	41 22	81.0	7 50	40 22	80.9	7 41	39 23	80.8	7 31	38 23	80.6	7 21	37 23	80.5	7 11	36 24	80.4	192 348
13 167	8 39	41 16	80.3	8 29	40 16	80.1	8 19	39 16	80.0	8 08	38 16	79.8	7 58	37 17	79.7	7 47	36 17	79.6	193 347
14 166	9 19	41 09	79.5	9 08	40 09	79.3	8 57	39 09	79.2	8 45	38 09	79.0	8 34	37 10	78.9	8 22	36 10	78.7	194 346
15 165	9 58	41 01	78.7	9 47	40 01	78.6	9 35	39 02	78.4	9 22	38 02	78.2	9 10	37 02	78.1	8 58	36 03	77.9	195 345
16 164	10 38	40 53	78.0	10 25	39 53	77.8	10 12	38 53	77.6	9 59	37 54	77.4	9 46	36 54	77.3	9 33	35 55	77.1	196 344
17 163	11 17	40 44	77.2	11 04	39 44	77.0	10 50	38 45	76.8	10 36	37 45	76.6	10 22	36 46	76.5	10 08	35 47	76.3	197 343
18 162	11 56	40 34	76.4	11 42	39 35	76.2	11 27	38 35	76.0	11 13	37 36	75.8	10 58	36 37	75.6	10 43	35 38	75.5	198 342
19 161	12 35	40 25	75.6	12 20	39 25	75.4	12 05	38 26	75.2	11 49	37 26	75.0	11 34	36 27	74.8	11 18	35 28	74.6	199 341
20 160	13 14	40 14	74.9	12 58	39 15	74.6	12 42	38 15	74.4	12 26	37 16	74.2	12 09	36 17	74.0	11 53	35 18	73.8	200 340
21 159	13 52	40 03	74.1	13 36	39 04	73.8	13 19	38 04	73.6	13 02	37 05	73.4	12 45	36 06	73.2	12 27	35 08	73.0	201 339
22 158	14 31	39 51	73.3	14 14	38 52	73.0	13 56	37 53	72.8	13 38	36 54	72.6	13 20	35 55	72.3	13 02	34 56	72.1	202 338
23 157	15 09	39 39	72.5	14 51	38 40	72.2	14 33	37 41	72.0	14 14	36 42	71.7	13 55	35 43	71.5	13 36	34 45	71.3	203 337
24 156	15 48	39 26	71.7	15 29	38 27	71.4	15 09	37 28	71.2	14 50	36 30	70.9	14 30	35 31	70.7	14 10	34 33	70.4	204 336
25 155	16 26	39 13	70.9	16 06	38 14	70.6	15 46	37 15	70.3	15 25	36 17	70.1	15 05	35 18	69.8	14 44	34 20	69.6	205 335
26 154	17 03	38 59	70.1	16 43	38 00	69.8	16 22	37 01	69.5	16 01	36 03	69.2	15 39	35 05	69.0	15 18	34 07	68.7	206 334
27 153	17 41	38 44	69.3	17 20	37 46	69.0	16 58	36 47	68.7	16 36	35 49	68.4	16 14	34 51	68.1	15 51	33 53	67.9	207 333
28 152	18 19	38 29	68.4	17 56	37 30	68.1	17 34	36 32	67.8	17 11	35 34	67.5	16 48	34 36	67.3	16 25	33 38	67.0	208 332
29 151	18 56	38 13	67.6	18 33	37 15	67.3	18 09	36 16	67.0	17 46	35 18	66.7	17 22	34 21	66.4	16 58	33 23	66.1	209 331
30 150	19 33	37 57	66.8	19 09	36 58	66.5	18 45	36 00	66.1	18 20	35 03	65.8	17 56	34 05	65.5	17 31	33 08	65.2	210 330
31 149	20 10	37 40	65.9	19 45	36 41	65.6	19 20	35 44	65.3	18 55	34 46	65.0	18 30	33 49	64.7	18 03	32 52	64.4	211 329
32 148	20 46	37 22	65.1	20 21	36 24	64.8	19 55	35 26	64.4	19 29	34 29	64.1	19 02	33 32	63.8	18 36	32 35	63.5	212 328
33 147	21 22	37 03	64.2	20 56	36 06	63.9	20 30	35 08	63.6	20 03	34 11	63.2	19 35	33 14	62.9	19 08	32 18	62.6	213 327
34 146	21 58	36 44	63.4	21 31	35 47	63.0	21 04	34 49	62.7	20 36	33 53	62.3	20 08	32 56	62.0	19 40	32 00	61.7	214 326
35 145	22 34	36 25	62.5	22 06	35 27	62.1	21 38	34 30	61.8	21 10	33 33	61.4	20 41	32 37	61.1	20 12	31 41	60.8	215 325
36 144	23 10	36 04	61.6	22 41	35 07	61.3	22 12	34 10	60.9	21 43	33 14	60.5	21 13	32 18	60.2	20 43	31 22	59.9	216 324
37 143	23 45	35 43	60.8	23 15	34 46	60.4	22 45	33 50	60.0	22 15	32 54	59.6	21 45	31 58	59.3	21 14	31 02	59.0	217 323
38 142	24 20	35 21	59.9	23 49	34 25	59.5	23 19	33 28	59.1	22 48	32 33	58.7	22 16	31 37	58.4	21 45	30 42	58.0	218 322
39 141	24 54	34 59	59.0	24 23	34 02	58.6	23 52	33 07	58.2	23 20	32 11	57.8	22 48	31 16	57.5	22 15	30 21	57.1	219 321
40 140	25 28	34 36	58.1	24 57	33 40	57.7	24 24	32 44	57.3	23 52	31 49	56.9	23 19	30 54	56.5	22 45	30 00	56.2	220 320
41 139	26 02	34 12	57.1	25 30	33 16	56.7	24 57	32 21	56.3	24 23	31 26	56.0	23 49	30 32	55.6	23 15	29 38	55.2	221 319
42 138	26 36	33 47	56.2	26 02	32 52	55.8	25 28	31 57	55.4	24 54	31 02	55.0	24 20	30 08	54.6	23 45	29 15	54.3	222 318
43 137	27 09	33 22	55.3	26 35	32 27	54.9	26 00	31 32	54.5	25 25	30 38	54.1	24 50	29 45	53.7	24 14	28 52	53.3	223 317
44 136	27 42	32 56	54.4	27 07	32 01	53.9	26 31	31 07	53.5	25 55	30 13	53.1	25 19	29 20	52.7	24 43	28 28	52.4	224 316
45 135	28 14	32 29	53.4	27 38	31 35	53.0	27 02	30 41	52.5	26 26	29 48	51.8	25 48	28 55	51.8	25 11	28 03	51.4	225 315

Lat./F		48°			49°			50°			51°			52°			53°			Lat./Ā
LHA/F		A/H	B/P	Z₁/Z₂	A/H	B/P	Z₁/Z₂	A/H	B/P	Z₁/Z₂	A/H	B/P	Z₁/Z₂	A/H	B/P	Z₁/Z₂	A/H	B/P	Z₁/Z₂	LHA	
45	135	28 14	32 29	53.4	27 38	31 35	53.0	27 02	30 41	52.5	26 25	29 48	52.1	25 48	28 55	51.8	25 11	28 03	51.4	225	315
46	134	28 46	32 01	52.4	28 10	31 08	52.0	27 32	30 14	51.6	26 55	29 22	51.2	26 17	28 29	50.8	25 39	27 38	50.4	226	314
47	133	29 18	31 33	51.4	28 40	30 40	51.0	28 02	29 47	50.6	27 24	28 55	50.2	26 46	28 03	49.8	26 07	27 12	49.4	227	313
48	132	29 49	31 04	50.5	29 11	30 11	50.0	28 32	29 19	49.6	27 53	28 27	49.2	27 14	27 36	48.8	26 34	26 46	48.4	228	312
49	131	30 20	30 34	49.5	29 41	29 42	49.0	29 01	28 50	48.6	28 21	27 59	48.2	27 41	27 08	47.8	27 01	26 18	47.4	229	311
50	130	30 50	30 04	48.5	30 10	29 12	48.0	29 30	28 20	47.6	28 49	27 30	47.2	28 08	26 40	46.8	27 27	25 51	46.4	230	310
51	129	31 20	29 32	47.5	30 39	28 41	47.0	29 58	27 50	46.6	29 17	27 00	46.2	28 35	26 11	45.8	27 53	25 22	45.4	231	309
52	128	31 49	29 00	46.4	31 08	28 09	46.0	30 26	27 19	45.6	29 44	26 30	45.2	29 01	25 41	44.8	28 19	24 53	44.4	232	308
53	127	32 18	28 27	45.4	31 36	27 37	45.0	30 53	26 48	44.5	30 10	25 59	44.1	29 27	25 11	43.7	28 44	24 24	43.3	233	307
54	126	32 46	27 53	44.4	32 03	27 04	43.9	31 20	26 15	43.5	30 36	25 27	43.1	29 52	24 40	42.7	29 08	23 53	42.3	234	306
55	125	33 14	27 19	43.3	32 30	26 30	42.9	31 46	25 42	42.4	31 02	24 55	42.0	30 17	24 08	41.6	29 32	23 23	41.2	235	305
56	124	33 42	26 44	42.2	32 57	25 55	41.8	32 12	25 08	41.4	31 27	24 22	41.0	30 41	23 36	40.6	29 56	22 51	40.2	236	304
57	123	34 08	26 07	41.1	33 23	25 20	40.7	32 37	24 34	40.3	31 51	23 48	39.9	31 05	23 03	39.5	30 19	22 19	39.1	237	303
58	122	34 34	25 30	40.1	33 48	24 44	39.6	33 02	23 58	39.2	32 15	23 14	38.8	31 28	22 29	38.4	30 41	21 46	38.0	238	302
59	121	35 00	24 53	39.0	34 13	24 07	38.5	33 26	23 22	38.1	32 39	22 38	37.7	31 51	21 55	37.3	31 03	21 13	37.0	239	301
60	120	35 25	24 14	37.8	34 37	23 30	37.4	33 50	22 46	37.0	33 02	22 03	36.6	32 13	21 20	36.2	31 25	20 39	35.9	240	300
61	119	35 49	23 35	36.7	35 01	22 51	36.3	34 12	22 08	35.9	33 24	21 26	35.5	32 35	20 45	35.1	31 46	20 04	34.8	241	299
62	118	36 13	22 55	35.6	35 24	22 12	35.2	34 35	21 30	34.8	33 45	20 49	34.4	32 56	20 09	34.0	32 06	19 29	33.7	242	298
63	117	36 36	22 14	34.4	35 46	21 32	34.0	34 56	20 51	33.6	34 06	20 11	33.3	33 16	19 32	32.9	32 26	18 53	32.5	243	297
64	116	36 58	21 32	33.3	36 08	20 52	32.9	35 17	20 12	32.5	34 27	19 33	32.1	33 36	18 54	31.8	32 45	18 17	31.4	244	296
65	115	37 20	20 50	32.1	36 29	20 10	31.7	35 38	19 32	31.3	34 47	18 54	31.0	33 55	18 16	30.6	33 03	17 40	30.3	245	295
66	114	37 41	20 07	30.9	36 49	19 28	30.5	35 58	18 51	30.2	35 06	18 14	29.8	34 13	17 38	29.5	33 21	17 02	29.1	246	294
67	113	38 01	19 23	29.7	37 09	18 46	29.4	36 17	18 09	29.0	35 24	17 33	28.6	34 31	16 59	28.3	33 38	16 24	28.0	247	293
68	112	38 21	18 38	28.5	37 28	18 02	28.2	36 35	17 27	27.8	35 42	16 53	27.5	34 48	16 19	27.1	33 55	15 46	26.8	248	292
69	111	38 40	17 53	27.3	37 46	17 18	27.0	36 53	16 44	26.6	35 59	16 11	26.3	35 05	15 38	26.0	34 11	15 07	25.7	249	291
70	110	38 58	17 07	26.1	38 04	16 33	25.7	37 10	16 01	25.4	36 15	15 29	25.1	35 21	14 58	24.8	34 26	14 27	24.5	250	290
71	109	39 15	16 20	24.9	38 20	15 48	24.5	37 26	15 17	24.2	36 31	14 46	23.9	35 36	14 16	23.6	34 41	13 47	23.3	251	289
72	108	39 31	15 33	23.6	38 36	15 02	23.3	37 41	14 32	23.0	36 46	14 03	22.7	35 50	13 34	22.4	34 55	13 07	22.1	252	288
73	107	39 47	14 45	22.4	38 51	14 16	22.1	37 56	13 47	21.8	37 00	13 19	21.5	36 04	12 52	21.2	35 08	12 25	20.9	253	287
74	106	40 02	13 56	21.1	39 06	13 28	20.8	38 10	13 01	20.5	37 13	12 35	20.3	36 17	12 09	20.0	35 21	11 44	19.8	254	286
75	105	40 16	13 07	19.8	39 19	12 41	19.5	38 23	12 15	19.3	37 26	11 50	19.0	36 29	11 26	18.8	35 33	11 02	18.5	255	285
76	104	40 29	12 17	18.5	39 32	11 53	18.3	38 35	11 28	18.0	37 38	11 05	17.8	36 41	10 42	17.6	35 44	10 20	17.3	256	284
77	103	40 41	11 27	17.3	39 44	11 04	17.0	38 47	10 41	16.8	37 49	10 19	16.5	36 52	9 58	16.3	35 54	9 37	16.1	257	283
78	102	40 53	10 36	16.0	39 55	10 15	15.7	38 57	9 54	15.5	38 00	9 33	15.3	37 02	9 14	15.1	36 04	8 54	14.9	258	282
79	101	41 04	9 45	14.7	40 05	9 25	14.4	39 07	9 06	14.2	38 09	8 47	14.0	37 11	8 29	13.9	36 13	8 11	13.7	259	281
80	100	41 13	8 53	13.3	40 15	8 35	13.2	39 16	8 17	13.0	38 18	8 00	12.8	37 19	7 44	12.6	36 21	7 27	12.5	260	280
81	99	41 22	8 01	12.0	40 23	7 45	11.9	39 25	7 29	11.7	38 26	7 13	11.5	37 27	6 58	11.4	36 28	6 43	11.2	261	279
82	98	41 30	7 09	10.7	40 31	6 54	10.5	39 32	6 40	10.4	38 33	6 26	10.3	37 34	6 12	10.1	36 35	5 59	10.0	262	278
83	97	41 37	6 16	9.4	40 38	6 03	9.2	39 39	5 50	9.1	38 39	5 38	9.0	37 40	5 26	8.9	36 41	5 15	8.7	263	277
84	96	41 43	5 23	8.1	40 44	5 12	7.9	39 44	5 01	7.8	38 45	4 50	7.7	37 45	4 40	7.6	36 46	4 30	7.5	264	276
85	95	41 48	4 29	6.7	40 49	4 20	6.6	39 49	4 11	6.5	38 49	4 02	6.4	37 50	3 54	6.3	36 50	3 45	6.3	265	275
86	94	41 52	3 36	5.4	40 53	3 28	5.3	39 53	3 21	5.2	38 53	3 14	5.1	37 53	3 07	5.1	36 54	3 01	5.0	266	274
87	93	41 56	2 42	4.0	40 56	2 36	4.0	39 56	2 31	3.9	38 56	2 26	3.9	37 56	2 20	3.8	36 56	2 16	3.8	267	273
88	92	41 58	1 48	2.7	40 58	1 44	2.6	39 58	1 41	2.6	38 58	1 37	2.6	37 58	1 34	2.5	36 58	1 30	2.5	268	272
89	91	42 00	0 54	1.3	41 00	0 52	1.3	40 00	0 50	1.3	39 00	0 49	1.3	38 00	0 47	1.3	37 00	0 45	1.3	269	271
90	90	42 00	0 00	0.0	41 00	0 00	0.0	40 00	0 00	0.0	39 00	0 00	0.0	38 00	0 00	0.0	37 00	0 00	0.0	270	270

N. Lat.: for LHA>180°....Zn = Z
for LHA<180°....Zn =360° − Z

S. Lat.: for LHA > 180°.... Zn =180° − Z
for LHA < 180°.... Zn =180° + Z

LATITUDE / Ā : 54° – 59°

B: (–) for 90°< LHA < 270°
Dec: (–) for Lat. contrary name

Z₁: same sign as B
Z₂: (–)for F > 90°

Lat./Ā LHA/F̄	F̄	54° A/H	54° B/P	54° Z₁/Z₂	55° A/H	55° B/P	55° Z₁/Z₂	56° A/H	56° B/P	56° Z₁/Z₂	57° A/H	57° B/P	57° Z₁/Z₂	58° A/H	58° B/P	58° Z₁/Z₂	59° A/H	59° B/P	59° Z₁/Z₂	Lat./Ā LHA
0	180	0 00	36 00	90.0	0 00	35 00	90.0	0 00	34 00	90.0	0 00	33 00	90.0	0 00	32 00	90.0	0 00	31 00	90.0	180
1	179	0 35	36 00	89.2	0 34	35 00	89.2	0 34	34 00	89.2	0 33	33 00	89.2	0 32	32 00	89.2	0 31	31 00	89.1	181
2	178	1 11	35 59	88.4	1 09	34 59	88.4	1 07	33 59	88.3	1 05	32 59	88.3	1 04	31 59	88.3	1 02	30 59	88.3	182
3	177	1 46	35 58	87.6	1 43	34 58	87.5	1 41	33 58	87.5	1 38	32 58	87.5	1 35	31 58	87.5	1 33	30 58	87.4	183
4	176	2 21	35 56	86.8	2 18	34 56	86.7	2 14	33 56	86.7	2 11	32 56	86.6	2 07	31 56	86.6	2 04	30 56	86.6	184
5	175	2 56	35 54	86.0	2 52	34 54	85.9	2 48	33 54	85.9	2 43	32 54	85.8	2 39	31 54	85.8	2 34	30 54	85.7	185
6	174	3 31	35 51	85.1	3 26	34 51	85.1	3 21	33 51	85.0	3 16	32 51	85.0	3 11	31 52	84.9	3 05	30 52	84.9	186
7	173	4 06	35 48	84.3	4 00	34 48	84.3	3 54	33 48	84.2	3 48	32 48	84.1	3 42	31 48	84.1	3 36	30 49	84.0	187
8	172	4 42	35 44	83.5	4 34	34 44	83.4	4 28	33 44	83.4	4 21	32 45	83.3	4 14	31 45	83.2	4 07	30 45	83.1	188
9	171	5 17	35 40	82.7	5 09	34 40	82.6	5 01	33 40	82.5	4 53	32 41	82.4	4 45	31 41	82.3	4 37	30 41	82.3	189
10	170	5 51	35 35	81.9	5 43	34 35	81.8	5 34	33 36	81.7	5 26	32 36	81.6	5 17	31 36	81.5	5 08	30 37	81.4	190
11	169	6 26	35 30	81.1	6 17	34 30	81.0	6 08	33 31	80.8	5 58	32 31	80.7	5 48	31 31	80.6	5 38	30 32	80.5	191
12	168	7 01	35 24	80.2	6 51	34 24	80.1	6 41	33 25	80.0	6 30	32 25	79.9	6 20	31 26	79.8	6 09	30 27	79.7	192
13	167	7 36	35 18	79.4	7 25	34 18	79.3	7 14	33 19	79.2	7 02	32 19	79.0	6 51	31 20	78.9	6 39	30 21	78.8	193
14	166	8 11	35 11	78.6	7 59	34 12	78.5	7 46	33 12	78.3	7 34	32 13	78.2	7 22	31 14	78.1	7 09	30 15	77.9	194
15	165	8 45	35 04	77.8	8 32	34 04	77.6	8 19	33 05	77.5	8 06	32 06	77.3	7 53	31 07	77.2	7 40	30 08	77.1	195
16	164	9 19	34 56	76.9	9 06	33 57	76.8	8 52	32 58	76.6	8 38	31 58	76.5	8 24	31 00	76.3	8 10	30 01	76.2	196
17	163	9 54	34 47	76.1	9 39	33 48	75.9	9 25	32 49	75.8	9 10	31 50	75.6	8 55	30 52	75.5	8 40	29 53	75.3	197
18	162	10 28	34 39	75.3	10 13	33 40	75.1	9 57	32 41	74.9	9 41	31 42	74.8	9 25	30 43	74.6	9 09	29 45	74.4	198
19	161	11 02	34 29	74.4	10 46	33 30	74.2	10 29	32 32	74.1	10 13	31 33	73.9	9 56	30 35	73.7	9 39	29 36	73.6	199
20	160	11 36	34 19	73.6	11 19	33 21	73.4	11 02	32 22	73.2	10 44	31 24	73.0	10 27	30 25	72.8	10 09	29 27	72.7	200
21	159	12 10	34 09	72.7	11 52	33 10	72.5	11 34	32 12	72.3	11 15	31 14	72.2	10 57	30 15	72.0	10 38	29 17	71.8	201
22	158	12 43	33 58	71.9	12 24	33 00	71.7	12 06	32 01	71.5	11 46	31 03	71.3	11 27	30 05	71.1	11 07	29 07	70.9	202
23	157	13 17	33 46	71.0	12 57	32 48	70.8	12 37	31 50	70.6	12 17	30 52	70.4	11 57	29 54	70.2	11 37	28 57	70.0	203
24	156	13 50	33 34	70.2	13 29	32 36	70.0	13 09	31 38	69.7	12 48	30 41	69.5	12 27	29 43	69.3	12 06	28 46	69.1	204
25	155	14 23	33 22	69.3	14 02	32 24	69.1	13 40	31 26	68.8	13 18	30 29	68.6	12 56	29 31	68.4	12 34	28 34	68.2	205
26	154	14 56	33 09	68.5	14 34	32 11	68.2	14 11	31 14	68.0	13 49	30 16	67.8	13 26	29 19	67.5	13 03	28 22	67.3	206
27	153	15 29	32 55	67.6	15 06	31 58	67.3	14 42	31 00	67.1	14 19	30 03	66.9	13 55	29 06	66.6	13 31	28 09	66.4	207
28	152	16 01	32 41	66.7	15 37	31 44	66.5	15 13	30 47	66.3	14 49	29 50	66.0	14 24	28 53	65.7	14 00	27 57	65.5	208
29	151	16 33	32 26	65.8	16 09	31 29	65.6	15 44	30 32	65.3	15 19	29 36	65.1	14 53	28 39	64.8	14 28	27 43	64.6	209
30	150	17 05	32 11	65.0	16 40	31 14	64.7	16 14	30 17	64.4	15 48	29 21	64.2	15 22	28 25	63.9	14 55	27 29	63.7	210
31	149	17 37	31 55	64.1	17 11	30 58	63.8	16 44	30 02	63.5	16 17	29 06	63.3	15 50	28 10	63.0	15 23	27 15	62.7	211
32	148	18 09	31 38	63.2	17 42	30 42	62.9	17 14	29 46	62.6	16 47	28 51	62.4	16 19	27 55	62.1	15 50	27 00	61.8	212
33	147	18 40	31 21	62.3	18 12	30 25	62.0	17 44	29 30	61.7	17 15	28 34	61.4	16 47	27 39	61.2	16 17	26 45	60.9	213
34	146	19 11	31 04	61.4	18 42	30 08	61.1	18 13	29 13	60.8	17 44	28 18	60.5	17 14	27 23	60.2	16 44	26 29	60.0	214
35	145	19 42	30 46	60.5	19 12	29 50	60.2	18 42	28 55	59.9	18 12	28 01	59.6	17 42	27 06	59.3	17 11	26 12	59.0	215
36	144	20 13	30 27	59.6	19 42	29 32	59.2	19 11	28 37	58.9	18 40	27 43	58.6	18 09	26 49	58.4	17 37	25 55	58.1	216
37	143	20 43	30 07	58.6	20 12	29 13	58.3	19 40	28 19	58.0	19 08	27 25	57.7	18 36	26 31	57.4	18 03	25 38	57.1	217
38	142	21 13	29 48	57.7	20 41	28 53	57.4	20 08	27 59	57.1	19 35	27 06	56.8	19 02	26 13	56.5	18 29	25 20	56.2	218
39	141	21 43	29 27	56.8	21 10	28 33	56.4	20 36	27 40	56.1	20 03	26 47	55.8	19 29	25 54	55.5	18 55	25 02	55.2	219
40	140	22 12	29 06	55.8	21 38	28 13	55.5	21 04	27 20	55.2	20 30	26 27	54.9	19 55	25 35	54.6	19 20	24 43	54.3	220
41	139	22 41	28 44	54.9	22 06	27 51	54.5	21 31	26 59	54.2	20 56	26 07	53.9	20 21	25 15	53.6	19 45	24 24	53.3	221
42	138	23 10	28 22	53.9	22 34	27 29	53.6	21 58	26 37	53.3	21 22	25 46	52.9	20 46	24 55	52.6	20 10	24 04	52.3	222
43	137	23 38	27 59	53.0	23 02	27 07	52.6	22 25	26 15	52.3	21 48	25 24	52.0	21 11	24 34	51.7	20 34	23 43	51.4	223
44	136	24 06	27 36	52.0	23 29	26 44	51.7	22 51	25 53	51.3	22 14	25 02	51.0	21 36	24 12	50.7	20 58	23 23	50.4	224
45	135	24 34	27 11	51.0	23 56	26 20	50.7	23 17	25 30	50.3	22 39	24 40	50.0	22 00	23 50	49.7	21 21	23 01	49.4	225

Lat. / Ā		54°			55°			56°			57°			58°			59°			Lat. / Ā	
LHA/F		A/H	B/P	Z₁/Z₂	A/H	B/P	Z₁/Z₂	A/H	B/P	Z₁/Z₂	A/H	B/P	Z₁/Z₂	A/H	B/P	Z₁/Z₂	A/H	B/P	Z₁/Z₂	LHA	
45	135	24 34	27 11	51.0	23 56	26 20	50.7	23 17	25 30	50.3	22 39	24 40	50.0	22 00	23 50	49.7	21 21	23 01	49.4	225	315
46	134	25 01	26 47	50.0	24 24	25 56	49.7	23 43	25 06	49.4	23 04	24 17	49.0	22 24	23 28	48.7	21 45	22 39	48.4	226	314
47	133	25 28	26 22	49.1	24 48	25 32	48.7	24 08	24 42	48.4	23 28	23 53	48.0	22 48	23 05	47.7	22 08	22 17	47.4	227	313
48	132	25 54	25 56	48.1	25 14	25 06	47.7	24 33	24 17	47.4	23 53	23 29	47.0	23 11	22 41	46.7	22 30	21 54	46.4	228	312
49	131	26 20	25 29	47.1	25 39	24 40	46.7	24 58	23 52	46.4	24 16	23 05	46.0	23 34	22 17	45.7	22 52	21 31	45.4	229	311
50	130	26 46	25 02	46.0	26 04	24 14	45.7	25 22	23 26	45.3	24 40	22 39	45.0	23 57	21 53	44.7	23 14	21 07	44.4	230	310
51	129	27 11	24 34	45.0	26 28	23 47	44.7	25 45	23 00	44.3	25 02	22 14	44.0	24 19	21 28	43.7	23 36	20 43	43.4	231	309
52	128	27 36	24 06	44.0	26 52	23 19	43.6	26 09	22 33	43.3	25 25	21 48	43.0	24 41	21 03	42.7	23 57	20 18	42.3	232	308
53	127	28 00	23 37	43.0	27 16	22 51	42.6	26 32	22 06	42.3	25 47	21 21	41.9	25 02	20 37	41.6	24 17	19 53	41.3	233	307
54	126	28 24	23 07	41.9	27 39	22 23	41.6	26 54	21 38	41.2	26 09	20 54	40.9	25 23	20 10	40.6	24 37	19 27	40.3	234	306
55	125	28 47	22 37	40.9	28 01	21 53	40.5	27 16	21 09	40.2	26 30	20 26	39.9	25 44	19 43	39.5	24 57	19 01	39.2	235	305
56	124	29 10	22 07	39.8	28 24	21 23	39.5	27 37	20 40	39.1	26 50	19 57	38.8	26 04	19 16	38.5	25 17	18 34	38.2	236	304
57	123	29 32	21 35	38.8	28 45	20 52	38.4	27 58	20 10	38.1	27 11	19 29	37.8	26 23	18 48	37.4	25 35	18 07	37.1	237	303
58	122	29 54	21 03	37.7	29 06	20 21	37.3	28 19	19 40	37.0	27 31	18 59	36.7	26 42	18 19	36.4	25 54	17 40	36.1	238	302
59	121	30 15	20 31	36.6	29 27	19 50	36.3	28 38	19 09	35.9	27 50	18 30	35.6	27 01	17 50	35.3	26 12	17 12	35.0	239	301
60	120	30 36	19 58	35.5	29 47	19 18	35.2	28 58	18 38	34.9	28 09	18 00	34.5	27 19	17 21	34.2	26 29	16 43	34.0	240	300
61	119	30 56	19 24	34.4	30 07	18 45	34.1	29 17	18 06	33.8	28 27	17 29	33.5	27 37	16 51	33.2	26 46	16 14	32.9	241	299
62	118	31 16	18 50	33.3	30 26	18 12	33.0	29 35	17 34	32.7	28 45	16 57	32.4	27 54	16 21	32.1	27 03	15 45	31.8	242	298
63	117	31 35	18 15	32.2	30 44	17 38	31.9	29 53	17 02	31.6	29 02	16 26	31.3	28 10	15 50	31.0	27 19	15 15	30.7	243	297
64	116	31 53	17 40	31.1	31 02	17 04	30.8	30 10	16 28	30.5	29 19	15 53	30.2	28 27	15 19	29.9	27 35	14 45	29.6	244	296
65	115	32 11	17 04	30.0	31 19	16 29	29.7	30 27	15 55	29.4	29 35	15 21	29.1	28 42	14 48	28.8	27 50	14 15	28.5	245	295
66	114	32 29	16 28	28.8	31 36	15 54	28.5	30 43	15 20	28.2	29 50	14 48	28.0	28 57	14 16	27.7	28 04	13 44	27.4	246	294
67	113	32 45	15 51	27.7	31 52	15 18	27.4	30 59	14 46	27.1	30 05	14 14	26.8	29 12	13 43	26.6	28 18	13 13	26.3	247	293
68	112	33 01	15 14	26.5	32 08	14 42	26.3	31 14	14 11	26.0	30 20	13 40	25.7	29 26	13 10	25.5	28 31	12 41	25.2	248	292
69	111	33 17	14 36	25.4	32 23	14 05	25.1	31 28	13 35	24.8	30 34	13 06	24.6	29 39	12 37	24.4	28 44	12 09	24.1	249	291
70	110	33 32	13 57	24.2	32 37	13 28	24.0	31 42	12 59	23.7	30 47	12 31	23.5	29 52	12 04	23.2	28 57	11 37	23.0	250	290
71	109	33 46	13 18	23.1	32 51	12 51	22.8	31 55	12 23	22.6	31 00	11 56	22.3	30 04	11 30	22.1	29 09	11 04	21.9	251	289
72	108	33 59	12 39	21.9	33 04	12 13	21.6	32 08	11 46	21.4	31 12	11 20	21.2	30 16	10 56	21.0	29 20	10 31	20.8	252	288
73	107	34 12	12 00	20.7	33 16	11 34	20.5	32 20	11 09	20.2	31 23	10 45	20.0	30 27	10 21	19.8	29 30	9 58	19.6	253	287
74	106	34 24	11 19	19.5	33 28	10 55	19.3	32 31	10 32	19.1	31 34	10 09	18.9	30 37	9 46	18.7	29 41	9 24	18.5	254	286
75	105	34 36	10 39	18.3	33 39	10 16	18.1	32 42	9 54	17.9	31 44	9 32	17.7	30 47	9 11	17.5	29 50	8 50	17.4	255	285
76	104	34 46	9 58	17.1	33 49	9 37	16.9	32 52	9 16	16.7	31 54	8 56	16.6	30 57	8 36	16.4	29 59	8 16	16.2	256	284
77	103	34 56	9 17	15.9	33 59	8 57	15.7	33 01	8 38	15.6	32 03	8 19	15.4	31 05	8 00	15.2	30 07	7 42	15.1	257	283
78	102	35 06	8 35	14.7	34 08	8 17	14.5	33 10	7 59	14.4	32 11	7 41	14.2	31 13	7 24	14.1	30 15	7 07	13.9	258	282
79	101	35 14	7 54	13.5	34 16	7 37	13.3	33 18	7 20	13.2	32 19	7 04	13.0	31 21	6 48	12.9	30 22	6 32	12.8	259	281
80	100	35 22	7 11	12.3	34 24	6 56	12.1	33 25	6 41	12.0	32 26	6 26	11.9	31 27	6 12	11.7	30 29	5 57	11.6	260	280
81	99	35 29	6 29	11.1	34 30	6 15	10.9	33 32	6 01	10.8	32 33	5 48	10.7	31 34	5 35	10.6	30 35	5 22	10.5	261	279
82	98	35 36	5 46	9.9	34 37	5 34	9.7	33 37	5 22	9.6	32 38	5 10	9.5	31 39	4 58	9.4	30 40	4 47	9.3	262	278
83	97	35 41	5 04	8.6	34 42	4 53	8.5	33 43	4 42	8.4	32 43	4 32	8.3	31 44	4 21	8.2	30 45	4 11	8.2	263	277
84	96	35 46	4 21	7.4	34 47	4 11	7.3	33 47	4 02	7.2	32 48	3 53	7.1	31 48	3 44	7.1	30 49	3 36	7.0	264	276
85	95	35 51	3 37	6.2	34 51	3 30	6.1	33 51	3 22	6.0	32 52	3 14	5.9	31 52	3 07	5.9	30 52	3 00	5.8	265	275
86	94	35 54	2 54	4.9	34 54	2 48	4.9	33 54	2 42	4.8	32 55	2 36	4.8	31 55	2 30	4.7	30 55	2 24	4.7	266	274
87	93	35 57	2 11	3.7	34 57	2 06	3.7	33 57	2 01	3.6	32 57	1 57	3.6	31 57	1 52	3.5	30 57	1 48	3.5	267	273
88	92	35 58	1 27	2.5	34 59	1 24	2.4	33 59	1 21	2.4	32 59	1 18	2.4	31 59	1 15	2.4	30 59	1 12	2.3	268	272
89	91	36 00	0 44	1.2	35 00	0 42	1.2	34 00	0 40	1.2	33 00	0 39	1.2	32 00	0 37	1.2	31 00	0 36	1.2	269	271
90	90	36 00	0 00	0.0	35 00	0 00	0.0	34 00	0 00	0.0	33 00	0 00	0.0	32 00	0 00	0.0	31 00	0 00	0.0	270	270

N. Lat.: for LHA>180°... Zn = Z
for LHA<180°... Zn =360° − Z

S. Lat.: for LHA > 180°.... Zn =180° − Z
for LHA < 180°.... Zn =180° + Z

LATITUDE/Ā : 60° – 65°

B: (–) for 90° < LHA < 270°
Dec: (–) for Lat. contrary name

Z₁: same sign as B
Z₂: (–) for F > 90°

Lat./Ā		60°			61°			62°			63°			64°			65°			Lat./Ā	
LHA/F	Ā	A/H	B/P	Z₁/Z₂	A/H	B/P	Z₁/Z₂	A/H	B/P	Z₁/Z₂	A/H	B/P	Z₁/Z₂	A/H	B/P	Z₁/Z₂	A/H	B/P	Z₁/Z₂	Ā	LHA
0	180	0 00	30 00	90.0	0 00	29 00	90.0	0 00	28 00	90.0	0 00	27 00	90.0	0 00	26 00	90.0	0 00	25 00	90.0	180	360
1	179	0 30	30 00	89.1	0 29	29 00	89.1	0 28	28 00	89.1	0 27	27 00	89.1	0 26	26 00	89.1	0 25	25 00	89.1	181	359
2	178	1 00	29 59	88.3	0 58	28 59	88.3	0 56	27 59	88.2	0 54	26 59	88.2	0 53	25 59	88.2	0 51	24 59	88.2	182	358
3	177	1 30	29 58	87.4	1 27	28 58	87.4	1 24	27 58	87.4	1 22	26 58	87.3	1 19	25 58	87.3	1 16	24 58	87.3	183	357
4	176	2 00	29 56	86.5	1 56	28 56	86.5	1 53	27 57	86.5	1 49	26 57	86.4	1 45	25 57	86.4	1 41	24 57	86.4	184	356
5	175	2 30	29 54	85.7	2 25	28 54	85.6	2 21	27 55	85.6	2 16	26 55	85.5	2 11	25 55	85.5	2 07	24 55	85.5	185	355
6	174	3 00	29 52	84.8	2 54	28 52	84.7	2 49	27 52	84.7	2 43	26 52	84.6	2 38	25 53	84.6	2 32	24 53	84.6	186	354
7	173	3 30	29 49	83.9	3 23	28 49	83.9	3 17	27 49	83.8	3 10	26 50	83.8	3 04	25 50	83.7	2 57	24 50	83.7	187	353
8	172	3 59	29 45	83.1	3 52	28 46	83.0	3 45	27 46	82.9	3 37	26 46	82.9	3 30	25 47	82.8	3 22	24 47	82.7	188	352
9	171	4 29	29 42	82.2	4 21	28 42	82.1	4 13	27 42	82.0	4 04	26 43	82.0	3 56	25 43	81.9	3 47	24 44	81.8	189	351
10	170	4 59	29 37	81.3	4 50	28 38	81.2	4 41	27 38	81.2	4 31	26 39	81.1	4 22	25 39	81.0	4 13	24 40	80.9	190	350
11	169	5 28	29 33	80.4	5 18	28 33	80.4	5 08	27 34	80.3	4 58	26 34	80.2	4 48	25 35	80.1	4 38	24 36	80.0	191	349
12	168	5 58	29 27	79.6	5 47	28 28	79.5	5 36	27 29	79.4	5 25	26 29	79.3	5 14	25 30	79.2	5 02	24 31	79.1	192	348
13	167	6 27	29 22	78.7	6 16	28 22	78.6	6 04	27 23	78.5	5 52	26 23	78.4	5 40	25 25	78.4	5 27	24 26	78.2	193	347
14	166	6 57	29 15	77.8	6 44	28 16	77.7	6 31	27 17	77.6	6 18	26 18	77.5	6 05	25 20	77.4	5 52	24 21	77.3	194	346
15	165	7 26	29 09	76.9	7 13	28 10	76.8	6 59	27 11	76.7	6 45	26 12	76.6	6 31	25 14	76.5	6 17	24 15	76.4	195	345
16	164	7 55	29 02	76.1	7 41	28 03	75.9	7 26	27 04	75.8	7 11	26 06	75.7	6 56	25 07	75.5	6 41	24 09	75.4	196	344
17	163	8 24	28 54	75.2	8 09	27 56	75.0	7 53	26 57	74.9	7 38	25 59	74.8	7 22	25 00	74.6	7 06	24 02	74.5	197	343
18	162	8 53	28 46	74.3	8 37	27 48	74.1	8 20	26 50	74.0	8 04	25 51	73.9	7 47	24 53	73.7	7 30	23 55	73.6	198	342
19	161	9 22	28 38	73.4	9 05	27 40	73.2	8 48	26 41	73.1	8 30	25 43	73.0	8 12	24 45	72.8	7 55	23 48	72.7	199	341
20	160	9 51	28 29	72.5	9 33	27 31	72.3	9 14	26 33	72.2	8 56	25 35	72.0	8 37	24 37	71.9	8 19	23 40	71.7	200	340
21	159	10 19	28 19	71.6	10 00	27 22	71.4	9 41	26 24	71.3	9 22	25 26	71.1	9 02	24 29	71.0	8 43	23 32	70.8	201	339
22	158	10 48	28 10	70.7	10 28	27 12	70.5	10 08	26 15	70.4	9 48	25 17	70.2	9 27	24 20	70.0	9 07	23 23	69.9	202	338
23	157	11 16	27 59	69.8	10 55	27 02	69.6	10 34	26 05	69.5	10 13	25 08	69.3	9 52	24 11	69.1	9 30	23 14	69.0	203	337
24	156	11 44	27 49	68.9	11 22	26 51	68.7	11 00	25 54	68.5	10 38	24 58	68.4	10 16	24 01	68.2	9 54	23 04	68.0	204	336
25	155	12 12	27 37	68.0	11 49	26 40	67.8	11 27	25 44	67.6	11 04	24 48	67.4	10 41	23 51	67.3	10 17	22 55	67.1	205	335
26	154	12 40	27 26	67.1	12 16	26 29	66.9	11 53	25 33	66.7	11 29	24 36	66.5	11 05	23 40	66.3	10 41	22 44	66.2	206	334
27	153	13 07	27 13	66.2	12 43	26 17	66.0	12 18	25 21	65.8	11 54	24 25	65.6	11 29	23 29	65.4	11 04	22 34	65.2	207	333
28	152	13 35	27 01	65.3	13 09	26 05	65.1	12 44	25 09	64.9	12 18	24 13	64.7	11 53	23 18	64.5	11 27	22 23	64.3	208	332
29	151	14 02	26 48	64.4	13 36	25 52	64.1	13 09	24 56	63.9	12 43	24 01	63.7	12 16	23 06	63.5	11 49	22 11	63.3	209	331
30	150	14 29	26 34	63.4	14 02	25 39	63.2	13 35	24 43	63.0	13 07	23 49	62.8	12 40	22 54	62.6	12 12	21 59	62.4	210	330
31	149	14 55	26 20	62.5	14 28	25 25	62.3	14 00	24 30	62.1	13 31	23 36	61.8	13 03	22 41	61.6	12 34	21 47	61.4	211	329
32	148	15 22	26 05	61.6	14 53	25 11	61.3	14 25	24 16	61.1	13 55	23 22	60.9	13 26	22 28	60.7	12 56	21 35	60.5	212	328
33	147	15 48	25 50	60.6	15 19	24 56	60.4	14 49	24 02	60.2	14 19	23 08	59.9	13 49	22 15	59.7	13 18	21 22	59.5	213	327
34	146	16 14	25 35	59.7	15 44	24 41	59.5	15 13	23 47	59.2	14 42	22 54	59.0	14 11	22 01	58.8	13 40	21 08	58.6	214	326
35	145	16 40	25 19	58.8	16 09	24 25	58.5	15 37	23 32	58.3	15 06	22 39	58.0	14 34	21 47	57.8	14 02	20 54	57.6	215	325
36	144	17 05	25 02	57.8	16 33	24 09	57.6	16 01	23 17	57.3	15 29	22 24	57.1	14 56	21 32	56.9	14 23	20 40	56.6	216	324
37	143	17 31	24 45	56.9	16 58	23 53	56.6	16 25	23 00	56.4	15 51	22 09	56.1	15 18	21 17	55.9	14 44	20 26	55.6	217	323
38	142	17 56	24 28	55.9	17 22	23 36	55.7	16 48	22 44	55.4	16 14	21 53	55.2	15 39	21 01	54.9	15 05	20 11	54.7	218	322
39	141	18 20	24 10	55.0	17 46	23 18	54.7	17 11	22 27	54.4	16 36	21 36	54.2	16 01	20 46	54.0	15 26	19 55	53.7	219	321
40	140	18 45	23 52	54.0	18 09	23 00	53.7	17 34	22 10	53.5	16 58	21 19	53.2	16 22	20 29	53.0	15 46	19 39	52.7	220	320
41	139	19 09	23 33	53.0	18 33	22 42	52.8	17 56	21 52	52.5	17 20	21 02	52.2	16 43	20 13	52.0	16 06	19 23	51.8	221	319
42	138	19 33	23 13	52.1	18 56	22 23	51.8	18 19	21 34	51.5	17 41	20 44	51.3	17 03	19 55	51.0	16 26	19 07	50.8	222	318
43	137	19 56	22 54	51.1	19 18	22 04	50.8	18 40	21 15	50.5	18 02	20 26	50.3	17 24	19 38	50.0	16 45	18 50	49.8	223	317
44	136	20 19	22 33	50.1	19 41	21 44	49.8	19 02	20 56	49.5	18 23	20 08	49.3	17 44	19 20	49.0	17 04	18 33	48.8	224	316
45	135	20 42	22 12	49.1	20 03	21 24	48.8	19 23	20 36	48.6	18 43	19 49	48.3	18 03	19 02	48.1	17 23	18 15	47.8	225	315

LHA/F	F	60° A/H	60° B/P	60° Z_1/Z_2	61° A/H	61° B/P	61° Z_1/Z_2	62° A/H	62° B/P	62° Z_1/Z_2	63° A/H	63° B/P	63° Z_1/Z_2	64° A/H	64° B/P	64° Z_1/Z_2	65° A/H	65° B/P	65° Z_1/Z_2	Ā	LHA
45	135	20 42	22 12	49.1	20 03	21 24	48.8	19 23	20 36	48.6	18 43	19 49	48.3	18 03	19 02	48.1	17 23	18 15	47.8	315	225
46	134	21 05	21 51	48.1	20 25	21 04	47.8	19 44	20 16	47.6	19 04	19 29	47.3	18 23	18 43	47.1	17 42	17 57	46.8	314	226
47	133	21 27	21 30	47.1	20 46	20 43	46.8	20 05	19 56	46.6	19 24	19 10	46.3	18 42	18 24	46.1	18 00	17 39	45.8	313	227
48	132	21 49	21 07	46.1	21 07	20 21	45.8	20 25	19 35	45.6	19 43	18 50	45.3	19 01	18 04	45.1	18 18	17 20	44.8	312	228
49	131	22 10	20 45	45.1	21 28	19 59	44.8	20 45	19 14	44.6	20 02	18 29	44.3	19 19	17 45	44.0	18 36	17 01	43.8	311	229
50	130	22 31	20 22	44.1	21 48	19 37	43.8	21 05	18 52	43.5	20 21	18 08	43.3	19 37	17 24	43.0	18 53	16 41	42.8	310	230
51	129	22 52	19 58	43.1	22 08	19 14	42.8	21 24	18 30	42.5	20 40	17 47	42.3	19 55	17 04	42.0	19 10	16 21	41.8	309	231
52	128	23 12	19 34	42.1	22 28	18 51	41.7	21 43	18 08	41.5	20 58	17 25	41.2	20 13	16 43	41.0	19 27	16 01	40.8	308	232
53	127	23 32	19 10	41.0	22 47	18 27	40.7	22 01	17 45	40.5	21 15	17 03	40.2	20 30	16 21	40.0	19 44	15 41	39.7	307	233
54	126	23 52	18 45	40.0	23 06	18 03	39.7	22 19	17 21	39.4	21 33	16 40	39.2	20 46	16 00	39.0	20 00	15 20	38.7	306	234
55	125	24 11	18 19	39.0	23 24	17 38	38.7	22 37	16 58	38.4	21 50	16 17	38.2	21 03	15 38	37.9	20 15	14 58	37.7	305	235
56	124	24 29	17 54	37.9	23 42	17 13	37.6	22 54	16 34	37.4	22 07	15 54	37.1	21 19	15 15	36.9	20 31	14 37	36.7	304	236
57	123	24 48	17 27	36.9	23 59	16 48	36.6	23 11	16 09	36.3	22 23	15 31	36.1	21 34	14 53	35.8	20 46	14 15	35.6	303	237
58	122	25 05	17 01	35.8	24 17	16 22	35.5	23 28	15 44	35.3	22 39	15 07	35.0	21 49	14 29	34.8	21 00	13 53	34.6	302	238
59	121	25 23	16 34	34.8	24 33	15 56	34.5	23 44	15 19	34.2	22 54	14 42	34.0	22 04	14 06	33.8	21 14	13 30	33.5	301	239
60	120	25 40	16 06	33.7	24 50	15 29	33.4	23 59	14 53	33.2	23 09	14 18	32.9	22 19	13 42	32.7	21 28	13 07	32.5	300	240
61	119	25 56	15 38	32.6	25 05	15 03	32.4	24 15	14 27	32.1	23 24	13 53	31.9	22 33	13 18	31.7	21 42	12 44	31.5	299	241
62	118	26 12	15 10	31.5	25 21	14 35	31.3	24 29	14 01	31.1	23 38	13 27	30.8	22 46	12 54	30.6	21 55	12 21	30.4	298	242
63	117	26 27	14 41	30.5	25 36	14 08	30.2	24 44	13 34	30.0	23 52	13 01	29.8	22 59	12 29	29.5	22 07	11 57	29.3	297	243
64	116	26 42	14 12	29.4	25 50	13 39	29.1	24 57	13 07	28.9	24 05	12 35	28.7	23 12	12 04	28.5	22 19	11 33	28.3	296	244
65	115	26 57	13 43	28.3	26 04	13 11	28.1	25 11	12 40	27.8	24 18	12 09	27.6	23 25	11 39	27.4	22 31	11 09	27.2	295	245
66	114	27 11	13 13	27.2	26 17	12 42	27.0	25 24	12 12	26.8	24 30	11 43	26.6	23 36	11 13	26.4	22 43	10 44	26.2	294	246
67	113	27 24	12 43	26.1	26 30	12 13	25.9	25 36	11 44	25.7	24 42	11 16	25.5	23 48	10 47	25.3	22 54	10 20	25.1	293	247
68	112	27 37	12 12	25.0	26 43	11 44	24.8	25 48	11 16	24.6	24 54	10 48	24.4	23 59	10 21	24.2	23 04	9 55	24.0	292	248
69	111	27 50	11 41	23.9	26 55	11 14	23.7	26 00	10 47	23.5	25 05	10 21	23.3	24 09	9 55	23.1	23 14	9 29	23.0	291	249
70	110	28 01	11 10	22.8	27 06	10 44	22.6	26 11	10 18	22.4	25 15	9 53	22.2	24 20	9 28	22.0	23 24	9 04	21.9	290	250
71	109	28 13	10 39	21.7	27 17	10 14	21.5	26 21	9 49	21.3	25 25	9 25	21.1	24 29	9 01	21.0	23 33	8 38	20.8	289	251
72	108	28 24	10 07	20.6	27 27	9 43	20.4	26 31	9 20	20.2	25 35	8 57	20.0	24 38	8 34	19.9	23 42	8 12	19.7	288	252
73	107	28 34	9 35	19.4	27 37	9 12	19.3	26 41	8 50	19.1	25 44	8 28	18.9	24 47	8 07	18.8	23 50	7 46	18.6	287	253
74	106	28 44	9 03	18.3	27 47	8 41	18.2	26 50	8 20	18.0	25 52	8 00	17.8	24 55	7 39	17.7	23 58	7 19	17.6	286	254
75	105	28 53	8 30	17.2	27 55	8 10	17.0	26 58	7 50	16.9	26 01	7 31	16.7	25 03	7 12	16.6	24 06	6 53	16.5	285	255
76	104	29 01	7 57	16.1	28 04	7 38	15.9	27 06	7 20	15.8	26 08	7 02	15.6	25 10	6 44	15.5	24 13	6 26	15.4	284	256
77	103	29 09	7 24	14.9	28 11	7 06	14.8	27 13	6 49	14.7	26 15	6 32	14.5	25 17	6 16	14.4	24 19	5 59	14.3	283	257
78	102	29 17	6 51	13.8	28 18	6 34	13.7	27 20	6 19	13.5	26 22	6 03	13.4	25 23	5 47	13.3	24 25	5 32	13.2	282	258
79	101	29 24	6 17	12.7	28 25	6 02	12.5	27 27	5 48	12.4	26 28	5 33	12.3	25 29	5 19	12.2	24 31	5 05	12.1	281	259
80	100	29 30	5 44	11.5	28 31	5 30	11.4	27 32	5 17	11.3	26 33	5 03	11.1	25 35	4 50	11.1	24 36	4 38	11.0	280	260
81	99	29 36	5 10	10.4	28 37	4 57	10.3	27 38	4 45	10.2	26 38	4 33	10.1	25 39	4 22	10.0	24 40	4 10	9.9	279	261
82	98	29 41	4 36	9.2	28 41	4 25	9.1	27 42	4 14	9.0	26 43	4 03	9.0	25 44	3 53	8.9	24 44	3 43	8.8	278	262
83	97	29 45	4 01	8.1	28 46	3 52	8.0	27 46	3 42	7.9	26 47	3 33	7.8	25 48	3 24	7.8	24 48	3 15	7.7	277	263
84	96	29 49	3 27	6.9	28 50	3 19	6.9	27 50	3 11	6.8	26 50	3 03	6.7	25 51	2 55	6.7	24 51	2 47	6.6	276	264
85	95	29 52	2 53	5.8	28 53	2 46	5.7	27 53	2 39	5.7	26 53	2 33	5.6	25 54	2 26	5.6	24 54	2 20	5.5	275	265
86	94	29 55	2 18	4.6	28 55	2 13	4.6	27 56	2 07	4.5	26 56	2 02	4.5	25 56	1 57	4.4	24 56	1 52	4.4	274	266
87	93	29 57	1 44	3.5	28 57	1 40	3.4	27 57	1 36	3.4	26 58	1 32	3.4	25 58	1 28	3.3	24 58	1 24	3.3	273	267
88	92	29 59	1 09	2.3	28 59	1 06	2.3	27 59	1 04	2.3	26 59	1 01	2.2	25 59	0 59	2.2	24 59	0 56	2.2	272	268
89	91	30 00	0 35	1.2	28 59	0 33	1.1	28 00	0 32	1.1	27 00	0 31	1.1	26 00	0 29	1.1	25 00	0 28	1.1	271	269
		30 00	0 00	0.0	29 00	0 00	0.0	28 00	0 00	0.0	27 00	0 00	0.0	26 00	0 00	0.0	25 00	0 00	0.0	270	270

N. Lat.: for LHA>180°....Zn=Z
          for LHA<180°....Zn=360°−Z

S. Lat.: for LHA>180°.... Zn=180°−Z
          for LHA<180°.... Zn=180°+Z

LATITUDE/Ā: 66° – 71°

B: (−) for 90° < LHA < 270°
Dec: (−) for Lat. contrary name

Z₁: same sign as B
Z₂: (−) for F > 90°

Lat./Ā	66°			67°			68°			69°			70°			71°			Lat./Ā
LHA/F̄	A/H	B/P	Z₁/Z₂	A/H	B/P	Z₁/Z₂	A/H	B/P	Z₁/Z₂	A/H	B/P	Z₁/Z₂	A/H	B/P	Z₁/Z₂	A/H	B/P	Z₁/Z₂	LHA
0	0 00	24 00	90.0	0 00	23 00	90.0	0 00	22 00	90.0	0 00	21 00	90.0	0 00	20 00	90.0	0 00	19 00	90.0	180
1	0 24	24 00	89.1	0 23	23 00	89.1	0 22	22 00	89.1	0 22	21 00	89.1	0 21	20 00	89.1	0 20	19 00	89.1	181
2	0 49	23 59	88.2	0 47	22 59	88.2	0 45	21 59	88.1	0 43	20 59	88.1	0 41	19 59	88.1	0 39	18 59	88.1	182
3	1 13	23 58	87.3	1 10	22 58	87.2	1 07	21 58	87.2	1 04	20 58	87.2	1 02	19 58	87.2	0 59	18 59	87.2	183
4	1 38	23 57	86.3	1 34	22 57	86.3	1 30	21 57	86.3	1 26	20 57	86.3	1 22	19 57	86.2	1 18	18 57	86.2	184
5	2 02	23 55	85.4	1 57	22 55	85.4	1 52	21 55	85.4	1 47	20 56	85.3	1 42	19 56	85.3	1 38	18 56	85.3	185
6	2 26	23 53	84.5	2 20	22 53	84.5	2 15	21 53	84.4	2 09	20 54	84.4	2 03	19 54	84.4	1 57	18 54	84.3	186
7	2 50	23 50	83.6	2 44	22 51	83.6	2 37	21 51	83.5	2 30	20 51	83.5	2 23	19 52	83.4	2 16	18 52	83.4	187
8	3 15	23 48	82.7	3 07	22 48	82.6	2 59	21 48	82.6	2 52	20 49	82.5	2 44	19 49	82.5	2 36	18 50	82.4	188
9	3 39	23 44	81.8	3 30	22 45	81.7	3 22	21 45	81.6	3 13	20 46	81.6	3 04	19 46	81.5	2 55	18 47	81.5	189
10	4 03	23 41	80.8	3 53	22 41	80.8	3 44	21 42	80.7	3 34	20 42	80.7	3 24	19 43	80.6	3 14	18 44	80.5	190
11	4 27	23 36	79.9	4 17	22 37	79.9	4 06	21 38	79.8	3 55	20 39	79.7	3 45	19 40	79.6	3 34	18 41	79.6	191
12	4 51	23 32	79.0	4 40	22 33	78.9	4 28	21 34	78.8	4 16	20 35	78.8	4 05	19 36	78.7	3 53	18 37	78.6	192
13	5 15	23 27	78.1	5 03	22 28	78.0	4 50	21 29	77.9	4 37	20 30	77.8	4 25	19 32	77.8	4 12	18 33	77.7	193
14	5 39	23 22	77.2	5 25	22 23	77.1	5 12	21 24	77.0	4 58	20 26	76.9	4 45	19 27	76.8	4 31	18 28	76.7	194
15	6 03	23 16	76.2	5 48	22 18	76.1	5 34	21 19	76.1	5 19	20 21	76.0	5 05	19 22	75.9	4 50	18 24	75.8	195
16	6 26	23 10	75.3	6 11	22 12	75.2	5 56	21 13	75.1	5 40	20 15	75.0	5 25	19 17	74.9	5 09	18 19	74.8	196
17	6 50	23 04	74.4	6 34	22 06	74.3	6 17	21 08	74.2	6 01	20 09	74.1	5 44	19 11	74.0	5 28	18 14	73.9	197
18	7 13	22 57	73.5	6 56	21 59	73.3	6 39	21 01	73.2	6 21	20 03	73.1	6 04	19 06	73.0	5 46	18 08	72.9	198
19	7 37	22 50	72.5	7 19	21 52	72.4	7 00	20 54	72.3	6 42	19 57	72.2	6 24	18 59	72.1	6 05	18 02	72.0	199
20	8 00	22 42	71.6	7 41	21 45	71.4	7 22	20 47	71.4	7 02	19 50	71.2	6 43	18 53	71.1	6 24	17 56	71.0	200
21	8 23	22 34	70.7	8 03	21 37	70.5	7 43	20 40	70.4	7 23	19 43	70.3	7 02	18 46	70.2	6 42	17 49	70.1	201
22	8 46	22 26	69.7	8 25	21 29	69.6	8 04	20 32	69.5	7 43	19 35	69.3	7 22	18 39	69.2	7 00	17 42	69.1	202
23	9 09	22 17	68.8	8 47	21 21	68.7	8 25	20 24	68.7	8 03	19 28	68.4	7 41	18 31	68.3	7 19	17 35	68.1	203
24	9 31	22 08	67.9	9 09	21 12	67.7	8 46	20 16	67.6	8 23	19 19	67.4	8 00	18 24	67.3	7 37	17 28	67.2	204
25	9 54	21 58	66.9	9 30	21 03	66.8	9 07	20 07	66.6	8 43	19 11	66.5	8 19	18 15	66.3	7 55	17 20	66.2	205
26	10 16	21 49	66.0	9 52	20 53	65.8	9 27	19 57	65.7	9 02	19 02	65.5	8 37	18 07	65.4	8 12	17 12	65.2	206
27	10 38	21 38	65.0	10 13	20 43	64.9	9 48	19 48	64.7	9 22	18 53	64.6	8 56	17 58	64.4	8 30	17 03	64.3	207
28	11 00	21 28	64.1	10 34	20 33	63.9	10 08	19 38	63.8	9 41	18 43	63.6	9 14	17 49	63.5	8 48	16 55	63.3	208
29	11 22	21 17	63.1	10 55	20 22	63.0	10 28	19 28	62.8	10 00	18 34	62.6	9 33	17 39	62.5	9 05	16 46	62.3	209
30	11 44	21 05	62.2	11 16	20 11	62.0	10 48	19 17	61.8	10 19	18 23	61.7	9 51	17 30	61.5	9 22	16 36	61.4	210
31	12 06	20 53	61.2	11 37	20 00	61.1	11 07	19 06	60.9	10 38	18 13	60.7	10 09	17 20	60.5	9 39	16 27	60.4	211
32	12 27	20 41	60.3	11 57	19 48	60.1	11 27	18 55	59.9	10 57	18 02	59.7	10 26	17 09	59.6	9 56	16 17	59.4	212
33	12 48	20 29	59.3	12 17	19 36	59.1	11 46	18 43	58.9	11 15	17 51	58.8	10 44	16 58	58.6	10 13	16 06	58.4	213
34	13 09	20 16	58.4	12 37	19 23	58.2	12 06	18 31	58.0	11 34	17 39	57.8	11 02	16 47	57.6	10 29	15 56	57.5	214
35	13 29	20 02	57.4	12 57	19 10	57.2	12 24	18 19	57.0	11 52	17 27	56.8	11 19	16 36	56.7	10 46	15 45	56.5	215
36	13 50	19 49	56.4	13 17	18 57	56.2	12 43	18 06	56.0	12 10	17 15	55.9	11 36	16 24	55.7	11 02	15 34	55.5	216
37	14 10	19 34	55.5	13 36	18 44	55.3	13 02	17 53	55.1	12 27	17 03	54.9	11 53	16 12	54.7	11 18	15 23	54.5	217
38	14 30	19 20	54.5	13 55	18 30	54.3	13 20	17 40	54.1	12 45	16 50	53.9	12 09	16 00	53.7	11 34	15 11	53.5	218
39	14 50	19 05	53.5	14 14	18 15	53.3	13 38	17 26	53.1	13 02	16 37	52.9	12 26	15 48	52.7	11 49	14 59	52.6	219
40	15 09	18 50	52.5	14 33	18 01	52.3	13 56	17 12	52.1	13 19	16 23	51.9	12 42	15 35	51.7	12 05	14 47	51.6	220
41	15 29	18 34	51.5	14 51	17 46	51.3	14 14	16 57	51.1	13 36	16 09	50.9	12 58	15 22	50.8	12 20	14 34	50.6	221
42	15 48	18 18	50.6	15 09	17 30	50.3	14 31	16 43	50.1	13 52	15 55	49.9	13 14	15 08	49.8	12 35	14 21	49.6	222
43	16 06	18 02	49.6	15 27	17 15	49.4	14 48	16 28	49.2	14 09	15 41	49.0	13 29	14 54	48.8	12 50	14 08	48.6	223
44	16 25	17 46	48.6	15 45	16 59	48.4	15 05	16 12	48.2	14 25	15 26	48.0	13 45	14 40	47.8	13 05	13 55	47.6	224
45	16 43	17 29	47.6	16 02	16 42	47.4	15 22	15 57	47.2	14 41	15 11	47.0	14 00	14 26	46.8	13 19	13 41	46.6	225

LHA/F	F	66° A/H	66° B/P	66° Z_1/Z_2	67° A/H	67° B/P	67° Z_1/Z_2	68° A/H	68° B/P	68° Z_1/Z_2	69° A/H	69° B/P	69° Z_1/Z_2	70° A/H	70° B/P	70° Z_1/Z_2	71° A/H	71° B/P	71° Z_1/Z_2	Ā	LHA
45	135	16 43	17 29	47.6	16 02	16 42	47.4	15 22	15 57	47.2	14 41	15 11	47.0	14 00	14 26	46.8	13 19	13 41	46.6	225	315
46	134	17 01	17 11	46.6	16 19	16 26	46.4	15 38	15 41	46.2	14 56	14 56	46.0	14 15	14 11	45.8	13 33	13 27	45.6	226	314
47	133	17 18	16 53	45.6	16 36	16 09	45.4	15 54	15 24	45.2	15 12	14 40	45.0	14 29	13 56	44.8	13 46	13 13	44.6	227	313
48	132	17 36	16 35	44.6	16 53	15 51	44.4	16 10	15 08	44.2	15 27	14 24	44.0	14 43	13 41	43.8	14 00	12 58	43.6	228	312
49	131	17 53	16 17	43.6	17 09	15 34	43.4	16 25	14 51	43.2	15 42	14 08	43.0	14 58	13 26	42.8	14 13	12 44	42.6	229	311
50	130	18 09	15 58	42.6	17 25	15 16	42.4	16 41	14 33	42.1	15 56	13 52	41.9	15 11	13 10	41.8	14 27	12 29	41.6	230	310
51	129	18 26	15 39	41.6	17 41	14 57	41.3	16 56	14 16	41.1	16 10	13 35	40.9	15 25	12 54	40.8	14 39	12 14	40.6	231	309
52	128	18 42	15 20	40.5	17 56	14 39	40.3	17 10	13 58	40.1	16 24	13 18	39.9	15 38	12 38	39.7	14 52	11 58	39.6	232	308
53	127	18 57	15 00	39.5	18 11	14 20	39.3	17 24	13 40	39.1	16 38	13 00	38.9	15 51	12 21	38.7	15 04	11 42	38.6	233	307
54	126	19 13	14 40	38.5	18 26	14 01	38.3	17 39	13 22	38.1	16 51	12 43	37.9	16 04	12 05	37.7	15 16	11 26	37.5	234	306
55	125	19 28	14 20	37.5	18 40	13 41	37.3	17 52	13 03	37.1	17 04	12 25	36.9	16 16	11 48	36.7	15 28	11 10	36.5	235	305
56	124	19 42	13 59	36.4	18 54	13 21	36.2	18 06	12 44	36.0	17 17	12 07	35.8	16 28	11 30	35.7	15 40	10 54	35.5	236	304
57	123	19 57	13 38	35.4	19 08	13 01	35.2	18 19	12 25	35.0	17 29	11 49	34.8	16 40	11 13	34.6	15 51	10 37	34.5	237	303
58	122	20 11	13 17	34.4	19 21	12 41	34.2	18 31	12 05	34.0	17 42	11 30	33.8	16 52	10 55	33.6	16 02	10 20	33.5	238	302
59	121	20 24	12 55	33.3	19 34	12 20	33.1	18 44	11 45	32.9	17 53	11 11	32.8	17 03	10 37	32.6	16 12	10 03	32.4	239	301
60	120	20 37	12 33	32.3	19 47	11 59	32.1	18 56	11 25	31.9	18 05	10 52	31.7	17 14	10 19	31.5	16 23	9 46	31.4	240	300
61	119	20 50	12 11	31.2	19 59	11 38	31.1	19 08	11 05	30.9	18 16	10 33	30.7	17 24	10 00	30.5	16 33	9 29	30.4	241	299
62	118	21 03	11 48	30.2	20 11	11 16	30.0	19 19	10 44	29.8	18 27	10 13	29.7	17 35	9 42	29.5	16 42	9 11	29.4	242	298
63	117	21 15	11 26	29.2	20 23	10 54	29.0	19 30	10 24	28.8	18 37	9 53	28.6	17 45	9 23	28.5	16 52	8 53	28.3	243	297
64	116	21 27	11 03	28.1	20 34	10 32	28.0	19 41	10 03	27.7	18 47	9 33	27.6	17 54	9 04	27.4	17 01	8 35	27.3	244	296
65	115	21 38	10 39	27.0	20 44	10 10	26.9	19 51	9 41	26.7	18 57	9 13	26.5	18 03	8 45	26.4	17 10	8 17	26.2	245	295
66	114	21 49	10 16	26.0	20 55	9 48	25.8	20 01	9 20	25.7	19 07	8 52	25.5	18 12	8 25	25.4	17 18	7 58	25.2	246	294
67	113	21 59	9 52	24.9	21 05	9 25	24.7	20 11	8 58	24.6	19 16	8 32	24.5	18 21	8 06	24.3	17 26	7 40	24.2	247	293
68	112	22 09	9 28	23.9	21 14	9 02	23.7	20 19	8 36	23.5	19 24	8 11	23.4	18 29	7 46	23.3	17 34	7 21	23.1	248	292
69	111	22 19	9 04	22.8	21 24	8 39	22.6	20 28	8 14	22.5	19 33	7 50	22.4	18 37	7 26	22.2	17 42	7 02	22.1	249	291
70	110	22 28	8 40	21.7	21 32	8 16	21.6	20 37	7 52	21.4	19 41	7 29	21.3	18 45	7 06	21.2	17 49	6 43	21.1	250	290
71	109	22 37	8 15	20.7	21 41	7 52	20.5	20 45	7 30	20.4	19 48	7 07	20.2	18 52	6 45	20.1	17 56	6 24	20.0	251	289
72	108	22 45	7 50	19.6	21 49	7 28	19.4	20 52	7 07	19.3	19 56	6 46	19.2	18 59	6 25	19.1	18 02	6 04	19.0	252	288
73	107	22 53	7 25	18.5	21 56	7 04	18.4	21 00	6 44	18.2	20 03	6 24	18.1	19 05	6 04	18.0	18 08	5 45	17.9	253	287
74	106	23 01	7 00	17.4	22 04	6 40	17.3	21 06	6 21	17.2	20 09	6 02	17.1	19 12	5 44	17.0	18 14	5 25	16.9	254	286
75	105	23 08	6 34	16.3	22 10	6 16	16.2	21 13	5 58	16.1	20 15	5 40	16.0	19 17	5 23	15.9	18 20	5 06	15.8	255	285
76	104	23 15	6 09	15.3	22 17	5 52	15.2	21 19	5 35	15.0	20 21	5 18	15.0	19 23	5 02	14.9	18 25	4 46	14.8	256	284
77	103	23 21	5 43	14.2	22 23	5 27	14.1	21 24	5 12	14.0	20 26	4 56	13.9	19 28	4 41	13.8	18 30	4 26	13.7	257	283
78	102	23 27	5 17	13.1	22 28	5 03	13.0	21 30	4 48	12.9	20 31	4 34	12.8	19 33	4 20	12.7	18 34	4 06	12.7	258	282
79	101	23 32	4 51	12.0	22 33	4 38	11.9	21 35	4 24	11.8	20 36	4 11	11.8	19 37	3 58	11.7	18 38	3 46	11.6	259	281
80	100	23 37	4 25	10.9	22 38	4 13	10.8	21 39	4 01	10.8	20 40	3 49	10.7	19 41	3 37	10.6	18 42	3 25	10.6	260	280
81	99	23 41	3 59	9.8	22 42	3 48	9.8	21 43	3 37	9.7	20 44	3 26	9.6	19 45	3 16	9.5	18 45	3 05	9.5	261	279
82	98	23 45	3 33	8.7	22 46	3 23	8.7	21 46	3 13	8.6	20 47	3 03	8.6	19 48	2 54	8.5	18 48	2 45	8.5	262	278
83	97	23 49	3 06	7.7	22 49	2 58	7.6	21 50	2 49	7.5	20 50	2 41	7.5	19 51	2 32	7.4	18 51	2 24	7.4	263	277
84	96	23 52	2 40	6.6	22 52	2 32	6.5	21 52	2 25	6.5	20 53	2 18	6.4	19 53	2 11	6.4	18 54	2 04	6.3	264	276
85	95	23 54	2 13	5.5	22 54	2 07	5.4	21 55	2 01	5.4	20 55	1 55	5.4	19 55	1 49	5.3	18 55	1 43	5.3	265	275
86	94	23 56	1 47	4.4	22 56	1 42	4.3	21 57	1 37	4.3	20 57	1 32	4.3	19 57	1 27	4.3	18 57	1 23	4.2	266	274
87	93	23 58	1 20	3.3	22 58	1 16	3.3	21 58	1 13	3.2	20 58	1 09	3.2	19 58	1 05	3.2	18 58	1 02	3.2	267	273
88	92	23 59	0 53	2.2	22 59	0 51	2.2	21 59	0 48	2.1	20 59	0 46	2.1	19 59	0 44	2.1	18 59	0 41	2.1	268	272
89	91	24 00	0 27	1.1	23 00	0 25	1.1	22 00	0 24	1.1	21 00	0 23	1.1	20 00	0 22	1.1	19 00	0 21	1.1	269	271
90	90	24 00	0 00	0.0	23 00	0 00	0.0	22 00	0 00	0.0	21 00	0 00	0.0	20 00	0 00	0.0	19 00	0 00	0.0	270	270

N. Lat.: for LHA > 180° .... Zn = Z
for LHA < 180° .... Zn = 360° − Z

S. Lat.: for LHA > 180° .... Zn = 180° − Z
for LHA < 180° .... Zn = 180° + Z

B: (−) for 90° < LHA < 270°
Dec: (−) for Lat. contrary name

Z₁ : same sign as B
Z₂ : (−)for F > 90°

LHA/F	72° A/H	72° B/P	72° Z₁/Z₂	73° A/H	73° B/P	73° Z₁/Z₂	74° A/H	74° B/P	74° Z₁/Z₂	75° A/H	75° B/P	75° Z₁/Z₂	76° A/H	76° B/P	76° Z₁/Z₂	77° A/H	77° B/P	77° Z₁/Z₂	LHA
0	0 00	18 00	90.0	0 00	17 00	90.0	0 00	16 00	90.0	0 00	15 00	90.0	0 00	14 00	90.0	0 00	13 00	90.0	180
1	0 19	18 00	89.0	0 18	17 00	89.0	0 17	16 00	89.0	0 16	15 00	89.0	0 15	14 00	89.0	0 13	13 00	89.0	181
2	0 37	17 59	88.1	0 35	16 59	88.1	0 33	15 59	88.1	0 31	14 59	88.1	0 29	13 59	88.1	0 27	13 00	88.1	182
3	0 56	17 59	87.1	0 53	16 59	87.1	0 50	15 59	87.1	0 47	14 59	87.1	0 44	13 58	87.1	0 40	12 59	87.1	183
4	1 14	17 58	86.2	1 10	16 58	86.2	1 06	15 58	86.2	1 02	14 58	86.1	0 58	13 58	86.1	0 54	12 58	86.1	184
5	1 33	17 56	85.2	1 28	16 56	85.2	1 23	15 57	85.2	1 18	14 57	85.2	1 12	13 57	85.1	1 07	12 57	85.1	185
6	1 51	17 54	84.3	1 45	16 55	84.3	1 39	15 55	84.2	1 33	14 55	84.2	1 27	13 56	84.2	1 21	12 56	84.2	186
7	2 09	17 52	83.3	2 03	16 53	83.3	1 56	15 53	83.3	1 48	14 54	83.2	1 41	13 54	83.2	1 34	12 54	83.2	187
8	2 28	17 50	82.4	2 20	16 51	82.3	2 12	15 51	82.3	2 04	14 52	82.3	1 56	13 52	82.2	1 48	12 53	82.2	188
9	2 46	17 48	81.4	2 37	16 48	81.4	2 28	15 49	81.3	2 19	14 49	81.3	2 10	13 50	81.3	2 01	12 51	81.2	189
10	3 05	17 45	80.5	2 55	16 45	80.5	2 45	15 46	80.4	2 35	14 47	80.3	2 24	13 48	80.3	2 14	12 49	80.3	190
11	3 23	17 41	79.5	3 12	16 42	79.5	3 01	15 43	79.4	2 50	14 44	79.4	2 39	13 45	79.3	2 28	12 46	79.3	191
12	3 41	17 38	78.6	3 29	16 39	78.6	3 17	15 40	78.5	3 05	14 41	78.4	2 53	13 42	78.3	2 41	12 44	78.3	192
13	3 59	17 34	77.6	3 46	16 35	77.6	3 33	15 37	77.5	3 20	14 38	77.4	3 07	13 39	77.4	2 54	12 41	77.3	193
14	4 17	17 30	76.7	4 03	16 31	76.6	3 49	15 33	76.5	3 35	14 34	76.5	3 21	13 36	76.4	3 07	12 38	76.3	194
15	4 35	17 25	75.7	4 20	16 27	75.7	4 05	15 29	75.6	3 50	14 31	75.5	3 35	13 32	75.4	3 20	12 34	75.4	195
16	4 53	17 21	74.7	4 37	16 23	74.7	4 21	15 25	74.6	4 05	14 27	74.5	3 49	13 29	74.4	3 33	12 31	74.4	196
17	5 11	17 16	73.8	4 54	16 18	73.7	4 37	15 20	73.6	4 20	14 22	73.5	4 03	13 25	73.5	3 46	12 27	73.4	197
18	5 29	17 10	72.8	5 11	16 13	72.7	4 53	15 15	72.7	4 35	14 18	72.6	4 17	13 20	72.5	3 59	12 23	72.4	198
19	5 46	17 05	71.9	5 28	16 07	71.8	5 09	15 10	71.7	4 50	14 13	71.6	4 31	13 16	71.5	4 12	12 19	71.5	199
20	6 04	16 59	70.9	5 44	16 02	70.8	5 25	15 05	70.7	5 05	14 08	70.6	4 45	13 11	70.5	4 25	12 14	70.5	200
21	6 21	16 52	69.9	6 01	15 56	69.8	5 40	14 59	69.7	5 19	14 03	69.7	4 58	13 06	69.6	4 37	12 10	69.5	201
22	6 39	16 46	69.0	6 17	15 50	68.9	5 56	14 53	68.8	5 34	13 57	68.7	5 12	13 01	68.6	4 50	12 05	68.5	202
23	6 56	16 39	68.0	6 34	15 43	67.9	6 11	14 47	67.8	5 48	13 51	67.7	5 25	12 56	67.6	5 03	12 00	67.5	203
24	7 13	16 32	67.1	6 50	15 36	66.9	6 26	14 41	66.9	6 03	13 45	66.7	5 39	12 50	66.6	5 15	11 55	66.5	204
25	7 30	16 25	66.1	7 06	15 29	66.0	6 41	14 34	65.9	6 17	13 39	65.8	5 52	12 44	65.7	5 27	11 49	65.6	205
26	7 47	16 17	65.1	7 22	15 22	65.0	6 56	14 27	64.9	6 31	13 32	64.8	6 05	12 38	64.7	5 40	11 43	64.6	206
27	8 04	16 09	64.1	7 38	15 14	64.0	7 11	14 20	63.9	6 45	13 26	63.8	6 18	12 32	63.7	5 52	11 37	63.6	207
28	8 20	16 00	63.2	7 53	15 06	63.0	7 26	14 12	62.9	6 59	13 19	62.8	6 31	12 25	62.7	6 04	11 31	62.6	208
29	8 37	15 52	62.2	8 09	14 58	62.1	7 41	14 05	61.9	7 13	13 11	61.8	6 44	12 18	61.7	6 16	11 25	61.6	209
30	8 53	15 43	61.2	8 24	14 50	61.1	7 55	13 57	61.0	7 26	13 04	60.9	6 57	12 11	60.7	6 27	11 18	60.6	210
31	9 09	15 34	60.3	8 40	14 41	60.1	8 10	13 49	60.0	7 40	12 56	59.9	7 09	12 04	59.8	6 39	11 11	59.7	211
32	9 25	15 24	59.3	8 55	14 32	59.1	8 24	13 40	59.0	7 53	12 48	58.9	7 22	11 56	58.8	6 51	11 05	58.7	212
33	9 41	15 15	58.3	9 10	14 23	58.2	8 38	13 31	58.0	8 06	12 40	57.9	7 34	11 49	57.8	7 02	10 57	57.7	213
34	9 57	15 05	57.3	9 25	14 13	57.2	8 52	13 22	57.0	8 19	12 31	56.9	7 46	11 41	56.8	7 14	10 50	56.7	214
35	10 13	14 54	56.3	9 39	14 04	56.2	9 06	13 13	56.1	8 32	12 23	55.9	7 59	11 33	55.8	7 25	10 43	55.7	215
36	10 28	14 44	55.4	9 54	13 54	55.2	9 19	13 04	55.1	8 45	12 14	54.9	8 11	11 24	54.8	7 36	10 35	54.7	216
37	10 43	14 33	54.4	10 08	13 43	54.2	9 33	12 54	54.1	8 58	12 05	53.9	8 22	11 16	53.8	7 47	10 27	53.7	217
38	10 58	14 22	53.4	10 22	13 33	53.2	9 46	12 44	53.1	9 10	11 55	53.0	8 34	11 07	52.8	7 58	10 19	52.7	218
39	11 13	14 10	52.4	10 36	13 22	52.3	9 59	12 34	52.1	9 22	11 46	52.0	8 45	10 58	51.8	8 08	10 11	51.7	219
40	11 27	13 59	51.4	10 50	13 11	51.3	10 12	12 23	51.1	9 35	11 36	51.0	8 57	10 49	50.8	8 19	10 02	50.7	220
41	11 42	13 47	50.4	11 04	13 00	50.3	10 25	12 13	50.1	9 47	11 26	50.0	9 08	10 39	49.9	8 29	9 53	49.7	221
42	11 56	13 34	49.4	11 17	12 48	49.3	10 38	12 02	49.1	9 58	11 16	49.0	9 19	10 30	48.9	8 39	9 44	48.7	222
43	12 10	13 22	48.4	11 30	12 36	48.3	10 50	11 51	48.1	10 10	11 06	48.0	9 30	10 20	47.9	8 49	9 35	47.7	223
44	12 24	13 09	47.4	11 43	12 24	47.3	11 02	11 39	47.1	10 21	10 55	47.0	9 40	10 10	46.9	8 59	9 26	46.7	224
45	12 37	12 56	46.4	11 56	12 12	46.3	11 14	11 28	46.1	10 33	10 44	46.0	9 51	10 00	45.9	9 09	9 16	45.7	225

Lat./Ā

B: (−) for 90° < LHA < 270°
Dec: (−) for Lat. contrary name

Lat. / Ā		72°			73°			74°			75°			76°			77°		Lat. / Ā	
	LHA/F	A/H	B/P	Z₁/Z₂	A/H	B/P	Z₁/Z₂	A/H	B/P	Z₁/Z₂	A/H	B/P	Z₁/Z₂	A/H	B/P	Z₁/Z₂	A/H	B/P	Z₁/Z₂	LHA	
45	135	12 37	12 56	46.4	11 56	12 12	46.3	11 14	11 28	46.1	10 33	10 44	46.0	9 51	10 00	45.9	9 09	9 16	45.7	225	315
46	134	12 51	12 43	45.4	12 08	11 59	45.3	11 26	11 16	45.1	10 44	10 33	45.0	10 01	9 50	44.9	9 19	9 07	44.7	226	314
47	133	13 04	12 30	44.4	12 21	11 47	44.3	11 38	11 04	44.1	10 55	10 21	44.0	10 11	9 39	43.9	9 28	8 57	43.7	227	313
48	132	13 17	12 16	43.4	12 33	11 34	43.3	11 49	10 52	43.1	11 06	10 10	43.0	10 21	9 28	42.9	9 37	8 47	42.7	228	312
49	131	13 29	12 02	42.4	12 45	11 21	42.3	12 00	10 39	42.1	11 16	9 58	42.0	10 31	9 17	41.9	9 46	8 37	41.7	229	311
50	130	13 42	11 48	41.4	12 57	11 07	41.3	12 11	10 27	41.1	11 26	9 46	41.0	10 41	9 06	40.9	9 55	8 26	40.7	230	310
51	129	13 54	11 33	40.4	13 08	10 53	40.3	12 22	10 14	40.1	11 36	9 34	40.0	10 50	8 55	39.8	10 04	8 16	39.7	231	309
52	128	14 06	11 19	39.4	13 19	10 40	39.2	12 33	10 01	39.1	11 46	9 22	39.0	10 59	8 44	38.8	10 13	8 05	38.7	232	308
53	127	14 17	11 04	38.4	13 30	10 26	38.2	12 43	9 47	38.1	11 56	9 10	38.0	11 08	8 32	37.8	10 21	7 55	37.7	233	307
54	126	14 29	10 49	37.4	13 41	10 11	37.2	12 53	9 34	37.1	12 05	8 57	36.9	11 17	8 20	36.8	10 29	7 44	36.7	234	306
55	125	14 40	10 33	36.4	13 51	9 57	36.2	13 03	9 20	36.1	12 14	8 44	35.9	11 26	8 08	35.8	10 37	7 33	35.7	235	305
56	124	14 51	10 18	35.3	14 02	9 42	35.2	13 13	9 07	35.1	12 23	8 31	34.9	11 34	7 56	34.8	10 45	7 21	34.7	236	304
57	123	15 01	10 02	34.3	14 12	9 27	34.2	13 22	8 53	34.0	12 32	8 18	33.9	11 42	7 44	33.8	10 52	7 10	33.7	237	303
58	122	15 12	9 46	33.3	14 21	9 12	33.2	13 31	8 38	33.0	12 41	8 05	32.9	11 50	7 32	32.8	11 00	6 59	32.7	238	302
59	121	15 22	9 30	32.3	14 31	8 57	32.1	13 40	8 24	32.0	12 49	7 51	31.9	11 58	7 19	31.8	11 07	6 47	31.7	239	301
60	120	15 31	9 14	31.3	14 40	8 41	31.1	13 49	8 10	31.0	12 57	7 38	30.9	12 06	7 06	30.8	11 14	6 35	30.6	240	300
61	119	15 41	8 57	30.2	14 49	8 26	30.1	13 57	7 55	30.0	13 05	7 24	29.8	12 13	6 54	29.7	11 21	6 23	29.6	241	299
62	118	15 50	8 40	29.2	14 58	8 10	29.1	14 05	7 40	28.9	13 13	7 10	28.8	12 20	6 41	28.7	11 27	6 11	28.6	242	298
63	117	15 59	8 23	28.2	15 06	7 54	28.0	14 13	7 25	27.9	13 20	6 56	27.8	12 27	6 27	27.7	11 34	5 59	27.6	243	297
64	116	16 08	8 06	27.2	15 14	7 38	27.0	14 21	7 09	26.9	13 27	6 42	26.8	12 34	6 14	26.7	11 40	5 47	26.6	244	296
65	115	16 16	7 49	26.1	15 22	7 22	26.0	14 28	6 55	25.9	13 34	6 28	25.8	12 40	6 01	25.7	11 46	5 34	25.6	245	295
66	114	16 24	7 32	25.1	15 29	7 05	25.0	14 35	6 39	24.9	13 41	6 13	24.7	12 46	5 47	24.6	11 52	5 22	24.6	246	294
67	113	16 32	7 14	24.1	15 37	6 49	23.9	14 42	6 24	23.8	13 47	5 59	23.7	12 52	5 34	23.6	11 57	5 09	23.5	247	293
68	112	16 39	6 56	23.0	15 44	6 32	22.9	14 48	6 08	22.8	13 53	5 44	22.7	12 58	5 20	22.6	12 02	4 57	22.5	248	292
69	111	16 46	6 39	22.0	15 50	6 15	21.9	14 55	5 52	21.8	13 59	5 29	21.7	13 03	5 06	21.6	12 07	4 44	21.5	249	291
70	110	16 53	6 20	20.9	15 57	5 58	20.8	15 01	5 36	20.7	14 05	5 14	20.6	13 08	4 52	20.6	12 12	4 31	20.5	250	290
71	109	16 59	6 02	19.9	16 03	5 41	19.8	15 06	5 20	19.7	14 10	4 59	19.6	13 13	4 38	19.5	12 17	4 18	19.5	251	289
72	108	17 05	5 44	18.9	16 09	5 24	18.8	15 12	5 04	18.7	14 15	4 44	18.6	13 18	4 24	18.5	12 21	4 05	18.4	252	288
73	107	17 11	5 26	17.8	16 14	5 06	17.7	15 17	4 48	17.6	14 20	4 29	17.6	13 23	4 10	17.5	12 25	3 52	17.4	253	287
74	106	17 17	5 07	16.8	16 19	4 49	16.7	15 22	4 31	16.6	14 24	4 13	16.5	13 27	3 56	16.5	12 29	3 38	16.4	254	286
75	105	17 22	4 48	15.7	16 24	4 31	15.7	15 26	4 15	15.6	14 29	3 58	15.5	13 31	3 42	15.4	12 33	3 25	15.4	255	285
76	104	17 27	4 30	14.7	16 29	4 14	14.6	15 31	3 58	14.5	14 33	3 43	14.5	13 35	3 27	14.4	12 36	3 12	14.4	256	284
77	103	17 31	4 11	13.6	16 33	3 56	13.6	15 35	3 41	13.5	14 36	3 27	13.4	13 38	3 13	13.4	12 40	2 58	13.3	257	283
78	102	17 36	3 52	12.6	16 37	3 38	12.5	15 38	3 25	12.5	14 40	3 11	12.4	13 41	2 58	12.4	12 43	2 45	12.3	258	282
79	101	17 39	3 33	11.6	16 41	3 20	11.5	15 42	3 08	11.4	14 43	2 56	11.4	13 44	2 43	11.3	12 45	2 31	11.3	259	281
80	100	17 43	3 14	10.5	16 44	3 02	10.4	15 45	2 51	10.4	14 46	2 40	10.3	13 47	2 29	10.3	12 48	2 18	10.3	260	280
81	99	17 46	2 55	9.5	16 47	2 44	9.4	15 48	2 34	9.4	14 49	2 24	9.3	13 49	2 14	9.3	12 50	2 04	9.2	261	279
82	98	17 49	2 35	8.4	16 50	2 26	8.4	15 50	2 17	8.3	14 51	2 08	8.3	13 52	1 59	8.2	12 52	1 50	8.2	262	278
83	97	17 52	2 16	7.4	16 52	2 08	7.3	15 53	2 00	7.3	14 53	1 52	7.2	13 54	1 44	7.2	12 54	1 37	7.2	263	277
84	96	17 54	1 57	6.3	16 54	1 50	6.3	15 55	1 43	6.2	14 55	1 36	6.2	13 55	1 30	6.2	12 56	1 23	6.2	264	276
85	95	17 56	1 37	5.3	16 56	1 32	5.2	15 56	1 26	5.2	14 56	1 20	5.2	13 57	1 15	5.2	12 57	1 09	5.1	265	275
86	94	17 57	1 18	4.2	16 57	1 13	4.2	15 58	1 09	4.2	14 58	1 04	4.1	13 58	1 00	4.1	12 58	0 55	4.1	266	274
87	93	17 58	0 58	3.2	16 59	0 55	3.1	15 59	0 52	3.1	14 59	0 48	3.1	13 59	0 45	3.1	12 59	0 42	3.1	267	273
88	92	17 59	0 39	2.1	16 59	0 37	2.1	15 59	0 34	2.1	14 59	0 32	2.1	13 59	0 30	2.1	13 00	0 28	2.1	268	272
89	91	18 00	0 19	1.1	17 00	0 18	1.0	16 00	0 17	1.0	15 00	0 16	1.0	14 00	0 15	1.0	13 00	0 14	1.0	269	271
90	90	18 00	0 00	0.0	17 00	0 00	0.0	16 00	0 00	0.0	15 00	0 00	0.0	14 00	0 00	0.0	13 00	0 00	0.0	270	270

N. Lat.: for LHA>180°....Zn = Z
for LHA<180°....Zn =360° − Z

S. Lat.: for LHA > 180°.... Zn =180° − Z
for LHA < 180° .... Zn = 180° + Z

B: (−) for 90°< LHA < 270°
Dec: (−)for Lat. contrary name

Z₁: same sign as B
Z₂: (−)for F > 90°

Lat./Ā		78°			79°			80°			81°			82°			83°			Lat./Ā
LHA/F	LHA/Ā	A/H	B/P	Z₁/Z₂	A/H	B/P	Z₁/Z₂	A/H	B/P	Z₁/Z₂	A/H	B/P	Z₁/Z₂	A/H	B/P	Z₁/Z₂	A/H	B/P	Z₁/Z₂	LHA
0	180	0 00	12 00	90.0	0 00	11 00	90.0	0 00	10 00	90.0	0 00	9 00	90.0	0 00	8 00	90.0	0 00	7 00	90.0	180	360
1	179	0 12	12 00	89.0	0 11	11 00	89.0	0 10	10 00	89.0	0 09	9 00	89.0	0 08	8 00	89.0	0 07	7 00	89.0	181	359
2	178	0 25	12 00	88.0	0 23	11 00	88.0	0 21	10 00	88.0	0 19	9 00	88.0	0 17	8 00	88.0	0 15	7 00	88.0	182	358
3	177	0 37	11 59	87.1	0 34	10 59	87.1	0 31	9 59	87.0	0 28	8 59	87.0	0 25	7 59	87.0	0 22	6 59	87.0	183	357
4	176	0 50	11 58	86.1	0 46	10 58	86.1	0 42	9 59	86.0	0 38	8 59	86.0	0 33	7 59	86.0	0 29	6 59	86.0	184	356
5	175	1 02	11 57	85.1	0 57	10 58	85.1	0 52	9 58	85.1	0 47	8 58	85.1	0 42	7 58	85.0	0 37	6 58	85.0	185	355
6	174	1 15	11 56	84.1	1 09	10 56	84.1	1 02	9 57	84.1	0 56	8 57	84.1	0 50	7 57	84.1	0 44	6 58	84.0	186	354
7	173	1 27	11 55	83.2	1 20	10 55	83.1	1 13	9 56	83.1	1 06	8 56	83.1	0 58	7 56	83.1	0 51	6 57	83.1	187	353
8	172	1 39	11 53	82.2	1 31	10 54	82.1	1 23	9 54	82.1	1 15	8 55	82.1	1 07	7 55	82.1	0 58	6 56	82.1	188	352
9	171	1 52	11 51	81.2	1 43	10 52	81.2	1 33	9 53	81.1	1 24	8 53	81.1	1 15	7 54	81.1	1 06	6 55	81.1	189	351
10	170	2 04	11 49	80.2	1 54	10 50	80.2	1 44	9 51	80.1	1 33	8 52	80.1	1 23	7 53	80.1	1 13	6 54	80.1	190	350
11	169	2 16	11 47	79.2	2 05	10 48	79.2	1 54	9 49	79.2	1 43	8 50	79.1	1 31	7 51	79.1	1 20	6 52	79.1	191	349
12	168	2 29	11 45	78.3	2 16	10 46	78.2	2 04	9 47	78.2	1 52	8 48	78.1	1 39	7 50	78.1	1 27	6 51	78.1	192	348
13	167	2 41	11 42	77.3	2 28	10 43	77.2	2 14	9 45	77.2	2 01	8 46	77.2	1 48	7 48	77.1	1 34	6 49	77.1	193	347
14	166	2 53	11 39	76.3	2 39	10 41	76.2	2 24	9 43	76.2	2 10	8 44	76.2	1 56	7 46	76.1	1 41	6 48	76.1	194	346
15	165	3 05	11 36	75.3	2 50	10 38	75.3	2 35	9 40	75.2	2 19	8 42	75.2	2 04	7 44	75.2	1 48	6 46	75.1	195	345
16	164	3 17	11 33	74.3	3 01	10 35	74.3	2 45	9 37	74.2	2 28	8 39	74.2	2 12	7 42	74.2	1 56	6 44	74.1	196	344
17	163	3 29	11 29	73.4	3 12	10 32	73.3	2 55	9 34	73.2	2 37	8 37	73.2	2 20	7 39	73.2	2 03	6 42	73.1	197	343
18	162	3 41	11 26	72.4	3 23	10 28	72.3	3 05	9 31	72.3	2 46	8 34	72.2	2 28	7 37	72.2	2 09	6 40	72.1	198	342
19	161	3 53	11 22	71.4	3 34	10 25	71.3	3 14	9 28	71.3	2 55	8 31	71.2	2 36	7 34	71.2	2 16	6 37	71.1	199	341
20	160	4 05	11 18	70.4	3 45	10 21	70.3	3 24	9 24	70.3	3 04	8 28	70.2	2 44	7 31	70.2	2 23	6 35	70.1	200	340
21	159	4 16	11 13	69.4	3 55	10 17	69.4	3 34	9 21	69.3	3 13	8 25	69.2	2 52	7 28	69.2	2 30	6 32	69.1	201	339
22	158	4 28	11 09	68.4	4 06	10 13	68.4	3 44	9 17	68.3	3 22	8 21	68.2	2 59	7 25	68.2	2 37	6 30	68.1	202	338
23	157	4 40	11 04	67.5	4 17	10 09	67.4	3 53	9 13	67.3	3 30	8 18	67.3	3 07	7 22	67.2	2 44	6 27	67.2	203	337
24	156	4 51	10 59	66.5	4 27	10 04	66.4	4 03	9 09	66.4	3 39	8 14	66.3	3 15	7 19	66.2	2 50	6 24	66.2	204	336
25	155	5 02	10 54	65.5	4 38	9 59	65.4	4 13	9 05	65.3	3 47	8 10	65.3	3 22	7 16	65.2	2 57	6 21	65.2	205	335
26	154	5 14	10 49	64.5	4 48	9 55	64.4	4 22	9 00	64.4	3 56	8 06	64.3	3 30	7 12	64.2	3 04	6 18	64.2	206	334
27	153	5 25	10 43	63.5	4 58	9 50	63.4	4 31	8 56	63.4	4 04	8 02	63.3	3 37	7 08	63.2	3 10	6 15	63.2	207	333
28	152	5 36	10 38	62.5	5 08	9 44	62.4	4 41	8 51	62.4	4 13	7 58	62.3	3 45	7 04	62.2	3 17	6 11	62.2	208	332
29	151	5 47	10 32	61.5	5 18	9 39	61.4	4 50	8 46	61.4	4 21	7 53	61.3	3 52	7 00	61.2	3 23	6 08	61.2	209	331
30	150	5 58	10 26	60.5	5 28	9 33	60.5	4 59	8 41	60.4	4 29	7 49	60.3	3 59	6 56	60.2	3 30	6 04	60.2	210	330
31	149	6 09	10 20	59.6	5 38	9 28	59.5	5 08	8 36	59.4	4 37	7 44	59.3	4 07	6 52	59.2	3 36	6 00	59.2	211	329
32	148	6 20	10 13	58.6	5 48	9 22	58.5	5 17	8 30	58.5	4 45	7 39	58.3	4 14	6 48	58.3	3 42	5 57	58.2	212	328
33	147	6 30	10 06	57.6	5 58	9 16	57.5	5 26	8 25	57.4	4 53	7 34	57.3	4 21	6 43	57.3	3 48	5 53	57.2	213	327
34	146	6 41	10 00	56.6	6 08	9 09	56.5	5 34	8 19	56.4	5 01	7 29	56.3	4 28	6 39	56.3	3 54	5 49	56.2	214	326
35	145	6 51	9 53	55.6	6 17	9 03	55.5	5 43	8 13	55.4	5 09	7 24	55.3	4 35	6 34	55.3	4 00	5 45	55.2	215	325
36	144	7 01	9 45	54.6	6 26	8 56	54.5	5 51	8 07	54.5	5 17	7 18	54.3	4 42	6 29	54.3	4 06	5 40	54.2	216	324
37	143	7 11	9 38	53.6	6 36	8 49	53.6	6 00	8 01	53.5	5 24	7 13	53.3	4 48	6 24	53.3	4 12	5 36	53.2	217	323
38	142	7 21	9 31	52.6	6 45	8 43	52.6	6 08	7 55	52.5	5 32	7 07	52.3	4 55	6 19	52.3	4 18	5 32	52.2	218	322
39	141	7 31	9 23	51.6	6 54	8 35	51.6	6 16	7 48	51.5	5 39	7 01	51.3	5 01	6 14	51.3	4 24	5 27	51.2	219	321
40	140	7 41	9 15	50.6	7 03	8 28	50.6	6 25	7 42	50.5	5 46	6 55	50.3	5 08	6 09	50.3	4 30	5 22	50.2	220	320
41	139	7 50	9 07	49.6	7 11	8 21	49.5	6 32	7 35	49.5	5 53	6 49	49.4	5 14	6 03	49.3	4 35	5 18	49.2	221	319
42	138	8 00	8 59	48.6	7 20	8 13	48.5	6 40	7 28	48.5	6 01	6 43	48.4	5 21	5 58	48.3	4 41	5 13	48.2	222	318
43	137	8 09	8 50	47.6	7 29	8 05	47.5	6 48	7 21	47.5	6 07	6 36	47.4	5 27	5 52	47.3	4 46	5 08	47.2	223	317
44	136	8 18	8 42	46.6	7 37	7 58	46.5	6 56	7 14	46.5	6 14	6 30	46.4	5 33	5 46	46.3	4 51	5 03	46.2	224	316
45	135	8 27	8 33	45.6	7 45	7 50	45.5	7 03	7 06	45.5	6 21	6 23	45.4	5 39	5 41	45.3	4 58	4 58	45.2	225	315

LHA	F	78° A/H	78° B/P	78° Z₁/Z₂	79° A/H	79° B/P	79° Z₁/Z₂	80° A/H	80° B/P	80° Z₁/Z₂	81° A/H	81° B/P	81° Z₁/Z₂	82° A/H	82° B/P	82° Z₁/Z₂	83° A/H	83° B/P	83° Z₁/Z₂	Ā	LHA
45	135	8 27	8 33	45.6	7 45	7 50	45.5	7 03	7 06	45.4	6 21	6 23	45.4	5 39	5 41	45.3	4 57	4 58	45.2	225	315
46	134	8 36	8 24	44.6	7 53	7 41	44.5	7 11	6 59	44.4	6 28	6 17	44.4	5 45	5 35	44.3	5 02	4 53	44.2	226	314
47	133	8 45	8 15	43.6	8 01	7 33	43.5	7 18	6 51	43.4	6 34	6 10	43.4	5 51	5 29	43.3	5 07	4 47	43.2	227	313
48	132	8 53	8 06	42.6	8 09	7 25	42.5	7 25	6 44	42.4	6 41	6 03	42.4	5 56	5 22	42.3	5 12	4 42	42.2	228	312
49	131	9 02	7 56	41.6	8 17	7 16	41.5	7 32	6 36	41.4	6 47	5 56	41.4	6 02	5 16	41.3	5 17	4 36	41.2	229	311
50	130	9 10	7 47	40.6	8 24	7 07	40.5	7 39	6 28	40.4	6 53	5 49	40.3	6 07	5 10	40.3	5 21	4 31	40.2	230	310
51	129	9 18	7 37	39.6	8 32	6 58	39.5	7 45	6 20	39.4	6 59	5 42	39.3	6 13	5 03	39.3	5 26	4 25	39.2	231	309
52	128	9 26	7 27	38.6	8 39	6 49	38.5	7 52	6 12	38.4	7 05	5 34	38.3	6 18	4 57	38.3	5 31	4 19	38.2	232	308
53	127	9 33	7 17	37.6	8 46	6 40	37.5	7 58	6 03	37.4	7 11	5 27	37.3	6 23	4 50	37.3	5 35	4 14	37.2	233	307
54	126	9 41	7 07	36.6	8 53	6 31	36.5	8 05	5 55	36.4	7 16	5 19	36.3	6 28	4 43	36.3	5 39	4 08	36.2	234	306
55	125	9 48	6 57	35.6	9 00	6 22	35.5	8 11	5 47	35.4	7 22	5 11	35.3	6 33	4 37	35.3	5 44	4 02	35.2	235	305
56	124	9 56	6 47	34.6	9 06	6 12	34.5	8 17	5 38	34.4	7 27	5 04	34.3	6 38	4 30	34.3	5 48	3 56	34.2	236	304
57	123	10 03	6 36	33.6	9 13	6 03	33.5	8 22	5 29	33.4	7 32	4 56	33.3	6 42	4 23	33.3	5 52	3 50	33.2	237	303
58	122	10 09	6 26	32.6	9 19	5 53	32.5	8 28	5 20	32.4	7 37	4 48	32.3	6 47	4 16	32.3	5 56	3 43	32.2	238	302
59	121	10 16	6 15	31.6	9 25	5 43	31.5	8 34	5 11	31.4	7 42	4 40	31.3	6 51	4 08	31.2	6 00	3 37	31.2	239	301
60	120	10 22	6 04	30.6	9 31	5 33	30.5	8 39	5 02	30.4	7 47	4 32	30.3	6 55	4 01	30.2	6 04	3 31	30.2	240	300
61	119	10 29	5 53	29.5	9 36	5 23	29.5	8 44	4 53	29.4	7 52	4 23	29.3	6 59	3 54	29.2	6 07	3 24	29.2	241	299
62	118	10 35	5 42	28.5	9 42	5 13	28.4	8 49	4 44	28.4	7 56	4 15	28.3	7 04	3 46	28.2	6 11	3 18	28.2	242	298
63	117	10 41	5 31	27.5	9 47	5 03	27.4	8 54	4 35	27.4	8 01	4 07	27.3	7 07	3 39	27.2	6 14	3 11	27.2	243	297
64	116	10 46	5 19	26.5	9 52	4 52	26.4	8 59	4 25	26.3	8 05	3 58	26.3	7 11	3 32	26.2	6 17	3 05	26.2	244	296
65	115	10 52	5 08	25.5	9 57	4 42	25.4	9 03	4 16	25.3	8 09	3 50	25.3	7 15	3 24	25.2	6 20	2 58	25.2	245	295
66	114	10 57	4 56	24.5	10 02	4 31	24.4	9 08	4 06	24.3	8 13	3 41	24.3	7 18	3 16	24.2	6 24	2 52	24.2	246	294
67	113	11 02	4 45	23.5	10 07	4 21	23.4	9 12	3 56	23.3	8 17	3 32	23.3	7 22	3 09	23.2	6 26	2 45	23.2	247	293
68	112	11 07	4 33	22.4	10 11	4 10	22.4	9 16	3 47	22.3	8 20	3 24	22.2	7 25	3 01	22.2	6 29	2 38	22.1	248	292
69	111	11 12	4 21	21.4	10 16	3 59	21.4	9 20	3 37	21.3	8 24	3 15	21.2	7 28	2 53	21.2	6 32	2 31	21.1	249	291
70	110	11 16	4 09	20.4	10 20	3 48	20.3	9 23	3 27	20.3	8 27	3 06	20.2	7 31	2 45	20.2	6 35	2 24	20.1	250	290
71	109	11 20	3 58	19.4	10 24	3 37	19.3	9 27	3 17	19.3	8 30	2 57	19.2	7 34	2 37	19.2	6 37	2 17	19.1	251	289
72	108	11 24	3 45	18.4	10 27	3 26	18.3	9 30	3 07	18.3	8 33	2 48	18.2	7 36	2 29	18.2	6 39	2 10	18.1	252	288
73	107	11 28	3 33	17.4	10 31	3 15	17.3	9 34	2 57	17.2	8 36	2 39	17.2	7 39	2 21	17.2	6 42	2 03	17.1	253	287
74	106	11 32	3 21	16.3	10 34	3 04	16.3	9 37	2 47	16.2	8 39	2 30	16.2	7 41	2 13	16.1	6 44	1 56	16.1	254	286
75	105	11 35	3 09	15.3	10 37	2 53	15.3	9 39	2 37	15.2	8 41	2 21	15.2	7 44	2 05	15.1	6 46	1 49	15.1	255	285
76	104	11 38	2 57	14.3	10 40	2 42	14.3	9 42	2 26	14.2	8 44	2 12	14.2	7 46	1 57	14.1	6 47	1 42	14.1	256	284
77	103	11 41	2 44	13.3	10 43	2 30	13.2	9 44	2 16	13.2	8 46	2 02	13.2	7 48	1 49	13.1	6 49	1 35	13.1	257	283
78	102	11 44	2 32	12.3	10 45	2 19	12.2	9 47	2 06	12.2	8 48	1 53	12.1	7 49	1 40	12.1	6 51	1 28	12.1	258	282
79	101	11 47	2 19	11.2	10 48	2 07	11.2	9 49	1 56	11.2	8 50	1 44	11.1	7 51	1 32	11.1	6 52	1 21	11.1	259	281
80	100	11 49	2 07	10.2	10 50	1 56	10.2	9 51	1 45	10.2	8 52	1 35	10.1	7 53	1 24	10.1	6 54	1 13	10.1	260	280
81	99	11 51	1 54	9.2	10 52	1 45	9.2	9 53	1 35	9.1	8 53	1 25	9.1	7 54	1 16	9.1	6 55	1 06	9.1	261	279
82	98	11 53	1 42	8.2	10 53	1 33	8.2	9 54	1 24	8.1	8 55	1 16	8.1	7 55	1 07	8.1	6 56	0 59	8.1	262	278
83	97	11 55	1 29	7.2	10 55	1 21	7.1	9 55	1 14	7.1	8 56	1 06	7.1	7 56	0 59	7.1	6 57	0 51	7.1	263	277
84	96	11 56	1 16	6.1	10 56	1 10	6.1	9 57	1 03	6.1	8 57	0 57	6.1	7 57	0 50	6.1	6 58	0 44	6.0	264	276
85	95	11 57	1 04	5.1	10 57	0 58	5.1	9 58	0 53	5.1	8 58	0 47	5.1	7 58	0 42	5.0	6 58	0 37	5.0	265	275
86	94	11 58	0 51	4.1	10 58	0 47	4.1	9 59	0 42	4.1	8 59	0 38	4.0	7 59	0 34	4.0	6 59	0 29	4.0	266	274
87	93	11 59	0 38	3.1	10 59	0 35	3.1	9 59	0 32	3.0	8 59	0 28	3.0	7 59	0 25	3.0	6 59	0 22	3.0	267	273
88	92	12 00	0 26	2.0	11 00	0 23	2.0	10 00	0 21	2.0	9 00	0 19	2.0	8 00	0 17	2.0	7 00	0 15	2.0	268	272
89	91	12 00	0 13	1.0	11 00	0 12	1.0	10 00	0 11	1.0	9 00	0 09	1.0	8 00	0 08	1.0	7 00	0 07	1.0	269	271
90	90	12 00	0 00	0.0	11 00	0 00	0.0	10 00	0 00	0.0	9 00	0 00	0.0	8 00	0 00	0.0	7 00	0 00	0.0	270	270

N. Lat.: for LHA>180°...Zn = Z
for LHA<180°...Zn =360° − Z

S. Lat.: for LHA > 180°...Zn =180° − Z
for LHA < 180°...Zn =180° + Z

LATITUDE/Ā : 84° – 89°

B: (−) for 90° < LHA < 270°
Dec: (−) for Lat. contrary name

Z₁; same sign as B
Z₂; (−)for F > 90°

Lat./Ā LHA/F̄	84° A/H	84° B/P	84° Z₁/Z₂	85° A/H	85° B/P	85° Z₁/Z₂	86° A/H	86° B/P	86° Z₁/Z₂	87° A/H	87° B/P	87° Z₁/Z₂	88° A/H	88° B/P	88° Z₁/Z₂	89° A/H	89° B/P	89° Z₁/Z₂	Lat./Ā LHA
0 180	0 00	6 00	90.0	0 00	5 00	90.0	0 00	4 00	90.0	0 00	3 00	90.0	0 00	2 00	90.0	0 00	1 00	90.0	180
1 179	0 06	6 00	89.0	0 05	5 00	89.0	0 04	4 00	89.0	0 03	3 00	89.0	0 02	2 00	89.0	0 01	1 00	89.0	181
2 178	0 13	6 00	88.0	0 10	5 00	88.0	0 08	4 00	88.0	0 06	3 00	88.0	0 04	2 00	88.0	0 02	1 00	88.0	182
3 177	0 19	6 00	87.0	0 16	4 59	87.0	0 13	3 59	87.0	0 09	3 00	87.0	0 06	2 00	87.0	0 03	1 00	87.0	183
4 176	0 25	5 59	86.0	0 21	4 59	86.0	0 17	3 59	86.0	0 13	3 00	86.0	0 08	2 00	86.0	0 04	1 00	86.0	184
5 175	0 31	5 59	85.0	0 26	4 59	85.0	0 21	3 59	85.0	0 16	2 59	85.0	0 10	2 00	85.0	0 05	1 00	85.0	185
6 174	0 38	5 58	84.0	0 31	4 58	84.0	0 25	3 59	84.0	0 19	2 59	84.0	0 13	1 59	84.0	0 06	1 00	84.0	186
7 173	0 44	5 57	83.0	0 37	4 58	83.0	0 29	3 58	83.0	0 22	2 59	83.0	0 15	1 59	83.0	0 07	1 00	83.0	187
8 172	0 50	5 57	82.0	0 42	4 57	82.0	0 33	3 58	82.0	0 25	2 58	82.0	0 17	1 59	82.0	0 08	0 59	82.0	188
9 171	0 56	5 56	81.0	0 47	4 56	81.0	0 38	3 57	81.0	0 28	2 58	81.0	0 19	1 59	81.0	0 09	0 59	81.0	189
10 170	1 02	5 55	80.1	0 52	4 55	80.0	0 42	3 56	80.0	0 31	2 57	80.0	0 21	1 58	80.0	0 10	0 59	80.0	190
11 169	1 09	5 53	79.1	0 57	4 55	79.1	0 46	3 56	79.0	0 34	2 57	79.0	0 23	1 58	79.0	0 11	0 59	79.0	191
12 168	1 15	5 52	78.1	1 02	4 53	78.1	0 50	3 55	78.0	0 37	2 56	78.0	0 25	1 57	78.0	0 12	0 59	78.0	192
13 167	1 21	5 51	77.1	1 07	4 52	77.1	0 54	3 54	77.0	0 40	2 55	77.0	0 27	1 57	77.0	0 13	0 58	77.0	193
14 166	1 27	5 49	76.1	1 12	4 51	76.1	0 58	3 53	76.0	0 44	2 55	76.0	0 29	1 56	76.0	0 15	0 58	76.0	194
15 165	1 33	5 48	75.1	1 18	4 50	75.1	1 02	3 52	75.0	0 47	2 54	75.0	0 31	1 56	75.0	0 16	0 58	75.0	195
16 164	1 39	5 46	74.1	1 23	4 48	74.1	1 06	3 51	74.0	0 50	2 53	74.0	0 33	1 55	74.0	0 17	0 58	74.0	196
17 163	1 45	5 44	73.1	1 28	4 47	73.1	1 10	3 50	73.0	0 53	2 52	73.0	0 35	1 55	73.0	0 18	0 57	73.0	197
18 162	1 51	5 43	72.1	1 33	4 45	72.1	1 14	3 48	72.0	0 56	2 51	72.0	0 37	1 54	72.0	0 19	0 57	72.0	198
19 161	1 57	5 41	71.1	1 38	4 44	71.1	1 18	3 47	71.0	0 59	2 50	71.0	0 39	1 53	71.0	0 20	0 57	71.0	199
20 160	2 03	5 38	70.1	1 42	4 42	70.1	1 22	3 46	70.0	1 02	2 49	70.0	0 41	1 53	70.0	0 21	0 56	70.0	200
21 159	2 09	5 36	69.1	1 47	4 40	69.1	1 26	3 44	69.0	1 04	2 48	69.0	0 43	1 52	69.0	0 22	0 56	69.0	201
22 158	2 15	5 34	68.1	1 52	4 38	68.1	1 30	3 43	68.0	1 07	2 47	68.0	0 45	1 51	68.0	0 22	0 56	68.0	202
23 157	2 20	5 32	67.1	1 57	4 36	67.1	1 34	3 41	67.1	1 10	2 46	67.0	0 47	1 50	67.0	0 23	0 55	67.0	203
24 156	2 26	5 29	66.1	2 02	4 34	66.1	1 38	3 39	66.1	1 13	2 44	66.0	0 49	1 50	66.0	0 24	0 55	66.0	204
25 155	2 32	5 26	65.1	2 07	4 32	65.1	1 41	3 38	65.1	1 16	2 43	65.0	0 51	1 49	65.0	0 25	0 54	65.0	205
26 154	2 38	5 24	64.1	2 11	4 30	64.1	1 45	3 36	64.1	1 19	2 42	64.0	0 53	1 48	64.0	0 26	0 54	64.0	206
27 153	2 43	5 21	63.1	2 16	4 27	63.1	1 49	3 34	63.1	1 22	2 40	63.0	0 54	1 47	63.0	0 27	0 53	63.0	207
28 152	2 49	5 18	62.1	2 21	4 25	62.1	1 53	3 32	62.1	1 24	2 39	62.0	0 56	1 46	62.0	0 28	0 53	62.0	208
29 151	2 54	5 15	61.1	2 25	4 23	61.1	1 56	3 30	61.1	1 27	2 37	61.0	0 58	1 45	61.0	0 29	0 52	61.0	209
30 150	3 00	5 12	60.1	2 30	4 20	60.1	2 00	3 28	60.1	1 30	2 36	60.0	1 00	1 44	60.0	0 30	0 52	60.0	210
31 149	3 05	5 09	59.1	2 34	4 17	59.1	2 04	3 26	59.1	1 33	2 34	59.0	1 02	1 43	59.0	0 31	0 51	59.0	211
32 148	3 11	5 06	58.1	2 39	4 15	58.1	2 07	3 24	58.1	1 35	2 33	58.0	1 04	1 42	58.0	0 32	0 51	58.0	212
33 147	3 16	5 02	57.1	2 43	4 12	57.1	2 11	3 21	57.1	1 38	2 31	57.0	1 05	1 41	57.0	0 33	0 50	57.0	213
34 146	3 21	4 59	56.1	2 48	4 09	56.1	2 14	3 19	56.1	1 41	2 29	56.0	1 07	1 39	56.0	0 34	0 50	56.0	214
35 145	3 26	4 55	55.1	2 52	4 06	55.1	2 18	3 17	55.1	1 43	2 27	55.0	1 09	1 38	55.0	0 34	0 49	55.0	215
36 144	3 31	4 52	54.1	2 56	4 03	54.1	2 21	3 14	54.1	1 46	2 26	54.0	1 11	1 37	54.0	0 35	0 49	54.0	216
37 143	3 36	4 48	53.2	3 00	4 00	53.1	2 24	3 12	53.1	1 48	2 24	53.0	1 12	1 36	53.0	0 36	0 48	53.0	217
38 142	3 41	4 44	52.2	3 05	3 57	52.1	2 28	3 09	52.1	1 51	2 22	52.0	1 14	1 35	52.0	0 37	0 47	52.0	218
39 141	3 46	4 40	51.2	3 09	3 53	51.1	2 31	3 07	51.1	1 53	2 20	51.0	1 16	1 33	51.0	0 38	0 47	51.0	219
40 140	3 51	4 36	50.2	3 13	3 50	50.1	2 34	3 04	50.1	1 56	2 18	50.0	1 17	1 32	50.0	0 39	0 46	50.0	220
41 139	3 56	4 32	49.2	3 17	3 47	49.1	2 37	3 01	49.1	1 58	2 16	49.0	1 19	1 31	49.0	0 39	0 45	49.0	221
42 138	4 01	4 28	48.2	3 21	3 43	48.1	2 41	2 58	48.1	2 00	2 14	48.0	1 20	1 29	48.0	0 40	0 45	48.0	222
43 137	4 05	4 24	47.2	3 24	3 40	47.1	2 44	2 56	47.1	2 03	2 12	47.0	1 22	1 28	47.0	0 41	0 44	47.0	223
44 136	4 10	4 19	46.2	3 28	3 36	46.1	2 47	2 53	46.1	2 05	2 10	46.0	1 23	1 26	46.0	0 42	0 43	46.0	224
45 135	4 14	4 15	45.2	3 32	3 32	45.1	2 50	2 50	45.1	2 07	2 07	45.0	1 25	1 25	45.0	0 42	0 42	45.0	225

Lat. / Ā	LHA/F̄	84° A/H	84° B/P	84° Z₁/Z₂	85° A/H	85° B/P	85° Z₁/Z₂	86° A/H	86° B/P	86° Z₁/Z₂	87° A/H	87° B/P	87° Z₁/Z₂	88° A/H	88° B/P	88° Z₁/Z₂	89° A/H	89° B/P	89° Z₁/Z₂	Lat. / Ā	LHA
45	135	4 14	4 15	45.2	3 32	3 32	45.1	2 50	2 50	45.1	2 07	2 07	45.0	1 25	1 25	45.0	0 42	0 42	45.0	225	315
46	134	4 19	4 11	44.2	3 36	3 29	44.1	2 53	2 47	44.1	2 09	2 05	44.0	1 26	1 23	44.0	0 43	0 42	44.0	226	314
47	133	4 23	4 06	43.2	3 39	3 25	43.1	2 55	2 44	43.1	2 12	2 03	43.0	1 28	1 22	43.0	0 44	0 41	43.0	227	313
48	132	4 27	4 01	42.2	3 43	3 21	42.1	2 58	2 41	42.1	2 14	2 01	42.0	1 29	1 20	42.0	0 45	0 40	42.0	228	312
49	131	4 31	3 57	41.2	3 46	3 17	41.1	3 01	2 38	41.1	2 16	1 58	41.0	1 31	1 19	41.0	0 45	0 39	41.0	229	311
50	130	4 36	3 52	40.2	3 50	3 13	40.1	3 04	2 34	40.1	2 18	1 56	40.0	1 32	1 17	40.0	0 46	0 39	40.0	230	310
51	129	4 40	3 47	39.2	3 53	3 09	39.1	3 06	2 31	39.1	2 20	1 53	39.0	1 33	1 16	39.0	0 47	0 38	39.0	231	309
52	128	4 43	3 42	38.2	3 56	3 05	38.1	3 09	2 28	38.1	2 22	1 51	38.0	1 35	1 14	38.0	0 47	0 37	38.0	232	308
53	127	4 47	3 37	37.2	3 59	3 01	37.1	3 12	2 25	37.1	2 24	1 48	37.0	1 36	1 12	37.0	0 48	0 36	37.0	233	307
54	126	4 51	3 32	36.1	4 03	2 57	36.1	3 14	2 21	36.1	2 26	1 46	36.0	1 37	1 11	36.0	0 49	0 35	36.0	234	306
55	125	4 55	3 27	35.1	4 06	2 52	35.1	3 17	2 18	35.1	2 27	1 43	35.0	1 38	1 09	35.0	0 49	0 34	35.0	235	305
56	124	4 58	3 22	34.1	4 09	2 48	34.1	3 19	2 14	34.1	2 29	1 41	34.0	1 39	1 07	34.0	0 50	0 34	34.0	236	304
57	123	5 02	3 17	33.1	4 12	2 44	33.1	3 21	2 11	33.1	2 31	1 38	33.0	1 41	1 05	33.0	0 50	0 33	33.0	237	303
58	122	5 05	3 11	32.1	4 14	2 39	32.1	3 23	2 07	32.1	2 33	1 35	32.0	1 42	1 04	32.0	0 51	0 32	32.0	238	302
59	121	5 08	3 06	31.1	4 17	2 35	31.1	3 26	2 04	31.1	2 34	1 33	31.0	1 43	1 02	31.0	0 51	0 31	31.0	239	301
60	120	5 12	3 00	30.1	4 20	2 30	30.1	3 28	2 00	30.1	2 36	1 30	30.0	1 44	1 00	30.0	0 52	0 30	30.0	240	300
61	119	5 15	2 55	29.1	4 22	2 26	29.1	3 30	1 56	29.1	2 37	1 27	29.0	1 45	0 58	29.0	0 52	0 30	29.0	241	299
62	118	5 18	2 49	28.1	4 25	2 21	28.1	3 32	1 53	28.1	2 39	1 25	28.0	1 46	0 56	28.0	0 53	0 29	28.0	242	298
63	117	5 21	2 44	27.1	4 27	2 16	27.1	3 34	1 49	27.1	2 40	1 22	27.0	1 47	0 54	27.0	0 53	0 28	27.0	243	297
64	116	5 23	2 38	26.1	4 30	2 12	26.1	3 36	1 45	26.1	2 42	1 19	26.0	1 48	0 53	26.0	0 54	0 27	26.0	244	296
65	115	5 26	2 33	25.1	4 32	2 07	25.1	3 37	1 42	25.1	2 43	1 16	25.0	1 49	0 51	25.0	0 54	0 26	25.0	245	295
66	114	5 29	2 27	24.1	4 34	2 02	24.1	3 39	1 38	24.1	2 44	1 13	24.0	1 50	0 49	24.0	0 55	0 25	24.0	246	294
67	113	5 31	2 21	23.1	4 36	1 57	23.1	3 41	1 34	23.1	2 46	1 10	23.0	1 50	0 47	23.0	0 55	0 24	23.0	247	293
68	112	5 34	2 15	22.1	4 38	1 53	22.1	3 42	1 30	22.0	2 47	1 07	22.0	1 51	0 45	22.0	0 56	0 23	22.0	248	292
69	111	5 36	2 09	21.1	4 40	1 48	21.1	3 44	1 26	21.0	2 48	1 05	21.0	1 52	0 43	21.0	0 56	0 22	21.0	249	291
70	110	5 38	2 04	20.1	4 42	1 43	20.1	3 46	1 22	20.0	2 49	1 02	20.0	1 53	0 41	20.0	0 56	0 21	20.0	250	290
71	109	5 40	1 58	19.1	4 44	1 38	19.1	3 47	1 18	19.0	2 50	0 59	19.0	1 53	0 39	19.0	0 57	0 20	19.0	251	289
72	108	5 42	1 52	18.1	4 45	1 33	18.1	3 48	1 14	18.0	2 51	0 56	18.0	1 54	0 37	18.0	0 57	0 19	18.0	252	288
73	107	5 44	1 46	17.1	4 47	1 28	17.1	3 49	1 10	17.0	2 52	0 53	17.0	1 54	0 35	17.0	0 58	0 18	17.0	253	287
74	106	5 46	1 40	16.1	4 48	1 23	16.1	3 51	1 06	16.0	2 53	0 50	16.0	1 55	0 33	16.0	0 58	0 17	16.0	254	286
75	105	5 48	1 33	15.1	4 50	1 18	15.1	3 52	1 02	15.0	2 54	0 47	15.0	1 56	0 31	15.0	0 58	0 16	15.0	255	285
76	104	5 49	1 27	14.1	4 51	1 13	14.1	3 53	0 58	14.0	2 55	0 44	14.0	1 56	0 29	14.0	0 58	0 15	14.0	256	284
77	103	5 51	1 21	13.1	4 52	1 08	13.0	3 54	0 54	13.0	2 55	0 41	13.0	1 57	0 27	13.0	0 58	0 13	13.0	257	283
78	102	5 52	1 15	12.1	4 53	1 03	12.0	3 55	0 50	12.0	2 56	0 37	12.0	1 57	0 25	12.0	0 59	0 12	12.0	258	282
79	101	5 53	1 09	11.1	4 54	0 57	11.0	3 56	0 46	11.0	2 57	0 34	11.0	1 58	0 23	11.0	0 59	0 11	11.0	259	281
80	100	5 55	1 03	10.1	4 55	0 52	10.0	3 56	0 42	10.0	2 57	0 31	10.0	1 58	0 21	10.0	0 59	0 10	10.0	260	280
81	99	5 56	0 57	9.0	4 56	0 47	9.0	3 57	0 38	9.0	2 58	0 28	9.0	1 59	0 19	9.0	0 59	0 09	9.0	261	279
82	98	5 56	0 50	8.0	4 57	0 42	8.0	3 58	0 33	8.0	2 58	0 25	8.0	1 59	0 17	8.0	0 59	0 08	8.0	262	278
83	97	5 57	0 44	7.0	4 58	0 37	7.0	3 58	0 29	7.0	2 59	0 22	7.0	1 59	0 15	7.0	1 00	0 07	7.0	263	277
84	96	5 58	0 38	6.0	4 58	0 31	6.0	3 59	0 25	6.0	2 59	0 19	6.0	1 59	0 13	6.0	1 00	0 06	6.0	264	276
85	95	5 58	0 31	5.0	4 59	0 26	5.0	3 59	0 21	5.0	2 59	0 16	5.0	2 00	0 10	5.0	1 00	0 05	5.0	265	275
86	94	5 59	0 25	4.0	4 59	0 21	4.0	3 59	0 17	4.0	2 59	0 13	4.0	2 00	0 08	4.0	1 00	0 04	4.0	266	274
87	93	5 59	0 19	3.0	5 00	0 16	3.0	4 00	0 13	3.0	3 00	0 09	3.0	2 00	0 06	3.0	1 00	0 03	3.0	267	273
88	92	6 00	0 13	2.0	5 00	0 10	2.0	4 00	0 08	2.0	3 00	0 06	2.0	2 00	0 04	2.0	1 00	0 02	2.0	268	272
89	91	6 00	0 06	1.0	5 00	0 05	1.0	4 00	0 04	1.0	3 00	0 03	1.0	2 00	0 02	1.0	1 00	0 01	1.0	269	271
90	90	6 00	0 00	0.0	5 00	0 00	0.0	4 00	0 00	0.0	3 00	0 00	0.0	2 00	0 00	0.0	1 00	0 00	0.0	270	270

N. Lat.: for LHA>180°.... Zn = Z
for LHA<180°.... Zn =360° − Z

S. Lat.: for LHA > 180°.... Zn =180° − Z
for LHA < 180°.... Zn =180° + Z

Auxiliary Table – CORRECTIONS FOR H

Top right: Sign of corr2 for A' →

F' + →	▪ 30	29 31	28 32	27 33	26 34	25 35	24 36	23 37	22 38	21 39	20 40	19 41	18 42	17 43	16 44	15 45	14 46	13 47	12 48	11 49	10 50	9 51	8 52	7 53	6 54	5 55	4 56	3 57	2 58	1 59	Z₂ − A' +
P 1	-	-	-	-	-	-	-	-	-	-	-	-	-	-	-	-	-	-	-	-	-	-	-	-	-	-	-	-	-	-	89
2	1	1	0	0	0	0	0	0	0	0	0	0	0	0	0	0	0	0	0	0	0	0	0	0	0	0	0	0	0	0	88
3	1	1	1	1	1	1	1	1	1	1	1	1	1	0	1	1	1	0	0	0	1	0	0	0	0	0	0	0	0	0	87
4	2	2	1	1	2	2	2	2	2	1	2	1	1	1	1	1	1	1	1	1	1	1	1	0	1	1	0	0	0	0	86
5	2	3	2	2	2	2	2	2	2	2	2	2	2	2	2	2	1	2	1	1	1	1	1	1	1	1	1	1	0	0	85
6	3	3	3	3	3	3	3	3	3	3	3	3	2	2	2	2	2	2	2	2	2	2	1	2	2	1	1	1	1	0	84
7	3	4	3	4	4	4	3	4	3	3	3	3	3	3	3	3	2	3	2	2	2	2	2	2	2	2	1	1	1	1	83
8	4	4	4	4	4	4	4	4	4	4	4	4	3	3	3	3	3	3	3	3	2	2	2	2	2	2	1	1	1	1	82
9	4	5	4	5	5	5	4	5	4	4	4	4	4	4	4	4	3	3	3	3	3	3	2	2	2	2	2	2	1	1	81
10	5	5	5	5	5	5	5	5	5	4	5	4	4	4	4	4	4	4	4	3	3	3	3	3	3	2	2	2	1	1	80
11	6	6	5	6	6	6	5	6	5	5	5	5	5	5	4	5	4	4	4	4	4	3	3	3	3	3	2	2	1	1	79
12	6	6	6	6	6	6	6	6	6	6	6	5	5	5	5	5	5	5	4	4	4	4	3	3	3	3	2	2	1	1	78
13	7	7	7	7	7	6	7	7	6	6	6	6	6	6	5	6	5	5	5	5	4	4	4	4	3	3	3	2	1	1	77
14	7	8	7	7	7	7	7	7	7	7	7	6	6	6	6	6	6	6	5	5	5	4	4	4	4	3	3	2	2	1	76
15	8	8	8	8	8	7	8	8	7	7	7	7	7	7	6	6	6	6	6	5	5	5	4	4	4	3	3	2	2	1	75
16	8	8	8	8	8	8	8	8	8	8	8	7	7	7	7	7	6	6	6	6	6	5	5	4	4	4	3	3	2	1	74
17	9	9	9	9	9	9	9	9	8	8	8	8	8	8	7	7	7	7	6	6	6	5	5	5	4	4	3	3	2	1	73
18	9	9	9	9	9	9	9	9	9	9	8	8	8	8	8	8	7	7	7	6	6	6	5	5	5	4	4	3	2	1	72
19	10	10	10	10	9	10	9	10	9	9	9	9	9	8	8	8	8	7	7	7	6	6	6	5	5	4	4	3	2	1	71
20	10	10	10	10	10	10	10	10	10	9	9	9	9	9	9	8	8	8	7	7	7	6	6	5	5	4	4	3	2	1	70
21	11	11	11	10	10	10	11	11	10	10	10	10	9	9	9	9	8	8	8	7	7	6	6	6	5	5	4	3	2	1	69
22	11	11	11	11	11	11	11	11	11	10	10	10	10	10	9	9	9	8	8	7	7	6	6	6	5	5	4	3	2	1	68
23	12	12	12	12	12	11	12	12	11	11	11	10	10	10	10	9	9	9	8	8	7	7	6	6	5	5	4	3	2	1	67
24	12	12	12	12	12	12	12	12	12	11	11	11	11	10	10	10	9	9	9	8	7	7	7	6	6	5	4	3	2	1	66
25	13	13	13	13	13	12	13	13	12	12	11	11	11	11	10	10	10	9	9	8	8	7	7	6	6	5	4	4	2	1	65
26	13	13	13	13	13	13	13	13	13	12	12	12	11	11	11	10	10	9	9	8	8	8	7	6	6	5	4	4	2	1	64
27	14	14	14	14	13	13	14	14	13	13	12	12	12	11	11	11	10	10	9	9	8	8	7	7	6	5	4	4	2	1	63
28	14	14	14	14	14	14	14	14	14	13	13	12	12	12	11	11	10	10	10	9	8	8	7	7	6	5	4	4	2	1	62
29	15	15	15	15	15	14	15	14	14	13	13	13	13	12	12	11	11	10	10	9	9	8	7	7	6	5	5	4	2	1	61
30	15	15	15	15	15	15	15	15	14	14	14	13	13	12	12	11	11	11	10	9	9	8	8	7	6	6	5	4	2	1	60
31	16	16	16	16	16	15	15	15	15	14	14	14	13	13	12	12	11	11	10	10	9	8	8	7	6	6	5	4	2	1	59
32	16	16	16	16	16	16	16	16	15	15	14	14	14	13	13	12	12	11	11	10	9	9	8	7	7	6	5	4	2	1	58
33	17	17	17	17	16	16	16	16	16	15	15	14	14	13	13	12	12	11	11	10	9	9	8	7	7	6	5	4	2	1	57
34	17	17	17	17	17	16	17	16	16	15	15	15	14	14	13	13	12	12	11	10	10	9	8	8	7	6	5	4	2	1	56
35	18	17	18	17	17	17	17	17	16	16	16	15	15	14	14	13	12	12	11	11	10	9	8	8	7	6	5	4	2	1	55
36	18	18	18	18	18	17	17	17	17	16	16	15	15	14	14	13	13	12	11	11	10	9	9	8	7	6	5	4	2	1	54
37	18	18	18	18	18	18	18	18	17	17	16	16	15	15	14	13	13	12	12	11	10	9	9	8	7	6	5	4	2	1	53
38	19	19	18	18	18	18	18	18	18	17	16	16	16	15	14	14	13	13	12	11	10	10	9	8	7	6	5	4	2	1	52
39	19	19	19	19	18	18	18	18	18	17	17	16	16	15	15	14	13	13	12	11	11	10	9	8	7	6	5	4	2	1	51
40	19	19	19	19	19	18	18	18	18	17	17	16	16	15	15	14	13	13	12	11	11	10	9	8	7	6	6	4	2	1	50

F' + −	1 59	2 58	3 57	4 56	5 55	6 54	7 53	8 52	9 51	10 50	11 49	12 48	13 47	14 46	15 45	16 44	17 43	18 42	19 41	20 40	21 39	22 38	23 37	24 36	25 35	26 34	27 33	28 32	29 31	■ 30	− + A'
$\bar{P}$																															$\bar{Z}_2$
41	1	1	2	3	3	4	5	5	6	7	7	8	9	9	10	10	11	12	12	13	14	14	15	16	16	17	18	18	19	20	49
42	1	1	2	3	3	4	5	5	6	7	7	8	9	9	10	11	11	12	13	13	14	15	15	16	17	17	18	19	19	20	48
43	1	1	2	3	3	4	5	5	6	7	8	8	9	10	10	11	12	12	13	14	14	15	16	16	17	18	18	19	20	20	47
44	1	1	2	3	3	4	5	6	6	7	8	8	9	10	10	11	12	13	13	14	15	15	16	17	17	18	19	19	20	21	46
45	1	1	2	3	4	4	5	6	6	7	8	8	9	10	11	11	12	13	13	14	15	16	16	17	18	18	19	20	21	21	45
46	1	1	2	3	4	4	5	6	6	7	8	9	9	10	11	12	12	13	14	14	15	16	17	17	18	19	19	20	21	22	44
47	1	1	2	3	4	4	5	6	7	7	8	9	10	10	11	12	12	13	14	15	15	16	17	18	18	19	20	20	21	22	43
48	1	1	2	3	4	4	5	6	7	7	8	9	10	10	11	12	13	13	14	15	16	16	17	18	19	19	20	21	22	22	42
49	1	2	2	3	4	5	5	6	7	8	8	9	10	11	11	12	13	14	14	15	16	17	17	18	19	20	20	21	22	23	41
50	1	2	2	3	4	5	5	6	7	8	8	9	10	11	11	12	13	14	15	15	16	17	18	18	19	20	21	21	22	23	40
51	1	2	2	3	4	5	5	6	7	8	9	9	10	11	12	12	13	14	15	16	16	17	18	19	19	20	21	22	23	23	39
52	1	2	2	3	4	5	6	6	7	8	9	9	10	11	12	13	13	14	15	16	17	17	18	19	20	20	21	22	23	24	38
53	1	2	2	3	4	5	6	6	7	8	9	10	10	11	12	13	14	14	15	16	17	18	18	19	20	21	22	22	23	24	37
54	1	2	2	3	4	5	6	6	7	8	9	10	11	11	12	13	14	15	15	16	17	18	19	19	20	21	22	23	23	24	36
55	1	2	2	3	4	5	6	7	7	8	9	10	11	11	12	13	14	15	16	16	17	18	19	20	20	21	22	23	24	25	35
56	1	2	2	3	4	5	6	7	7	8	9	10	11	12	12	13	14	15	16	17	17	18	19	20	21	22	22	23	24	25	34
57	1	2	3	3	4	5	6	7	8	8	9	10	11	12	13	13	14	15	16	17	18	18	19	20	21	22	23	23	24	25	33
58	1	2	3	3	4	5	6	7	8	8	9	10	11	12	13	14	14	15	16	17	18	19	20	20	21	22	23	24	25	25	32
59	1	2	3	3	4	5	6	7	8	9	9	10	11	12	13	14	15	15	16	17	18	19	20	21	21	22	23	24	25	26	31
60	1	2	3	3	4	5	6	7	8	9	10	10	11	12	13	14	15	16	16	17	18	19	20	21	22	23	23	24	25	26	30
61	1	2	3	3	4	5	6	7	8	9	10	10	11	12	13	14	15	16	17	17	18	19	20	21	22	23	24	24	25	26	29
62	1	2	3	4	4	5	6	7	8	9	10	11	11	12	13	14	15	16	17	18	19	19	20	21	22	23	24	25	26	26	28
63	1	2	3	4	4	5	6	7	8	9	10	11	12	12	13	14	15	16	17	18	19	20	20	21	22	23	24	25	26	27	27
64	1	2	3	4	4	5	6	7	8	9	10	11	12	13	13	14	15	16	17	18	19	20	21	22	22	23	24	25	26	27	26
65	1	2	3	4	5	5	6	7	8	9	10	11	12	13	14	15	15	16	17	18	19	20	21	22	23	24	24	25	26	27	25
66	1	2	3	4	5	5	6	7	8	9	10	11	12	13	14	15	16	16	17	18	19	20	21	22	23	24	25	26	26	27	24
67	1	2	3	4	5	6	6	7	8	9	10	11	12	13	14	15	16	17	17	18	19	20	21	22	23	24	25	26	27	28	23
68	1	2	3	4	5	6	6	7	8	9	10	11	12	13	14	15	16	17	18	19	19	20	21	22	23	24	25	26	27	28	22
69	1	2	3	4	5	6	7	7	8	9	10	11	12	13	14	15	16	17	18	19	20	21	21	22	23	24	25	26	27	28	21
70	1	2	3	4	5	6	7	8	8	9	10	11	12	13	14	15	16	17	18	19	20	21	22	23	23	24	25	26	27	28	20
71	1	2	3	4	5	6	7	8	9	9	10	11	12	13	14	15	16	17	18	19	20	21	22	23	24	25	26	26	27	28	19
72	1	2	3	4	5	6	7	8	9	10	10	11	12	13	14	15	16	17	18	19	20	21	22	23	24	25	26	27	28	29	18
73	1	2	3	4	5	6	7	8	9	10	11	11	12	13	14	15	16	17	18	19	20	21	22	23	24	25	26	27	28	29	17
74	1	2	3	4	5	6	7	8	9	10	11	12	12	13	14	15	16	17	18	19	20	21	22	23	24	25	26	27	28	29	16
75	1	2	3	4	5	6	7	8	9	10	11	12	13	14	14	15	16	17	18	19	20	21	22	23	24	25	26	27	28	29	15
76	1	2	3	4	5	6	7	8	9	10	11	12	13	14	15	16	16	17	18	19	20	21	22	23	24	25	26	27	28	29	14
77	1	2	3	4	5	6	7	8	9	10	11	12	13	14	15	16	17	18	19	19	20	21	22	23	24	25	26	27	28	29	13
78	1	2	3	4	5	6	7	8	9	10	11	12	13	14	15	16	17	18	19	20	21	22	22	23	24	25	26	27	28	29	12
79	1	2	3	4	5	6	7	8	9	10	11	12	13	14	15	16	17	18	19	20	21	22	23	24	25	26	27	27	28	29	11
80	1	2	3	4	5	6	7	8	9	10	11	12	13	14	15	16	17	18	19	20	21	22	23	24	25	26	27	28	29	30	10

For P > 80°, use 80°

For $Z_2 < 10°$, use 10°

CPSIA information can be obtained at www.ICGtesting.com
Printed in the USA
LVOW03*1938061213

364162LV00008B/315/P